ACC Library

W9-DII-520

DISCARDED

Single Imperfection

Medieval & Renaissance Literary Studies

General Editor:
Albert C. Labriola

Advisory Editor:
Foster Provost

Editorial Board:
Judith H. Anderson
Diana Treviño Benet
Donald Cheney
Ann Baynes Coiro
Mary T. Crane
Patrick Cullen
A. C. Hamilton
Margaret P. Hannay
A. Kent Hieatt
William B. Hunter
Michael Lieb
Thomas P. Roche Jr.
Mary Beth Rose
John T. Shawcross
John M. Steadman
Humphrey Tonkin
Susanne Woods

Single Imperfection

Milton, Marriage and Friendship

Thomas H. Luxon

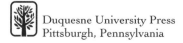

Duquesne University Press
Pittsburgh, Pennsylvania

Copyright © 2005 Duquesne University Press
All rights reserved

Published in the United States of America by:
DUQUESNE UNIVERSITY PRESS
600 Forbes Avenue
Pittsburgh, Pennsylvania 15282

No part of this book may be used or reproduced,
in any manner or form whatsoever,
without written permission from the publisher,
except in the case of short quotations
in critical articles or reviews.

Library of Congress Cataloging-in-Publication Data

Luxon, Thomas H., 1954–
    Single imperfection : Milton, marriage and friendship / Thomas H. Luxon.
      p. cm. — (Medieval & Renaissance literary studies)
    Includes bibliographical references and index.
    ISBN–13: 978–0–8207–0373–2 (cloth : acid-free paper)
    ISBN–10: 0–8207–0373–7 (cloth : acid-free paper)
    1. Milton, John, 1608–1674—Knowledge—Manners and customs. 2. Marriage
in literature. 3. Milton, John, 1608–1674—Political and social views. 4.
Literature and society—England—History—17th century. 5. Marriage—History
of doctrines—17th century. 6. Friendship—Religious aspects—Christianity. 7.
Divorce—Religious aspects—Christianity. 8. Friendship in literature. 9. Divorce
in literature. I. Title. II. Medieval and Renaissance literary studies
    PR3592.M3L89 2005
    821'.4—dc22

                                                    2005013665

∞Printed on acid-free paper.

"Milton's Wedded Love: Not About Sex (as We Know It)" by Thomas Luxon
is from MILTON STUDIES XL, ed. Albert C. Labriola, © 2002 by University
of Pittsburgh Press. Reprinted by permission of the University of Pittsburgh
Press.

To Barbara K. Lewalski

CONTENTS

Preface

It has long been recognized that Renaissance humanists and Protestant reformers changed forever the way Westerners think about marriage and its societal role. The literature on the early modern marriage and family, especially in England, is extensive and growing. This literature makes much of reformation doctrine and changes in the church, of an emerging bourgeois class, of advances in social mobility, manufacture, of huge economic shifts, political upheavals, and even concepts of sex and gender. Almost nothing, however, is made of friendship.

Sixteenth century humanists made much of the doctrines of classical friendship, not only those found in Aristotle and Cicero, but the newly recovered Platonic notions as well. As Laurie Shannon shows, discourses of friendship saturated early modern culture — schoolbooks, political treatises, epic poems, occasional essays and even marriage manuals.[1] In all the recent scholarship on early modern marriage, perhaps the single most pervasive aspect has been largely ignored: humanists, reformers, and puritans all tried to reinvent marriage as a friendship, using the nomenclature and discourses of classical friendship as a kind of template. This proved a successful, though difficult task, the difficulties of which have never been entirely acknowledged, even to this day. Marriage has indeed supplanted friendship as what we might call the default human relationship. Classical authors believed that friends served as second selves to each other, that they shared one soul in two bodies, and that the social fabric was woven on the warp of homo-social and homoerotic friendship. Friendship required sameness between partners — same status, same age, same wealth, same sex. Early modern humanists and reformers, John Milton chief among them, took on the huge project of reinterpreting heterosexual Christian marriage, what Genesis called two people made "one flesh," as a classical friendship. A homonormative model was recruited for the task of inventing a heteronormative world.

Few today ever doubt that marriage is the relationship that most defines one as human. This is one reason that states, like those in the United States, with a history of prizing and protecting human rights and liberties, are being pressured to allow gay men and lesbians to marry. Marriage is the *sine qua non* of adult human-ity. The humanists and reformers made this so. They also argued, against the demonized Roman Catholics of their day, that marriage is not principally about procreation, nor avoidance of lust, but about companionship, conversation and comradeship. In many reformed countries, England excepted, marriage fell out of church jurisdiction altogether and became entirely a civil affair. Some early modern radicals, mostly women, argued that marriage should also be about equality, that women and men were more the same than was usually allowed. Had they prevailed in this thinking, mar-riage would gradually have come to be even more like homonor-mative classical friendship than it has, but Pauline doctrines about women as the weaker vessel always trumped the friendship doc-trine before it could be taken too far.

Today, Western societies find themselves face-to-face with the contradictions and hitherto unacknowledged problematics involved with reinventing marriage as a friendship and insisting that mar-riage supersede friendship as the most human of all relations. These ambiguities and contradictions are now playing themselves out rather flagrantly in the United States. As I write this, 38 states in the United States have laws against recognizing same-sex marriages or civil unions as legal contracts, yet almost all of these laws are likely to be struck down as unconstitutional. In Vermont, the only state so far to create by law a special kind of same-sex union called a civil union, the first sentence of the statute enacting civil unions echoes the federal Defense of Marriage Act: "Civil marriage under Vermont's marriage statutes consists of a union between a man and a woman."[2] The act maintains a thin but prominent wall between homonormativity and heteronormativity. With every marriage license issued to same-sex couples by the Commonwealth of Massachusetts, another stone is torn from that wall.

I once saw a brief television interview with a man in the street who said that when gay men or lesbians in San Francisco or New Paltz, New York, marry, his heterosexual marriage is affected. Pressed by the interviewer to explain, he could not say just how it was affected, but he felt that it somehow was lessened or demeaned. I agree with him that same-sex marriage, finally emerging into the open, changes his own marriage. For better or for worse (mostly for better, I think), it is a change implied but denied in the early modern effort to rethink marriage as a friendship. Simply put, if marriage is a friendship, and marriage displaces friendship as the defining relationship of human society, then it only makes sense that friends will want to marry each other.[3] What appears as a kind of joke in Shakespeare and Fletcher's *Two Noble Kinsmen* has now finally become a serious inevitability. If marriage is only incidentally about procreation and not constitutively about sex, then sexual difference cannot be held to be a defining factor. Maybe this is the most important reason why Enlightenment and modern state constitutions do not stipulate sexual difference as crucial to marriage.

This book begins from a fairly straightforward observation: that John Milton devoted himself to one of the broadest Puritan efforts to transform social and cultural practice — the supersession of friendship by marriage as the most fundamental and most human of human relations, and that the failures and successes of that supersessionist project leave significant traces throughout Milton's work, traces that help us to understand the major poems in important new ways.

Most humanist authors suppressed the problems attendant upon redefining a heteroerotic relation using insistently homoerotic models. They tried to ignore these problems or invent work-arounds. My introduction lays out the difficulties, acknowledged and ignored, faced by this humanist project. Chapter 1 summarizes versions of the project from Erasmus, Luther, Calvin, the official Church of England homilies, and Edward Tilney's *Flower of Friendship*. Chapter 1 also presents a reading of Shakespeare's *Comedy of Errors* as an example of a comic treatment of the peculiar difficulties encountered by treating marriage as a friendship. That so many comedies poked fun at the project shows how pervasive an effort it was. It also demonstrates that problems like applying classical notions of self-identity and likeness across gender difference, translating the Bible's "one flesh" into friendship's "one soul," and trying to work around the principle of equality, could surface as jokes on the early modern stage, even as more serious writers tried to suppress or ignore them altogether.

Milton's work, especially the divorce tracts and the major poems, can very profitably be read as major documents in this struggle for redefinition and supersession. That reading, including several minor poems and letters, is the chief project of this book. Chapter 2 explicates and explores the problems of Milton's doctrine of marriage in the divorce tracts as "fit conversation" and produces a fresh reading of *Epitaphium Damonis* and several sonnets and elegies. It also challenges previous understandings of Milton's friendship and correspondence with Charles Diodati, whose death *Epitaphium Damonis* laments. Understanding their letters, sonnets and friendship in the light of classical and pastoral doctrines of friendship proves far more useful than thinking of them as protomodern homosexuals or schoolboy lovers.

Chapters 3 and 4 focus on *Paradise Lost* and its representations of both homoerotic and heteroerotic conversations. Here we can

see Milton's successes and, even more interesting, failures at trying to reimagine the first marriage as a classical friendship like those
celebrated by Plato and detailed by Aristotle and Cicero. Milton
intends to promote marriage as a friendship, but denies the relationship the mutual equality friendship doctrine requires. In-
advertently, I think, the poem depicts marriage, God's remedy for
Adam's loneliness, as just as much a barrier to as an icon of lost
Paradise. Conversations with God, with Raphael, and with Eve, all
become trapped in a Ciceronian elegiac version of friendship as
irrecoverable loss.

Chapter 5 re-reads Milton's Samson as a hero of and by divorce.
Milton offers a Samson who is insistently Hebrew, not Hellenized
as was usual, and insistently married, even though the Scripture
account says nothing of that. Milton uses Samson to imagine a pre-
Christian, old covenant attempt to reclaim the manly liberty lost
when Adam shamefully submitted to his fallen wife. Samson ulti-
mately fails, but he did one thing Adam could not manage: he
divorced an unfit wife. Finally, I reinterpret the temptation of the
Son in *Paradise Regain'd* as two forms of a classical pederastic temptation. Satan tempts the Son to take him on either as his philerast,
his beloved, or his pederast, his lover. In this way Milton completes
the demonization of Athenian homoerotics even as he presents the
Son as free of Adam's "single imperfection" — the need for a partner in conversation, male or female. Paradoxically (and unsatis-
factorily), Milton imagines that the Son restores a paradise of
manly dignity by demonstrating he has no need of any partner
aside from God his father, and so he restores humanity by doing
away with its chief defining trait — the need for a fit partner in
conversation.

Acknowledgments

This book owes many debts. I can acknowledge here only those I can remember; I know there are others I have forgotten or of which I have yet to become aware. Barbara K. Lewalski introduced me to Milton studies quite a long time ago, and since then I have wanted to write a book on Milton. I am certain that she will not endorse everything I say in this book, but I am just as certain that if I had never been her student this book would not exist. She remains a model for me of a teacher and a scholar. With deep gratitude for her inspiration and example, I dedicate this book to her.

Bits and pieces of this book have been presented in papers before Milton societies, both American and international, at the annual Modern Language Association conventions in Chicago (1995) and Philadelphia (2004) and at the International Symposiums held in Bangor, Wales (1995); York, England (1999); Beaufort, South Carolina (2002) and Grenoble, France (2005). At those events I particularly recall getting helpful advice from Stephen Fallon, Sharon Achinstein, Shari Zimmerman, Nigel Smith and Barbara Lewalski. The British Milton Seminar, hosted in Birmingham by Tom Corns, heard and commented upon an early version of chapter 3 in 1998, as did a group at Liverpool John Moore University that included Tamsin Spargo and Matthew Jordan. My early ideas about Milton and Plato's *Symposium* were helped along by the comments of scholars from the University of Strathclyde in 1998 and Dundee in 2000. I also benefited from reactions and suggestions from members of the UCLA Center for Medieval and Renaissance Studies in 2001. Chapter 4 first appeared in *Milton Studies* 40 (2001), after benefiting from suggestions made by William Hunter.

Jeffrey Shoulson, Len Tennenhouse, Linda Gregerson, Vera Camden, Peter Saccio, Elizabeth Sauer, Ivy Schweitzer and Jonathan Crewe have read large chunks of this book in early drafts and have contributed both ideas and notes of caution. Rachel Trubowitz read the whole book, parts of it more than once, and made many important suggestions, all of which I have adopted. An anonymous reader for the press saved me from an embarrassing error in prelapsarian chronology. For all of these and for the constructive ways Miltonists in general mix friendship and scholarship, I am deeply grateful. The errors that remain signify either my inattention or stubbornness.

I am grateful to the staff at the Baker/Berry Library and the Rauner Special Collections Library at Dartmouth College, and for those at the library of the University of Glasgow and Trinity College, Cambridge. The stunning collection of early Milton editions at Dartmouth prompted me to prepare the online edition of Milton's poetry that appears in *The Milton Reading Room*. Kathy Meyer did a fine job of editing.

Finally, I owe thanks to my family — Isaac Luxon, Bekah Schweitzer and, most of all, Ivy Schweitzer, my spouse and friend and colleague. They have tolerated this grouchy scholar and they have offered unrelenting support each and every day.

Introduction

But Man by number is to manifest
His single imperfection, and beget
Like of his like, his Image multipli'd,
In unitie defective, which requires
Collateral love, and deerest amitie.

(*Paradise Lost* 8.422–26)

Protestant Christianity, especially the brand we now call puritanism, both absorbed and reacted against the new humanism of the Renaissance. The same humanist principle that resurrected Plato's *Symposium* — return *ad fontes* — led Protestants to insist that according to Genesis the first human pair was a man and a wife, not a man and his friend, and that the original of human relations, therefore, must be heterosexual marriage, not homoerotic pederasty or amity. A society godly enough to welcome the Messiah's return and the reestablishment of human nature as God originally created it would, they believed, be a polis built upon heteroerotic marriage, not homoerotic friendship. Homoerotic friendship, once celebrated by urbane European humanists and poets, gradually suffered a Reformation devaluation as something puerile, an adolescent phase preparatory to adult marriage. Often it was also demonized as unfruitful sodomy. Plato's notion that the offspring born of homoerotic higher love must be more nearly immortal than children born of heteroerotic marriage survives in Milton's humanist texts, but beginning with the divorce tracts a new Miltonic project emerges — the effort to redefine heteroerotic marriage using the

1

terms and principles of classical friendship, and then to promote this newly dignified version of marriage as the originary human relation and, therefore, the bedrock of social and political culture in Protestant Christendom.

This supersession of friendship by marriage took time and involved many contradictions and negotiations, some explicit but most not. Milton was as dedicated to the classical principle of homonormativity ("Like of his Like, his Image multiplied") as he was to the emergent hegemony of heterosexual marriage in Protestant culture.[1] My purpose here is to pay close attention to these negotiations as they emerge in Milton's work, especially in his major poems. Reading Milton in light of this cultural negotiation exposes a strongly argued theme running through all his major poems, *Paradise Lost, Paradise Regain'd* and *Samson Agonistes*. Milton's Adam loses his originary manly liberty when he chooses to preserve his marriage at the cost of losing intimate conversation with heavenly beings and God; Milton's Samson begins the process of a manly recovery when he divorces his wife and resumes an intimacy, however vague, with God; Milton's Son of God fully recovers the manliness that draws strength from solitude and emerges alone but not lonely, a man who has transformed the "single imperfection" of loneliness into the site of recovered manliness, liberty and godliness. Milton argued, perhaps more strenuously than any other in his day, that marriage should be principally a friendship, and he did more than anyone else to rearticulate marriage according to the terms and theories of classical friendship doctrine, but in the end marriage in Milton's poems remains an epic obstacle rather than a locus of epic return or recovery. Milton's marriage theories finally fail to do the work he imagines for them because Milton withholds from his marriage theories the linchpin of classical and humanist friendship doctrine — equality.

Most of what passes for modern notions of friendship and marriage emerges from this period of cultural negotiation, with Milton as a chief negotiator. For Milton, it was not immediately obvious that marriage should be principally a friendship, "one soul in bodies twain" rather than two made "one flesh."[2] It was very hard for Puritanism, already overcommitted to the Pauline binary of flesh and spirit, to spiritualize a relation long considered very earthly and fleshly, and degrade a relation the ancients believed to be the most spiritual and truly human. Like the larger religious supersessions of Christianity over Judaism and Protestantism over Roman Catholicism, the emergent discourses and doctrines of companionate marriage borrow the vocabulary and values of classical friendship doctrines even as they claim to be reforming them root and branch. Milton, like many authors of his day, tried to reimagine marriage as friendship, even though this required radical revisions of friendship doctrine and, sometimes, a radical hermeneutics that reads Scripture against itself. This effort also ran a very high risk of introducing notions of sex and gender equality into marriage doctrine, and of appearing to value bodies, especially those of women and children, far more than could be supported by even the most creative readings of Pauline scriptures.

It is important to examine how we came to think of marriage and friendship as we do today. My purpose in tracing the history of these ideas is somewhat different from that pursued by traditional intellectual history. Traditional intellectual history attempts to teach us how to think correctly about the origins of our modern notions. It reminds us repeatedly of how different and distant the past is and upbraids us for projecting present concerns upon the past. I am far more interested in showing how modern notions came to be constructed as they are, than in trying to establish a single correct reading of the past. There will always be more than one reading of the past and each will always focus on concerns rooted very much in the present. Not only is there no way to see the past without reshaping it through present concerns, I believe those present concerns are what produce whatever counts as the past to begin with. Those concerns shape our questions about the past and determine in part what we can or cannot see there. I will be focusing not only on Milton's attempt to harness classical friendship theory to the task of reforming heterosexual Christian marriage, but also on what ideas and contradictions he and his contemporaries ignored or suppressed in the process. What problems remain unarticulated; what questions go unasked?

It may shock many to learn how much modern notions of marriage owe to Athenian doctrines of pederasty. It may comfort some to learn that heterosexual marriage has been regarded as the most fundamental human relationship for only a relatively short time. Neither feminists nor evangelicals will be overjoyed to learn how much equalist feminism owes to puritan formulations of companionate marriage. We need help remembering that the story of what was always so, or what is eternally true, is a story we human beings have always made up as we go along, and then projected onto our past as the "just-so story" of original truth. A little historical reflection exposes the constructedness of those stories and may allow us a glimpse of what those constructions hide, forget, submerge, ignore and transform. This is especially true of the early modern period, whose written record offers so many startling examples of emergent modern notions still hobbling around on what appear to us as ill-developed legs, notions that have come to appear natural only after centuries of practice at regarding them so. I also hope that the more we understand about how we tell ourselves the stories of what is true, the more we may tell better, more helpful, less harmful and more inclusive stories.

In Plato's *Symposium*, Pausanias advances an elaborate apologetic for Athenian pederasty based on "genuine friendship" between a man and a youth.[3] This relationship served as the bedrock of the polis. When formed for the correct reasons such partnerships would last a lifetime and the two would live together in love and dignity. Later in the dialogue Socrates advances an even more glorified version of homoerotic relations, imagining that when young men reach early adulthood, they are pregnant in their souls and long for a beautiful partner with whom to give birth to immortal offspring:

> And should he happen upon someone who has a beautiful, well-bred, and naturally gifted soul as well, he embraces the combination with

great enthusiasm and immediately engages in many conversations with this man about virtue, about what a good man should be like, and what he should make it his business to do; . . . When he attaches himself to someone beautiful, I believe, and associates with him, he gives birth and brings forth what he was pregnant with before, both while in that person's presence and while remembering him when he's absent. Together with him he nurtures the offspring produced, so that such men have much more to share with each other and a stronger friendship than that which comes from rearing children, since they share in the rearing of children who are more beautiful and immortal. (*Symposium,* 209b–c)

Aristotle places his discussion of friendship at the very center of his *Nicomachean Ethics.* He objects strongly to the inequalities of Athenian pederasty, insisting that the most virtuous friendships are those between equals, two men who share the same things with each other and are as similar as possible, each another self to his friend and "nothing," says Aristotle, "is as proper to friends as living together" and sharing all things equally.[4] I cite these three examples, which could be matched by scores of others from classical and Renaissance humanist authors, simply as an antidote to the modern, commonplace conviction that heterosexual marriage is the most natural human relation there is. Today many gay men and lesbian women want to enjoy the benefits and dignity our society confers upon marriage, but there was a time when homoerotic friendships were considered far more dignified, and far more typically human, than marriage. Plato's Socrates argued that friends produced immortal offspring — laws, societies, poems, philosophy, art and music; marriages produced only children.

Gendering Friendship and Marriage

In 1990 Louise Schleiner recommended that we reconsider Milton's marital ideal as an effort to adapt a homoerotic model — traditional male friendship — to a heteroerotic relation — Edenic marriage:

> Milton's accomplishment was a paradise of marital friendship that
> yet retained certain gender polarities; his writing strategy had been
> to exclude, to satanize courtly love (for centuries a primary literary
> means of construing male-female mutuality) and to write women
> into his own reconstituted textual system of the pastoral mode —
> reconstituted earlier in his career as a sustaining "space" of male
> friendship and sociability.[5]

Schleiner, building on Janet Halley's "Female Autonomy in Milton's Sexual Poetics," divides Milton's pastoral imaginary into
two periods, early and late.[6] Halley argues that the early pastoral
mode of *L'Allegro, Lycidas,* "*Epitaphium Damonis,*" and "*Elegy
VI*" is marked by a strenuous effort to banish the female figure from
"a homosocial sexual poetics" (Halley, 238), but that *Paradise Lost*
insists "on the incorporation of woman into its picture of social
and poetic harmony," constructing "a sexual poetics that can
accommodate rather than eliminate the female subject" (Halley,
243). Schleiner points out how much the "preveniently male intimacy" of Milton's early pastoral imaginary owes to classical discourses of friendship, and she appreciates the remarkable effort
entailed in trying to "write women" into this imaginary (Schleiner,
46). Halley concluded that Milton accommodated the female subject by subsuming it into male intention (Halley, 246), but Schleiner
wants to argue instead that "Milton's epic experimentally incorporates femaleness into a formerly and still pervasively male 'space'
of sociability" (Schleiner, 42).

One might be forgiven for not immediately appreciating the
distance between "incorporating the female voice and will only by
subsuming them in male intention" (Halley, 246) and incorporating femaleness into a social space "still pervasively male" (Schleiner,
42). Both formulations, however, point up the strains Milton
exerted in trying to bring the dignity of male homoerotic friendship doctrine to his reimagination of marriage without either rendering woman an honorary man or bestowing upon her the full
equality and dignity of complete humanity. Eve's version of her own
first experience with her reflection underscores her (and Milton's)

sense of the natural power of homonormative erotics. It takes the voice of God and the gently coercive hand of Adam to convince her that heteroerotics is even more natural than nature. (*PL* 4.449–91)

The predominant model in classical culture for human relationship was friendship. Every other relationship worthy of being dignified with the term "human" derived that dignity from its resemblance to this quintessentially human relation. Only very rarely in classical literature are married persons allowed to qualify as friends. Alcestis in Phaedrus's *Symposium* speech (179c) supplies the exception that proves the rule in Plato, and though Aristotle, in his *Nicomachean Ethics,* defines marriage in opposition to the more perfect "friendship of virtue," he allows that some marriages between particularly "decent" people — most likely older couples whose concerns for childbearing and sexual pleasure no longer predominate — "may also be a friendship for virtue" (*Nicomachean Ethics,* 1162a25). Neither Plato nor Aristotle pronounces women constitutionally unqualified for friendship; if they were considered so then wives could never form friendships, not even rarely, with their husbands. A wife does not fall short of perfect friendship simply because she is a woman, but because the husband-wife *relationship* is different from the "friendship of virtue." When the relations between husband and wife rise above concerns for pleasure and utility and focus clearly on each other's virtues, their relationship, Aristotle allows, may rise to the level of friendship. When this happens their friendship is something altogether apart from, and more dignifiedly human, than marriage. Classically speaking, marriage is a less dignified and less specifically human relation than friendship, but some particularly decent spouses might also qualify as friends.

Christianity, especially Protestant Christianity, understands Genesis as, among other things, the story of the first human relationship. According to Genesis 2, the first human relationship, established by God in Paradise, was heterosexual marriage. Moreover, Protestants like Milton, and those he refers to as "our authors," wanted to claim that marriage was originally established, like classical friendship, for reasons more dignified than childbearing (Aristotle's utility) and sexual pleasure. This is why, I believe, Protestant humanists tried to reimagine marriage as a friendship; friendship doctrine promised to restore a level of dignity to an institution that had suffered both derogation and mystification in the medieval Catholic Church. Genesis says God addressed Adam's loneliness by giving him a wife with whom he became "one flesh" (Gen. 2:24); classical philosophy taught that the most quintessentially human relation above family and marriage was friendship, in which two people saw each other as "another self" and loved each other as they loved themselves, sharing "one soul" in two bodies. The question arises then: what is more quintessentially human — to be "one flesh" with a woman or to share "one soul" with a fellow man? I put this question deliberately from a masculine perspective because that is precisely how it was put by thinkers and authors in the Renaissance.

Gregory Chaplin argues that "Milton's theory of marriage . . . represents the fusion of two discourses; Christian marriage, as modified by reformed theologians and humanist scholars, and Renaissance friendship — the practice of classical friendship revived by humanist educators and the dissemination of classical texts."[7] I will argue that this fusion never succeeded and that Milton's attempt to reimagine marriage as a heteroerotic version of the classical homoerotic ideal resulted instead in a very uneasy and temporizing supersession of friendship by marriage. Chaplin's attention to classical and Renaissance friendship doctrine allows him to understand Milton's relationship to Charles Diodati better than any other literary historian to date.[8] Milton and Diodati quite self-consciously modeled their friendship on the classical examples Spenser cites in the *Faerie Queene*'s "Legend of Friendship," men who loved each other with a chaste desire, all the more erotic for its commitment to sexual purity:

> But farre away from these, another sort
> Of louers lincked in true harts consent;

> Which loued not as these, for like intent,
> But on chast vertue grounded their desire,
> Farre from all fraud, or fayned blandishment;
> Which in their spirits kindling zealous fire,
> Braue thoughts and noble deedes did euermore aspire.
>
> Such were great *Hercules*, and *Hylas* deare;
> Trew *Ionathan*, and *Dauid* trustie tryde;
> Stout *Theseus*, and *Pirithous* his feare;
> *Pylades* and *Orestes* by his syde;
> Myld *Titus* and *Gesippus* without pryde;
> *Damon* and *Pythias* whom death could not seuer;
> All these and all that euer had bene tyde,
> In bands of friendship, there did liue for euer,
> Whose liues although decay'd, yet loues decayed neuer.

Spenser's Sir Scudamore follows a heteroerotic quest for Amoret, but even as he does, he envies these heroes of friendship their purer, less complicated, "homegeneal" relationships:

> I thought there was none other heauen then this;
> And gan their endlesse happinesse enuye,
> That being free from feare and gealosye,
> Might frankely there their loues desire possesse;
> Whilest I through paines and perlous ieopardie,
> Was forst to seeke my lifes deare patronesse.[9]

Chaplin regards Spenser's poem as presenting heterosexual marriage and homosocial friendship as two equal choices in a hero's life: "either relationship can be the gateway to this 'second paradise'" (Chaplin, 268). Laurie Shannon also calls our attention to the degree to which early modern authors regarded friendship and marriage as "competing normativities":

> Running athwart of the heterosexual organization of love and marriage, the powerfully homo-normative bias in Renaissance thought favors both self-likeness (constancy) and same-sex affects. Insofar as diverse logics rendering disparate phenomena "normal" can coincide, given cultural moments contain competing "normativities."[10]

Homosocial, even homoerotic, friendship certainly enjoyed in Spenser's day a reputation that rivaled marriage, but even then it was losing its competitive edge. The legend of Cambel and Telamond, though enjoying a central place in Spenser's great allegorical epic, absorbs neither the poet nor his readers as much as the legends of Redcrosse, Guyon, Britomart, Artegal and Calidore, all heroes on a heteroerotic trajectory. Competition is not the only, or even the best, way to think about the early modern discourses of marriage and friendship. Only as marriage began to be promoted as principally about friendship rather than just procreation and avoidance of sin, does something like a competition emerge. Once marriage, newly redefined as a friendship, displaces classical friendship, a heteroerotic normativity comes to supersede and then demonize what was once a homoerotic normativity. But of course, this oversimplifies the story.

In the 1580s Michel de Montaigne placed his essay on friendship near the center of his *Essais,* just as he regarded male friendship as the most centrally human aspect of his life. Montaigne finds all other relations — fathers and sons, brothers, lovers, and spouses — wanting in the spirituality and truly human dignity compared to friendship, but he anticipates Milton's efforts when he takes a moment to imagine what it would mean to find both spiritual and physical "jovissance" in a single relationship. Just as he concludes that women are normally not qualified for the "sacred bond" of friendship, he strays into a consideration of how fine it would be if they were sufficient:

> Seeing (to speake truely) that the ordinary sufficiencie of women, cannot answer this conference and communication, the nurse of this sacred bond: nor seeme their mindes strong enough to endure the pulling of a knot so hard, so fast, and durable. And truely, if without that, such a genuine and voluntarie acquaintance might be contracted, where not onely mindes had this entire jovissance, but also bodies, a share of the aliance, and where man might wholy be engaged: It is certaine, that friendship would thereby be more compleate and full: but this sexe could never yet by any example attaine

vnto it, and is by ancient schooles rejected thence. And this other Greeke licence is justly abhorred by our customes, which notwithstanding, because according to vse it had so necessarie a disparitie of ages, and difference of offices betweene lovers, did no more sufficiently answere the perfect vnion and agreement, which we here require. (Florio, 91–92)

A relationship in which a "man might wholly be engaged" body and soul would be a kind of paradise of jouissance. Unfortunately, concludes Montaigne, no woman is sufficient (not even exceptional women like Alcestis) for the mental part of this sacred bond, and "Greeke licence" is "justly abhorred by our customs." Montaigne objects to Athenian pederasty because it is founded upon and perpetuates inequality. His objection echoes Aristotle's in the *Nicomachean Ethics* where the philosopher stipulates that the best sort of friends "Must not be like the erotic lover and the boy he loves. For these do not take pleasure in the same things; the lover takes pleasure in seeing his beloved, while the beloved takes pleasure in being courted by his lover" (1157a6–8). Montaigne, like most Renaissance humanists, assumes that the higher love Socrates outlines in Plato's *Symposium* and the virtuous friendship Aristotle details in his *Ethics* have nothing whatever to do with the body's sensual pleasure. A man, he assumes, will either discipline bodily desires or satisfy them outside of friendship.

Spenser tried to commandeer the courtly love tradition for Protestant marriage, but Milton abandoned the courtly love model altogether. Milton wrote in the *Apology against a Pamphlet* (1642) that he learned about love from books, and he insists that he always preferred authors who linked eros to chastity. His favorite love poets from an early age were those "two famous renowners of *Beatrice* and *Laura*" because they never spoke anything "unworthy" of themselves or "unchaste of those names which before they had extoll'd."[11] "Sublime and pure thoughts, without transgression" — such was the love poetry young Milton preferred. From fables and romances, Milton learned "what a noble vertue chastity sure must be, to the defence of which so many worthies by such a deare adventure of themselves had sworne" (891). A true knight will swear to defend a virgin's chastity with his "best blood" or his life. Love's true heroes not only discipline their own bodies in restraint of sexual desire, they offer to sacrifice those disciplined bodies protecting virgins against other men's sexual desires. And if any knight in any romance ever broke his sacred promise to defend virgin chastity, if he ever succumbed to his own desire for the lady even in word, let alone deed, Milton says that even as a young man he "judg'd it the same fault of the Poet, as that which is attributed to *Homer*; to have written undecent things of the gods" (891). Any poet who might sing of a knight enjoying his lady's sexual favors was to Milton's way of thinking no better than a blasphemer.

When "riper years" led him to "the shady spaces of philosophy," Milton says he learned from Plato and Xenophon of "chastity and love" (891).[12] He learned to distinguish between true love and Circe's deadly poison. True love "begins and ends in the soule" rather than in the intoxicating pleasures of the body's appetites, and it produces by "divine generation" the "happy twins" of knowledge and virtue rather than the carnal fruits of sexual reproduction (892). Milton does not explicitly remind us, however, that the shady spaces of philosophy were explicitly homosocial spaces.

Both Plato's and Xenophon's *Symposium*s imagine men gathered together to talk about love, and the love they praise is homoerotic love. Once Plato's symposiasts agree not to drink to excess, they also agree that they can do without the flute girl as well and she is sent elsewhere to entertain the women. Eryximachus the physician draws an explicit division between the pleasures of wine and women on the one hand and the pleasures of conversation on the other: "the next thing I propose is that we dismiss the flute-girl who just came in. Let her play for herself or, if she prefers, for the women inside. We can entertain each other today with speeches" (*Symposium*, 176e). In Plato's Academy, the pleasures of conversation are pleasures shared between men. Dismissing the flute girl implies that the pleasures of academic conversation do not mix well with pleasures these men enjoy at other times. It won't quite do simply to say one type of pleasure is homoerotic and the other heteroerotic; both are strongly homoerotic. Men enjoying wine, women and song are still men enjoying these things together; though each man may take pleasure in gazing on the women, listening to the music and quaffing the wine, an even more profound pleasure arises from sharing such pleasures with other men. But speech making and academic conversation appear here as explicitly and even exclusively manly pleasures. Women not only cannot participate, their absence enables such pleasures and their presence may well hinder it. They must not go far away, as we shall see, and they really cannot be entirely absent. In one form or another — the exceptional Alcestis, the legendary Diotima, or the goddess Aphrodite — women remain significantly, maybe even necessarily, present. But for the serious conversation to get under way, Plato's men must have at least the appearance of male exclusivity.

Most of Plato's symposiasts use gender to help them distinguish between higher love and vulgar love. Pausanias takes what is probably the most traditional line when he distinguishes sharply between the heavenly and the earthly Aphrodite. The heavenly Aphrodite, he says, was "the motherless daughter of Uranus," while the earthly, vulgar, or "common" Aphrodite was produced by Zeus's extramarital passion for Dione (*Symposium,* 180d–e). Pausanias tries to ground his erotic ethics not in any particular action, in this case loving, but in the manner in which the action is performed — nobly or basely: "In actions it's the manner of the doing that determines the quality. When an action is done nobly and correctly, it becomes noble and beautiful, but if not done correctly, it becomes shameful. So, loving and Love are not in every case noble and deserving of praise, but the loving that points us in a noble direction is" (181a). A telltale difference between loving nobly and loving basely, as it turns out, has to do with the object of one's desire. Pausanias does not say that desire for women is vulgar and desire for boys is noble, but he does say that those men who "love women no less than boys" betray the carnality of their love, their overconcern with bodies rather than souls, both their own and those of their beloveds. Such men "love the most unintelligent people they can" (181b).

From what Pausanias says only two paragraphs later, we may justly suppose that he is married to a wife, so it would probably be wrong to conclude that Pausanias disapproves of what we would call heterosexuality or even bisexuality (181e–82a). The eros he describes and celebrates has nothing to do with marriage per se. For him marriage, presumably, is about fathering children, melding families, and caring properly for the body and worldly matters in general, but heavenly eros is about cultivating manly vigor and intellect, learning the only honorable way for one citizen (or protocitizen) to yield himself to another citizen's pleasure; it is about philosophy, sport, friendship and fellowship of the highest order (182b–c, 183a). All men, even the vulgar sort, marry and beget children; their love mixes male and female elements, just as the earthly Aphrodite was born of the union of Zeus and Dione. But only the noblest aristocrats form pederastic relations, though they may also have wives and children. And pederastic relations, when properly performed, are said to be purely male, springing as they do from "the heavenly Aphrodite," who "does not share in the female, but only in the male." This sort of love gravitates naturally toward male partners "cherishing what is by nature stronger and more intelligent" (181c).

Not every lover who gravitates toward boys does so in a heavenly manner, however. Some betray their earthly desires by loving boys before they begin to show intellectual promise, boys of as yet unknown quality. There should be a law, says Pausanias, to restrain such carnal lovers, just as there are laws to prevent them from preying upon "freeborn women," that is, the citizens' wives and daughters (182a). Pausanias's point is not that loving women is disgraceful or wrong. He does not say or even imply that. Rather, he insists that pederastic love is more noble, more peculiarly human and civilized than earthly love, that pederastic love must not be confused with earthly love, and that those who pursue pederastic love in the same manner as earthly lovers behave unethically and should be restrained. He also strongly implies that one way to know when pederastic relations are tainted with earthly desire is when they betray signs of the feminine, when the love object might just as well be a woman or a girl, when a lover does not really care about the difference. Higher love cares for the beloved's budding intellect and emerging virtue; to pursue a boy who does not yet show any such signs is to confuse the noble love of youths with a man's desire for women. Such confusion deserves blame.

It never occurs to Pausanias that one might form a pederastic relation with a woman, even one's wife. Presumably women's intellects never bud forth as those of young men, and whatever virtue they may possess does not merit the careful and deliberate cultivation promised by pederastic discipline.

Aristophanes's account of love is different, but not radically so. His just-so story about the original three sexes and their punishment by bisection for overweening ambition appears at first to locate the origins of human desire very much in the body. But it seems that some bodily desires are more elevated than others, and Aristophanes reserves his highest praises for a man's desire for a man. He ranks even his legendary original beings on a gender hierarchy: "The male was originally a progeny of the sun, the female of the earth, and the one that had a share in both was a progeny of the moon, since the moon also has a share in both" (190b). Aristophanes's story imagines three sexes, but only two genders — pure male, pure female, and mixed. The first hierarchy — sun, moon, earth — ranks male first and female last, with the mixed man-woman, or hermaphrodite, in between, but as Aristophanes goes on to describe how these origins account for the different kinds of erotic desire known among human beings, a different hierarchy emerges. This one appears to rank those lovers who were originally part of a man/woman or hermaphrodite as the least noble sort and those who were originally bisected from the hyperion males as the best. In the middle, more bracketed than actually ranked, fall the lesbian lovers:

Thus, each of us is the matching half of a human being, since we have been severed like a flatfish, two coming from one, and each part is always seeking its other half. Those men who are split from the mixed nature, which was then called "androgynous," are fond of women. Most adulterers come from this type, and those women who are fond of men and are adulteresses also come from this type. Those women who are split from a woman, however, have no interest at all in men, but rather are oriented toward women. This is the type lesbians come from. Those who are split from the male pursue males. While they are boys, since they are a slice off a male, they are fond of men and enjoy lying with men and becoming entwined with them. These are the best of the boys and young men, and at the same time are the most manly in nature. Anyone who says they are shameless is mistaken, for they do this, not from shamelessness, but from courage, manliness, and masculinity, welcoming what is like themselves. There is a definite proof of this: Only men of this sort are completely successful in the affairs of the city. When they become men, they are lovers of boys and by nature are not interested in marriage and having children, though they are forced into it by custom. (191e–192b)

Though according to Aristophanes's comic story, no man is more than half a man, some of those halves are more truly manly, virile, daring and public-spirited than others. Men who love women are best represented by adulterers, but really manly men prefer men, "welcoming what is like themselves." Aristotle, when he comes to write his discourse on friendship, will take his cue from Aristophanes and develop a whole theory of friendship based on likeness. Milton will come to regard much the same principle as fundamental to creation and metaphysics, as well as friendship.

Pausanias never mentions procreation, though he appears to assume that pederasts have wives and daughters. Aristophanes, however, addresses procreation explicitly if somewhat offhandedly. In his model of how love works among humans, procreation is more an accident than anything else. The original eight-limbed creatures who threatened to overthrow the gods did not procreate by having sex with each other. Each person had "two sets of genitals," one on each side opposite each other (190a). These beings "fathered and conceived, not in each other, but in the ground like cicadas" (191b). Presumably this means that in their ramblings across the earth, these original beings deposited gametes of one sort or another into the earth. Maybe females dropped eggs that were fertilized by randomly dropped sperm. We do not know because Aristophanes was not very concerned with procreation, which does not even figure, except accidentally, in the lives of his bisected men and women.

To be more precise, Aristophanes's story treats procreation as an accidental by-product of a bisected person's effort to find and embrace his or her original other half, but from Zeus's standpoint human reproduction by erotic means was deliberate. Zeus's punishment, bisecting the original beings, threatened humans with extinction. They yearned desperately for their other halves, longing to be reunited with them, but this erotics, according to the story, had nothing whatever to do with genitalia, since their "privy members" were located opposite their wounded side. Reuniting the bodies Zeus cut in two had nothing to do with the genitals. But Zeus later had the bright idea of linking erotics with genitalia and reproduction:

> Zeus took pity on them and came up with another good idea. He moved their genitals around to the front, for until then they had them on the back side, and they fathered and conceived, not on each other, but in the ground like cicadas. So, Zeus put their genitals around on the front side and thus made it possible for them to reproduce with each other with the male's genitals inside the female's. For this reason, whenever a male happened to encounter a female in their entwining, she would conceive and produce an offspring, and if a male encountered a male, at least they would get some satisfaction from their union and they would take a break, then return to their work and attend to the rest of life.
>
> It is from this situation, then, that love for one another developed in human beings. (191b–d)

The story's point is to show how originary (inestimably ancient) is mutual love, and it certainly sketches a theory of love that moves significantly away from Pausanias's classical pederasty. Pausanias's pederast and philerast, lover and darling, did not share a mutual love. They neither sought nor received the same things from each other. A generation later in the history of erotic theory, Aristotle will insist that such mutuality — seeking and getting the "same thing" from each other — distinguishes the best and most lasting friendships from the less durable and less noble pederastic relationships (*Nicomachean Ethics,* 1157a3–10). Aristophanes's story points toward the theories of sameness and mutuality we later find in Aristotle. Those original beings seek for another half of themselves, a lover who is the same age, once from the same body, sharing the same wound. This is likeness to the nth degree; the only mark of difference is Zeus's unkind cut, the cut that initiates difference from self-sameness and so literalizes the metaphor Aristotle and Cicero will later make famous — the other himself. Aristophanes's story even suggests that what we call heteroerotic desire is radically homoerotic, for what all beings desire is a missing part of an original self, the same piece once cut away long ago. The homoerotics of self-sameness takes priority over gender in this case, since even though the other half I desire may be female and I am male, that desire is for my other half, regardless of gender. Aristotle later will teach that friendship's roots lie in self-love (*Nicomachean Ethics,* 1166a), but Aristophanes's story grounds all erotics in the desire for a fully embodied self.

But the genitals are relatively unimportant for this embodied self. In this story carnal longing had nothing to do with sex until Zeus had the bright idea of transplanting the genitals onto the original "scar," thus linking desire for originary wholeness to copulation, reproduction and survival of the species. This story helps the symposiasts, and all erotic theorists who follow, to separate love from copulation and reproduction. This separation will be particularly important for Milton.

Milton did not care much for Aristophanes's just-so story about love. He had, of course, read Philo's and Leon Ebreo's ingenious attempts to reconcile part of Aristophanes's story with Genesis 1:27:

"So God created man in his own image, in the image of God created he him; male and female created he them." Both Philo and Ebreo suggested that perhaps the first Creation story told of the creation of a pure human being, male and female, a spiritual hermaphrodite, and Genesis 2 told the story of the creation of the earthly human being, formed from the dust, and divided by sex like Aristophanes's divided (and punished) hermaphrodite. This interpretation had the advantage not only of yoking biblical to classical stories, but also of solving the long-standing problem of Genesis's two conflicting Creation accounts.[13] But the Neoplatonists leave Aristophanes's other two sexes, all-male and all-female, entirely out of the account, as well as the homoerotics of all three types of love. Milton did not object to the Neoplatonist interpretation on that account. In his own peculiar rationalization of Plato and Genesis, he also, as we shall shortly see, suppresses the homoerotics of the *Symposium*. Milton's objection to what he sneeringly calls Jewish fables is that their interpretation would confer upon the first woman the inordinate dignity of being every bit as much an image of God as originary man. For all his high humanist education, Milton the Pauline puritan is still unwilling to take such a progressive road. He cites Paul to prove that women, even the first woman, were "not primarily and immediately the Image of God, but in reference to the Man":

> It might be doubted why he saith, *In the Image of God created he him*, not them, as well as *male and female* them; especially since that Image might be common to them both, but *male and female* could not, however the Jews fable, and please themselvs with the accidentall concurrence of *Plato's* wit, as if man at first had bin created *Hermaphrodite*: but then it must have bin male and female created he him. So had the Image of God bin equally common to them both, it had no doubt bin said, In the Image of God created he them. But *St. Paul* ends the controversie, by explaining that the Woman is not primarily and immediatly the Image of God, but in reference to the Man. *The head of the woman*, saith he, 1 *Cor.* 11. *is the man: he the image and glory of God, she the glory of the man:* he not for her, but she for him. Therefore his precept is, *Wives be subject to*

your husbands as is fit in the Lord, Coloss. 3. 18. In every thing, Eph.
5. 24. (Tetrachordon, YP 2:589)

And, of course, the Pauline misogyny upon which Milton grounds his argument is truer to the implicit misogyny of Plato's *Symposium* than either Philo's or Ebreo's redaction of Plato.

When Milton insists in his *Doctrine and Discipline of Divorce* that the chief end God intended in marriage was "the apt and cheerfull conversation of man with woman," he seeks to draw much the same division as Plato's symposiasts drew in their various ways between the satisfaction of carnal appetites and attention to intellectual and spiritual hunger (YP 2:235). He also implies that a woman — a wife — must have a place in the symposium, the conversation. Like Alcibiades she will be a latecomer, and like Alcibiades in his cups and besotted with desire for Socrates, her devotion to the carnal side of life will disrupt, for at least a moment, the shady groves of the Edenic Academy. Next to Adam's Socratic manliness and self-control (*Symposium*, 219d) she will feel much the same shame and humiliation the beribboned Alcibiades confesses to, but eventually she will learn, as Milton's Eve says she learned, to value inward beauty over outward charms, and the pleasures of conversation over the pleasures of the flesh:

> thy gentle hand
> Seisd mine, I yielded, and from that time see
> How beauty is excelld by manly grace
> And wisdom, which alone is truly fair.   (*Paradise Lost* 4.488–91)

The notion of rewriting the codes of classical friendship, even in its Renaissance pastoral forms, into a theory of marriage was not, as Schleiner implies, uniquely Milton's. I wish to show that throughout the sixteenth and early seventeenth centuries humanists of many stripes wrestled with the uncanny ways the doctrines of classical friendship echoed those of Christian marriage and vice versa. One doctrine had its roots in Plato, Aristotle, Xenophon, and its branches in Cicero and Plutarch — friends share one soul in bodies twain.

The other sprang from Genesis 2:24: "Therefore shall a man leave his father and his mother, and shall cleave unto his wife: and they shall be one flesh." One soul or one flesh — two radically different ways of imagining how two become one, yet in the project of installing heterosexual marriage at the center of human life, superseding and eventually demonizing homoerotic friendship, these two imaginary modes commingle quite fruitfully.

One

Classical Friendship and Humanist Marriage

Our laws of civil marriage do not privilege procreative heterosexual intercourse between married people above every other form of adult intimacy and every other means of creating a family . . . Fertility is not a condition of marriage, nor is it grounds for divorce. People who have never consummated their marriage, and never plan to, may be and stay married. . . . People who cannot stir from their deathbed may marry. . . . While it is certainly true that many, perhaps most, married couples have children together (assisted or unassisted), it is the exclusive and permanent commitment of the marriage partners to one another, not the begetting of children, that is the sine qua non of civil marriage.
— Justice C. J. Marshall, for the Supreme Judicial Court of Massachusetts, in *Goodridge et al. v. Department of Public Health et al.,* November 18, 2003

The doctrine of civil marriage that Justice Marshall articulates in the passage above has its intellectual roots in Renaissance and Reformation humanism. It has taken a long time to emerge and is still far from universally accepted. Justice Marshall spelled this out at some length in direct response to the Superior Court's earlier claim that "the state's interest in regulating marriage is based on the traditional concept that marriage's primary purpose is procreation." Roman Catholic marriage doctrine apparently survives on the bench in Massachusetts Superior court, and although Justice Marshall's more puritan doctrine has overturned the Superior Court's decision, federal courts and constitutional amendments could change all that in the future. Exactly what constitutes a marriage has never really been settled, even in law. Milton was a major player in the last widespread debate about what marriage truly is.[1]

The project of rethinking marriage with the theory, doctrines and terminology of classical friendship was underway long before Milton (motivated partly by personal concerns) joined the effort. Humanists like Erasmus, Protestants like Calvin and Luther, authors of conduct books and preachers, even popular playwrights like Shakespeare, participated in the discourse. Shakespeare's comedies provide particularly telling examples because in their characters' comic banter we can see that many of the knotty contradictions attendant upon rethinking heterosexual marriage within the doctrines and terms of homoerotic friendship were readily apparent to popular audiences some time before Milton set to work. The comedies simultaneously embrace and poke fun at the humanist project. Part of the humor is, of course, political satire aimed indirectly at the cluster of anxieties prompted by Queen Elizabeth's marriage plans around the time Shakespeare was born. The prospect of an English queen submitting in marriage to a foreign king was only slightly more frightening than the prospect of an English gentleman submitting in marriage to a royal wife. Elizabeth's "bizarre" proposal that her cousin Queen Mary of Scotland marry her own favorite, Robert Dudley, and come to England "to be conversant with her, Elizabeth, in this realm, and live with her" may well have been modeled on classical notions of amity.[2] As Elizabeth put the matter in her instructions to her ministers: "Nothing can more conserve the amity betwixt these two nations [England and Scotland] than that she [Mary] may marry with one of this nation. Seeing they two [Elizabeth and Mary] cannot be joined in marriage, the second degree to make them and their realms happy is that Mary marry him whom Elizabeth favours and loves as her brother."[3] All of the unresolved tensions and implicit contradictions involved in regarding marriage as a friendship were thrown into sharp relief as these two queens managed and mismanaged their marriages and non-marriages and pseudomarriages (including the startling proposal that they, in effect, share a household that would include the newly elevated Earl of Leicester as both quasi-brother and spouse) before a sometimes frightened and sometimes bemused public. By the time Shakespeare composed and performed his comedies, such tensions provided good grist for his sardonic humor.

This chapter will locate the marriage-as-friendship effort as a humanist project and then consider some of the ways this project appeared alternatively attractive, problematic, and sometimes ridiculous in Shakespeare's *Comedy of Errors,* which suits my purposes because it is early. It so clearly models itself on classical sources and, like the example of the two British queens, it plays humorously with issues of siblings, friends and spouses. Whether Milton ever saw the play performed is not really important. My point is that these issues were in the air already in the late sixteenth century and had been around long enough to take humorous shapes.

Shakespeare's comedies often appear to promote heterosexual marriage as the quintessential comic remedy for, or harmonic resolution of, whatever chaotic topsy-turvydom the world may dish out. This has been repeated so often that it is by now accepted orthodoxy. Not everyone, however, is prepared to agree that all of the comedies fully resolve or contain every disturbance or threatened subversion with marriage. Stephen Orgel demurs: "We are always told that the comedies end in marriages, and that this is normative. A few of Shakespeare's do, but the much more characteristic Shakespearean conclusion comes just before marriage, and sometimes, as in *Love's Labour's Lost* and *Twelfth Night,* with an entirely unexpected delay or postponement."[4] Laurie Shannon points out that *Two Noble Kinsmen*'s Emilia openly prefers homosocial friendship to marriage (*Sovereign Amity*, 112–22). She also marshals and interprets a range of evidence to support her argument that Renaissance articulations of nature as fundamentally homonormative and homoerotically inclined made single-sex friendship look more "natural," and certainly more distinctly human, to early modern humanists. She concludes that many Elizabethan comedies, including Shakespeare's, often "seem to take marriage itself as the thing that warrants explanation and accounting, rather than same-sex affects or connection. The ideological work of much comedy, then, is less to celebrate or to critique marriage . . . than to find a means to make it plausible or even thinkable in parity terms" ("Nature's Bias," 187).

For example, when Olivia in *Twelfth Night* finds herself smitten with Viola disguised as the young male Cesario, her desire follows several natural biases that also, from other perspectives, may count as unnatural. The natural attraction of like for like makes Olivia more attracted to Cesario's feminine qualities than to Orsino's overt manliness; the natural attraction of a sister for a brother registers another kind of sameness even as it raises the specter of unnatural conjunction. Perhaps Olivia senses Viola's grief for a lost sibling, a brother for whom she performs an elegiac impersonation, and this likeness draws on Olivia's affection. That, of course, is a likeness with a difference, for it is one thing to pine for a lost brother in suits of solemn woe (as Olivia does), and quite another to pretend to be him, or someone like him (as Viola does). Neither performance counts as altogether natural. Do these sisters love their brothers as they would love a sister, blood drawn to like blood? Or is their love heteroerotic across gender difference, or perversely heteroerotic in another way, across the boundary between the living and the dead? When is it right for such love to die, to submit to the attenuation caused by a gulf of difference? Nature's bias tends toward likeness and away from difference, but Shakespeare's play delights in reminding us that every likeness hobbles, and not every difference is naturally repellent.[5] Olivia mistook a woman for a young man, but her affections for Viola were not unnatural even though being "contracted to a maid" might evoke something considered highly so.

Even in *Paradise Lost* — a poem I argue engages energetically in the task of articulating the supersession of homonormative friendship by compulsory heteronormative marriage — both "competing normativities" are present, and both are crucial to Milton's imagination of Nature's origins in Creation:

> on the watrie calme
> His brooding wings the Spirit of God outspred,
> And vital vertue infus'd, and vital warmth
> Throughout the fluid Mass, but downward purg'd
> The black tartareous cold Infernal dregs
> Adverse to life: then founded, then conglob'd
> Like things to like, the rest to several place
> Disparted.   (*Paradise Lost* 7.234–41)

Milton imagines a Creation that is as much a product of the natural pairing of "Like things to like" as of the more obviously heteroerotic infusion of spiritual "vertue" into a material "fluid Mass." Nature in the seventeenth century had not yet been fully enlisted as an enforcer of compulsory heteroerotics, though I will argue that Milton played a large part in recruiting her for precisely that task. I will argue elsewhere that Milton's efforts to reimagine nature as principally heteroerotic succeed only partially. In his poetry, homonormativity and heteronormativity compete very seriously, but in Shakespeare's plays the competition is more playful and sometimes ranges more broadly without reaching, or even aiming for, a dogmatic conclusion. It will be useful, then, to attend to some of the ways this competition, very much alive in Reformation discourses of marriage and friendship, is performed in some of Shakespeare's plays.

Some of Shakespeare's comedies entertain audiences by satirizing the competing, oddly similar and often contradictory "normativities" of friendship and marriage.[6] Both discourses claim to make one out of two: in friendship two persons are said to share a single soul, and in marriage two persons are said to be made one flesh. By Shakespeare's day classical friendship had long been regarded as the most dignified and manly sort of human relation. Erasmus, Lyly, Lodge, Elyot, Sidney and Spenser all articulate what Shannon refers to as "the powerfully homo-normative bias in Renaissance thought" (*Sovereign Amity*, 55).[7] Following the classical tradition forged by Plato, Aristotle, Cicero and Plutarch, Montaigne calls friendship "the utmost drift" in the perfection of "societie," and asserts that "There is nothing to which Nature hath more addressed us than to societie" (Florio, 90). All other human relations, especially kinship relations, he regarded as "so much the less faire and generous, and so much the lesse true amities, in that they intermeddle other causes, scope, and fruite with friendship, then it selfe alone" (Florio, 90).

Other humanists and Protestant reformers, however, labored hard to recover wedded bliss from the antimarriage and misogynist discourses popular in late medieval Catholic Europe. Often this meant rearticulating marriage using the nomenclature of classical friendship theory. Protestants and Puritans read Genesis quite literally as the story of the first man and the first woman enjoying (and then spoiling) the first human relationship. According to this logic the only remedy for human loneliness explicitly approved, even instituted, by God is heterosexual marriage. Although reformers demoted marriage from its status as a Catholic sacrament, many of them energetically promoted it as proper for everyone, even (or especially) clergymen.[8]

Medieval Catholic antimarriage attitudes rooted themselves in Paul's apparent preference for pious abstention from women and the world: "It is good for a man not to touch a woman" (1 Cor. 7:1). When he advised the Corinthians, in an implicitly androcentric manner, "if they cannot contain, let them marry: for it is better to marry than to burn," he left the distinct impression that marriage is a second-best concession to postlapsarian lust — allowed, but hardly recommended, to those who cannot otherwise discipline their carnal desires. Catholic clergy and religious were therefore required to refrain from marriage, living in the world but distanced from it; they were to regard themselves as already married to Christ. Marriage to Christ, Catholic doctrine taught, would survive into the next world; heterosexual marriage would not.[9]

Protestants and humanist Catholics alike worked hard to shift this doctrine, teaching that marriage is proper and necessary for most men and virtually all women; only an exceptional few can successfully "contain" lust without it. When John Calvin paraphrases Adam's first recorded speech from Genesis 2:23 — "This is now bone of my bones, and flesh of my flesh: she shall be called Woman, because she was taken out of Man" — he borrows the most familiar term from the nomenclature of classical friendship: "Now at length I have obtained a suitable companion, who is part of the substance of my flesh, and in whom I behold, as it were, *another self.*"[10] Calvin puts classical and humanist words into Adam's mouth here; "another self" is the Aristotelian term for a special sort of friend — a friend not for use or pleasure, but a friend for virtue (*Nicomachean Ethics*, 1166a). Cicero's term for such a friend is *alter idem*, another the same, and it is this version that focuses Montaigne's discussion of why women are simply not qualified to be such friends to men and marriage can never hope to rise to the level of friendship (Florio, 91–92).[11] Aristotle allowed that some very exceptional marriages might rise to the level of friendship, but for the most part marriage was a relationship rooted in the usefulness of procreation and political alliances and the pleasures of sex. In general, classical teaching on friendship from Aristotle to Plutarch insisted that the most virtuous sorts of friendships could only grow between men similar in age, education, station and virtue. Difference, sexual difference included, was held to be inimical to friendship.

Augustine anticipated Montaigne's opinion when he asserted that God, if he had intended wives to be partners in conversation rather than breeders of children, would have made Adam another man for a companion rather than a woman: "How much more fitting, therefore, for living and conversing together would it be for two friends to live together equally than a man and a woman."[12] Protestants like Calvin disagreed with Montaigne, but few of them, including Calvin, spent much time worrying about the contradictions implicit in regarding marriage as a friendship. He imagines Adam employing terminology once reserved for describing homosocial and homoerotic relations, and so he hedges with "*as it were* another self" (my emphasis). Is marriage to be like friendship, a relationship between equals in virtue and in birth? Will sexual difference be rendered irrelevant, or does he believe, as Milton sometimes seems to, that Eve presents to Adam an outward expression in the flesh of his own inward and invisible likeness to God?[13]

Calvin did not press such questions as hard as Milton would more than a century later. Woven in and around his humanist tones, we hear vestiges of older popular misogynist attitudes toward marriage. For example, when he comments on "God's purpose in creating woman," it is not immediately clear whether he means us to regard woman as an end or a means, or both. Did God make Eve to remedy Adam's loneliness by being his companion or by bearing sons to become his companions?

> The commencement, therefore, involves a general principle, that man was formed to be a social animal. Now, the human race could not exist without the woman; and, therefore, in the conjunction of human beings, that sacred bond is especially conspicuous, by which the husband and the wife are combined in one body, and one soul; as nature itself taught Plato, and others of the sounder class of philosophers, to speak. (*Commentaries*, 1:128)

Calvin neatly combines the humanist emphasis on a wife as a companion, even adding "one soul" to Scripture's more flesh-focused language, with the more familiar Scholastic explanation of the wife's role as a means for producing new beings (men) capable of fully human conversation.[14] Milton's Adam virtually distills Calvin's prose in verse:

> But Man by number is to manifest
> His single imperfection, and beget
> Like of his like, his Image multipli'd,
> In unitie defective, which requires
> Collateral love, and deerest amitie. *(PL* 8.422–26)

Unlike God, man is in unity imperfect. The path to perfection requires that he reproduce himself and cultivate relations with "Like of his like." And the means to that reproduction, heteroerotic love, must also be regarded as "Collateral," a version of friendship between those alike in virtue — "deerest amitie."

But if the partners of this dearest amity are alike in virtue, why are they not considered also equals in all things? Calvin, like most Protestant reformers, will carry the recalculation of marriage as a friendship only so far. In the phrase "meet for him," he believes Moses intended to express not just similitude but also "some equality" *(Commentaries*, 1:131). Nevertheless, he concludes that both woman and marriage were created for the support of man and therefore "the order of nature implies that the woman should be the helper of the man" and not vice versa: "on this condition is the woman assigned as a help to the man, that he may fill the place of her head and leader" (1:129). Woman is not just a "necessary evil," as vulgar proverbs claimed, but she also has no claim to the perfect equality friendship doctrine insisted upon. Woman, like man, was made in the image of God, but "in the second degree" (1:129).

Finally, Calvin believes that God, in his infinite wisdom and foresight, also intended for marriage, after sin had depraved Adam's appetite, to serve as a remedy for lust. Unlike Milton, he is not prepared either to ignore or to rewrite Paul's "better to marry than to burn" theory of marriage. (1 Cor. 7:9):

> One thing more is to be noted, that, when the woman is here called the help of the man, no allusion is made to that necessity to which we are reduced since the fall of Adam; for the woman was ordained to be the man's helper, even though he had stood in his integrity. But now, since the depravity of appetite also requires a remedy, we

have from God a double benefit: but the latter is accidental. (*Commentaries*, 1:130)

Other humanist Bible commentators also began to regard marriage as principally about procreation and companionship and only secondarily as a remedy for lust. Milton takes the boldest step in this Protestant revaluation of marriage when he denies that Paul meant to speak about lust at all; the burning referred to in 1 Corinthians 7:9, Milton insists, is the "rationall burning" of a manly soul for fit conversation (*Doctrine and Discipline of Divorce*, YP 2:250–51). Heterosexual marriage has gradually developed since the Renaissance into what is now very widely (and largely without question) regarded as the most paradigmatic, natural and originary of human relationships.[15] In Calvin's words, "among the offices pertaining to human society, this is the principal, and as it were the most sacred, that a man should cleave unto his wife" (*Commentaries*, 1:136). Heterosexual marriage has taken the place once reserved in classical philosophy for friendship, a homosocial and homoerotic relation between men. Indeed, heterosexual marriage is today considered so natural and central to human society that men who remain unmarried are liable to be regarded as immature, or just plain "queer," whether they are homosexual or not.

Martin Luther sounds more like Erasmus than Calvin when he talks of marriage, especially Adam and Eve's marriage in Paradise, but unlike either of them, Luther taught that the original marriage united two equal beings. Eve's subjection to Adam, and thereafter the subjection of all wives to their husbands, is not a state of affairs inscribed or implied in the order of Creation, but an effect, says Luther, of original sin.[16] Husbands and wives originally were meant to be the same in all things except sex:

> Whatever the husband has, this the wife has and possesses in its entirety. Their partnership involves not only their means but children, food, bed, and dwelling; their purposes, too, are the same. The result is that the husband differs from the wife in no other respect than in sex; otherwise the woman is altogether a man. . . .

Also of this fellowship we observe some remnants today, although pitiable ones, if we look back to the first beginning. For if the wife is honorable, virtuous, and pious, she shares in all the cares, endeavors, duties, and functions of her husband. With this end in view she was created in the beginning; and for this reason she is called woman, or, if we were able to say so in Latin, a "she-man." (*Works*, 1:137)

No Protestant authors, as far as I know, taught a more progressive doctrine of companionate marriage. Not even Milton, though modern Miltonists have tried to imagine he did. Luther regarded the Pauline rationale for female subjection — "because the woman came from the man and not the man from the woman" (*Works*, 1:137; 1 Tim. 2:13) — as mistaken. He believed that wifely subjection proceeds not from the creation of woman but from the punishment meted out to Eve for the first sin (Gen. 3:16). He urges Christian husbands and wives, therefore, to try to imitate prelapsarian marriage by practicing household gender equality: "she is a mistress of the house just as you are its master." The terminology he employs — all possessions in common, common powers and virtues, fellowship, partnership, living together and equality — is largely the nomenclature of classical friendship applied to heterosexual marriage, and retro-projected onto Adam and Eve.

Luther embraces the Vulgate's word for woman in Genesis 2:23: *virago*, meaning man-woman or she-man. In Paradise, "the management would have been equally divided, just as Adam prophesies here that Eve must be called 'she-man,' or 'virago' because she performs similar activities in the home" (*Works*, 1:138). Calvin rejects everything implied by *virago*, alleging that "a deficiency in the Latin language has compelled the ancient interpreter to render the Hebrew 'ishah' as *virago*. It is, however, to be remarked, that the Hebrew term means nothing else than the female of the man" (*Commentaries*, 1:135). Man remains, of course, the default state of humanity, but Luther has reduced sexual inequality in marriage to a very narrow margin. For Luther, man and wife can almost qualify as alike enough in virtue to be friends in a classical sense.

Early proponents of equalist feminism, authors known pseudo-nymously as Jane Anger, Esther Sowernam and Mary Tattlewell, received no encouragement from Calvin, but plenty from Luther.[17] From the evidence of his letters to his wife, Luther's own marriage appears to have aimed at equality, at least in household matters. He tended to children when he was at home, changed diapers, and held his dying daughter in his arms. In letters he addressed his wife, Katherine, as "deeply learned lady," "my gracious consort," "doc-toress," "saintly," "owner of Zulsdorf" — their Wittenberg home — and "my gracious dear wife." He shared with her his professional as well as personal concerns. Her education was almost as dear to him as his own. Katherine enjoyed the conjugal respect typical of only the most enlightened (and usually aristocratic) humanist husbands.[18]

Edmund Tilney's quasi-Erasmian colloquy, *The Flower of Friendshippe* (1568), labels marriage a friendship, but only briefly flirts with the idea that spouses, like friends, could be equals. Humanist reformers like Tilney are keen to think of marriage as something more dignified than simply a means to "bring foorth fruite, and to avoyde fornication," two of the three chief purposes specified in the 1563 official "Homilie on the State of Matrimony." And since the classics teach that friendship is the most dignified and virtuous of human relations, humanists like Tilney are eager to reimagine marriage as a friendship. The youngest female speaker in Tilney's *Flower*, Ladie Isabella, dares to pursue the application of friendship doctrine to its logical conclusions — equality between man and wife:

> I know not, quoth the Lady *Isabella*, what we are bound to do, but as meete is it, that the husband obey the wife, as the wife the hus-band, or at the least that there be no superioritie between them, as the auncient philosophers have defended. For women have soules as wel as men, they have wits as wel as men, and more apt for pro-creation of children than men. What reason is it then, that they should be bound, whom nature hath made free.[19]

But, of course, the Lady Julia and Master Erasmus, the two domi-nant voices in the *Flower*, correct young Isabella by restating the familiar orthodoxy that laws both divine and human, supported by both reason and "our religion," "giveth the man absolute auc-thoritie, over the woman in all places" (134). Men that suffer their wives to command them for the sake of companionship come close to being cuckolds (134). Tilney can use Isabella to ventrilo-quize the emergent idea of sexual equality, and then he can con-tain that emergent idea with the paired authorities of his own Erasmus figure and Lady Julia.

The official *Homilie on Marriage*, published first in 1563, defined marriage as a "perpetuall frendly felowshyp" between a man and a woman.[20] In 1623, this language was changed (perhaps by Bishop George Abbot) to "a perpetuall friendship."[21] Calling marriage "friendship" applied a progressive humanist spin to a doctrine and legal canon that remained strictly orthodox and, as Milton later alleged, overly concerned with the fleshly aspects of marriage:

> It is instituted of GOD, to the intent that man and woman should live lawfully in a perpetuall friendship, to bring foorth fruite, and to avoide fornication. By which meane a good conscience might be pre-served on both parties, in brideling the corrupt inclinations of the flesh, within the limites of honestie. (*Homilie* 1623, 239)

Like Tilney's *Flower*, the homily energetically denies any notions of equality that the term "friendship" might suggest, repeating all the familiar formulas about the "weaker vessel" (241) and the Pauline injunctions on wifely subjection (242).

The ancients praised friendship; the Hebrew Bible privileges marriage. It made sense to Reformation humanists to try to reimag-ine and rewrite marriage as friendship, but almost no one would allow classical notions of equality between friends to trump the Pauline teaching about women's subjection and inferiority. Luther is an important exception, and Tilney may have imagined the bold Lady Isabella as a representative of Luther's attitude, one that needed to be quashed by higher authorities like Erasmus and the orthodox woman, Lady Julia. Being married still meant being made "one flesh" with a woman; being friends with a woman would have meant sharing "one soul in bodies twain," a relationship that supposedly transcended the flesh and lasted forever, even (some might say, especially) beyond the grave. For friendship, flesh was regarded as an impediment; for marriage, flesh seemed inescapably fundamental.

Marriage is allowed to be a friendship, is described as principally a matter of souls and only secondarily of bodies, but woman is the "weaker vessel" in this relationship and as such she willingly subordinates herself to her husband. In this account the "other self" of marriage is the undervalued term of a binary distinction rather than a true soul-twin. One cannot love an inferior, especially an ontological inferior, in exactly the same way one loves one's self, wishing for her the same things, the same pleasures, the same joys. Loving a "weaker vessel" is not like the self-love Aristotle insisted underpins the best sort of friendship, unless the self in this equation is the body rather than the soul. Pauline teaching implied as much: "So ought men to love their wives as they love their own bodies" (Eph. 5:28). Just as a man's soul was held responsible to discipline and care for (husband) bodies to maintain a proper *sophrosyne* (self-control), so husbands should discipline and care for what might well be termed their lesser halves — their wives. Those, like Milton, who try to avoid such disingenuousness and really proclaim marriage as the first and best gift of God and the original of all human friendships find they have an enormous task trying to avoid granting women the equality, even the full humanity, required of virtuous friends according to the classical friendship doctrine.

The Comedy of Errors

Shakespeare's *Comedy of Errors* borrows the structure of a Plautine twin comedy — *Menaechmi* — to humorously probe the contradictions and uncomfortable corollaries implied by these competing discourses of other selfhood. The extreme case of another self, of course, would be a twin. In fact, Montaigne would have disqualified twins as proper friends because siblings, though they answer very nicely to the traditional requirements of similarity between friends, fall short on the requirement of embracing friendship freely, and basing their love on souls rather than flesh. Montaigne insisted that the best of friends ground their relation in nothing other than their love for each other — no blood, no contracts, bonds or formalities of any sort (Florio, 90–91). His was an extreme position. Many other authors celebrated the friendships of brothers, cousins and blood brothers who made formal, if private, oaths of fidelity like that between Shakespeare's Palamon and Arcite in *Two Noble Kinsmen*. Finding themselves in prison together, shut off from the hopes of marriage and carnal offspring, the two cousins avail themselves of classical friendship theory blended with stoicism and pledge themselves to a higher love, untouched by the feminine:

> [Palamon] 'Tis a main goodnes Cosen, that our fortunes
> Were twyn'd together; tis most true, two soules
> Put in two noble Bodies, let 'em suffer
> The gaule of hazard, so they grow together,
> Will never sincke.   (2.2.63–67)
>
> . . . .
>
> [Arcite] And heere being thus together,
> We are an endles mine to one another;
> We are one anothers wife, ever begetting
> New birthes of love; we are father, friends, acquaintance,
> We are in one another, Families,
> I am your heire, and you are mine: This place
> Is our Inheritance: no hard Oppressour
> Dare take this from us; here with a little patience
> We shall live long, and loving: No surfeits seeke us.[22]   (2.2.78–86)

Arcite's speech is funny in large part because he calls attention to the anxieties lurking in the emergent humanist habit of talking about marriage as a friendship by reversing the discourse. Here is a legend of classical friendship talking about friendship as if it were an ersatz marriage. The effect risks making both humanists and the ancients appear ridiculous. They seem to design their friendship on Socrates's outline of enlightened pederasty in Plato's *Symposium*, except Socrates believes noble men would always value such higher love over marriage, while Palamon and Arcite appear to have been cornered into choosing higher love by adverse circumstances, thus making that higher love appear almost contemptible. Their love and its fruits will survive their mortal deaths and, says Arcite, "after death our spirits shall be led / To those that love eternally," much as Milton's Thyrsis imagined his beloved Damon enjoying the virgin honors and immortal nuptials reserved for those men whose love never succumbed to carnality (*Epitaphium Damonis*, 212–19). The extremity of their situation and of their rhetoric of love sets the stage for Emily's humorous entrance. One look at Emily and the neoclassical friendship dissolves into a bitter heterosexual rivalry.

Identical twins present another sort of extreme case; they are linked by birth and blood, even sprung from the same ovum. Identical twin brothers offer a limit case of the concept of a second self. One loves one's friend as one loves one's self, according to the orthodox friendship doctrine. Twins push the doctrine of similarity between friends to the asymptotic limit of absolute sameness; an absolute sameness that threatens to expose some of the problematics of identity. A twin even *looks* the same. Does he or she think the same, behave the same? Where is the threshold between the intersubjectivity of friendship and a shared subjectivity of identity? At what point does loving one's twin friend become exactly like loving one's self? Does similarity of body guarantee similarity of soul, or virtue? Won't such a friendship slide inevitably into narcissism? The more completely one's friend meets the requirements of similarity and other selfhood, the more friendship risks appearing as a kind of sanctioned narcissism.

I am certainly not the first critic to suggest that *The Comedy of Errors* prompts interesting questions about identity and difference or sameness and equality. René Girard is a good example:

In *The Comedy of Errors,* and more generally in all comedies of twins, the characters deal with each other on the assumption that all of them are unique and immediately identifiable as such. If they did not cling to this assumption in the face of contrary evidence they would not become so confused. It takes more than the presence of undistinguishable twins, I repeat, to generate the comic effects; it takes this persistent refusal to acknowledge the possibility of beings, human or divine, less different from each other than we would like them to be. . . .

The Comedy of Errors develops along the same lines as the other comedies and the tragedies. The unperceived substitutions of twins trigger a local failure in the system of differences upon which all human communication and intercourse is based.[23]

My reading of classical and Renaissance friendship doctrine suggests that the dominant discourses about human relations emphasize sameness rather than difference. There is far more talk in the age about sharing souls and seeing one's self in another than anything like a stubborn refusal to acknowledge the possibility of sameness. Girard appears to retroject distinctly late modern notions about individual identity onto an early modern age that was quite ready to believe souls could be shared, that marriage literally made two into "one flesh," and even that spirits both benign and malign could occupy one's body against one's will. The play even offers examples of these popular beliefs, and though I agree with Richard Strier that the play encourages skepticism about witchcraft, demon possession and exorcism, it would make no sense to offer such encouragement to an audience that unreflectively assumes the integrity of an autonomous individual. Early modern audiences probably, unlike modern audiences, made no such assumption.

"What is needed in *Errors,*" says Strier, "is neither faith nor ritual but ordinary common sense" (175). I agree, but even as the play ridicules popular superstition, it implies that some very orthodox formulations about friendship and marriage (formulations it does not dismissively ridicule) often remind one of superstitious supernaturalism — one soul in bodies twain, two people made one flesh.

As humanists took to describing marriage as a friendship, even the *first* friendship in creation, similar questions arose concerning husband and wife. How literally may we understand the notion of "one flesh" from Genesis 2:24? If friendship requires full inter-subjective equality to be truly a virtuous friendship, then must not husband and wife be regarded as equal as well? If a wife is to be a friend, must we not grant wives the status of full human dignity and equality? But will this not then conflict with traditional interpretations of 1 Corinthians 7, 14:34, Ephesians 5, and 1 Timothy 2:11–12, all of which teach women to submit to men? Shakespeare's early play takes on these issues with humor, sometimes irenic, sometime caustic.

In *The Comedy of Errors*, women take the lead in preaching marriage doctrine. One of the most effective devices of humanist pro-marriage rhetoric was to represent intelligent and interesting women articulating marriage theory, including the doctrine of wifely subordination. Erasmus's Eulalia, Edmund Tilney's Julia, Shakespeare's Katharine in *Taming of the Shrew*, and eventually Milton's Eve are all women we are invited to admire as the best any woman can be, and all of them embrace and endorse wifely subjection as natural, godly and satisfying.

In *Errors* matters are not so clear at the start. The principal female characters — Adriana, her unmarried sister Luciana, and the abbess — articulate familiar orthodoxies about marriage, but there is something unsettling about the way each delivers these orthodoxies. Luciana upbraids her sister's impatience (her husband is tardy for dinner and lately has appeared inattentive) with a homily on the natural and divinely ordained subjection of females to males:

> There's nothing situate vnder heauens eye,
> But hath his bound in earth, in sea, in skie.
> The beasts, the fishes, and the winged fowles
> Are their males subiects, and at their controules:
> Man more diuine, the Master of all these,
> Lord of the wide world, and wilde watry seas,
> Indued with intellectuall sence and soules,
> Of more preheminence then fish and fowles,

Are masters to their females, and their Lords:
Then let your will attend on their accords.[24]   (290–99)

Luciana's preaching sounds more than a bit out of place for a private conversation between sisters. Adriana's sharp retort: "This seruitude makes you to keepe vnwed," might well be taken to suggest that there is something unattractively servile about such abjection, however orthodox. Even more to the point, Adriana accuses her sister of speaking by the book rather than from experience:

A wretched soule bruis'd with aduersitie,
We bid be quiet when we heare it crie.
But were we burdned with like waight of paine,
As much, or more, we should our selues complaine:
So thou that hast no vnkinde mate to greeue thee,
With vrging helpelesse patience would releeue me;
But if thou liue to see like right bereft,
This foole-beg'd patience in thee will be left.   (308–15)

Audiences find Luciana's response — "Well, I will marry one day but to trie" — worse than lame (316). She betrays such a shallow grasp of marriage that it makes her little homily on obedience, however eloquent and orthodox, sound hollow.

Adriana is a shrewish nag, but not entirely without some cause. Her husband, Antipholus of Ephesus, has not been the attentive lover he once was and she is bold enough to call him on it. What sounds at first like the stereotypical nagging of the jealous wife familiar from popular medieval misogyny rapidly morphs into an articulate (if somewhat Scholastic) exposition on "one-flesh" marriage theory:

I, I, *Antipholus*, looke strange and frowne,
Some other Mistresse hath thy sweet aspects:
I am not *Adriana*, nor thy wife.
The time was once, when thou vn-vrg'd wouldst vow,
That neuer words were musicke to thine eare,
That neuer obiect pleasing in thine eye,
That neuer touch well welcome to thy hand,

That neuer meat sweet-sauour'd in thy taste,
Vnlesse I spake, or look'd, or touch'd, or caru'd to thee.   (504–12)

The time Adriana refers to is apparently a prenuptial period of courtship, the time perhaps when Antipholus of Ephesus swore love to her in a suitor's tones. That it takes nothing more than a strange look and a frown to prompt such complaints from Adriana suggests that her husband has abandoned his lover's language toward her for some time, long enough anyway to prompt her to be jealous on what appears to be a fairly slim excuse. He is late for dinner and apparently will not respond to any summons — this is enough to prompt Adriana to suspect that "his eye doth homage other-where" (380). She projects upon her absent husband the kind of complaints she hears that husbands make about their wives after years of marriage: age has taken her youthful fairness; her conversation and wit have turned dull (365–66). Then, without denying such flaws, she blames him as their cause:

That's not my fault, hee's master of my state.
What ruines are in me that can be found,
By him not ruin'd? Then is he the ground
Of my defeatures. My decayed faire
A sunnie look of his, would soone repaire.   (371–75)

So the play offers no challenge to the conventional notion that the ardent love and devotion typical of wooers lose their energy over time, that they fade in response to a wife's fading beauty and wit. In other words, time and familiarity breed, if not contempt, at least a desire to look elsewhere for beauty and conversation. Neither does the play challenge the misogynist stereotype of the unhappy, hard to satisfy, nagging and overly suspicious wife. But it does reflect the newer humanist attitude toward marriage by having Adriana argue that the reason women get to be that way is largely men's fault. Wives turn into sharp-tongued suspicious nags because men treat them badly and fail to shine on them with the sunny looks and Petrarchan exaggerations typical of courtship rhetoric.

More to the point, humanist marriage theory implies that a husband's absolute authority carries with it the responsibility for any problems that arise. The wise husband wields his authority more like a clever parent than a cruel tyrant. He must, in Tilney's words, "deale with his wyfe, rather by subtiltie, than by crueltie" (*Flower*, 795). He must take the same care for his apparently unruly wife that he takes for his often unruly flesh — firm but gentle discipline, with love rather than severe punishment or worse.

Adriana pushes the "two shall become one flesh" principle toward an impossibly literal sense (Gen. 2:24). When Antipholus throws her a strange look, she reads it not just as her husband treating her as a stranger, but that he has become estranged from himself. Not to know her — and Antipholus of Syracuse does not know her because he has only just arrived in Ephesus in search of his long-lost twin brother — is tantamount, she suggests, to not knowing himself, for husband and wife are one flesh. If she is a stranger to him, then he must be a stranger to himself:

> How comes it now, my Husband, oh, how comes it,
> That thou art then estranged from thy selfe?
> Thy selfe I call it, being strange to me:
> That vndividable, Incorporate,
> Am better than thy deere selfes better part.
> Ah, doe not teare away thy selfe from me.   (514–19)

Adriana's point is a strange one, for self-knowledge, as in the ancient imperative, *nosce teipsum*, is normally thought of as a largely spiritual affair. The underlying assumption is that we keep many truths about ourselves secret not only from others, but even from ourselves, and self-knowledge may only be achieved by those who can look at themselves, their inward selves, with brutal honesty. One hardly expects to gain something as dear or deep as self-knowledge by studying one's flesh. But flesh, according to a literal reading of Genesis, is the substance of wedded self-sameness — "they shall become one flesh." Genesis says nothing of one spirit.

The joke falls, initially, on Adriana, who, in mistaking her husband's brother for her husband, apparently fails to know her own

flesh. But only a moment after we have our laugh at Adriana's
expense, we find ourselves acknowledging that if brothers are one
flesh, and twins spring from a single fleshly act, then is not this
Antipholus, after all, one flesh with Adriana? Was it not precisely
such one-fleshness that led Queen Elizabeth's father to abhor his
first wife, Catherine, because she had been his brother's wife
before? In Shakespeare's chief source, Plautus's *Menaechmi*, the
stranger brother shares a meal and perhaps something more with
his citizen twin's courtesan friend. *Errors* shifts the dinner scene
to the citizen's own home, where the stranger eats his brother's dinner but apparently refuses his brother's wife's more intimate attentions. Immediately after what must have been an unquiet dinner,
Luciana upbraids Antipholus for his unhusbandlike demeanor at
the board with words that pun toward the bed: "And may it be that
you haue quite forgot / A husbands office? shall *Antipholus*, / Euen
in the spring of Love, thy Love-springs rot?" (785–87). If twins
enjoy a kind of fleshly sameness, why does Antipholus not naturally desire his brother's wife? In seeking his brother, has he not
succeeded in finding his brother's "better part"? His brother's
flesh? And yet he not only does not recognize his brother's flesh
but he does not find it attractive. Instead, he finds his brother's wife's
sister more attractive and calls her "mine own selfes better part;
/ Mine eies cleere eie, my deere hearts deerer heart" (850–51). The
erotic equation spreads the sameness over just enough different indi-
viduals to shift threatening images of illicit desire (thy brother's
wife, thy brother's flesh) into something more licit: brothers mar-
rying sisters, not their own of course, but each other's.[25] Thus, the
play tucks safely away the very specters of incest (both hetero- and
homoerotic) and narcissism it evokes. The play's humor dances
awfully close to things just beyond the humorous.

Adriana accuses her husband of not knowing his own flesh,
what she calls his "better part." In this she is unorthodox in precisely the way the popular misogyny of the period says women are
apt to be — valuing the flesh over the spirit. And, of course, she is
mistaken; this Antipholus is not her husband but her brother-in-

law. An audience familiar with Plautus's play will anticipate, for at least a moment, a scene of unwitting incest when Adriana presses this man home to dinner, but Shakespeare's play refrains from the punch line it evokes. Plautus prompts us to ask: wouldn't a woman know, in the act of sexual intimacy, her husband from his twin? Are spouse-knowledge and self-knowledge no deeper than the flesh? Shakespeare's play puts the same question in a more progressive humanist way: wouldn't a woman know, in the intimacy of dinner conversation, her husband from another man who looks just like him? If not, then it seems the attempt to reinvent marriage as a friendly conversation stumbles over the persistent carnality of incorporate fleshliness. Does Adriana betray herself, as Milton's Eve will later, as her husband's "outside," mistaking that corporal self for his "better part"? In dining away from home, or even worse, having carnal knowledge of another, he forgets his own flesh, his wife, his "undividable, incorporate" self, but is that truly his better part?

The play, after all, is a comedy about twins; much of the broad humor rests on the premise that you *cannot* identify a man by his outward flesh. Antipholus of Syracuse looks exactly like his twin, that is to say, his body is identical. No one, not even the Ephesian Antipholus's oldest companion, Dromio, whom he refers to as his living "almanacke" (206), can detect that another man is now before him. A man is not, after all, just his body; you can know the body and not know the man. As long as marriage is considered principally a matter of being one flesh, husbands and wives remain, in the senses most crucial to the friendship doctrine, strangers to each other.

The two Antipholuses are, in one literal sense, one flesh. Their identical bodies emerged from the same womb at the same time, begotten by one father upon a single ovum, and they have been strangers to each other all their lives. Are they one flesh in the same literal sense that marriage makes two into one flesh? A man leaves his father and mother and becomes "one flesh" with his wife. Does this mean marriage displaces or mimics kinship? Maybe "one flesh" should be taken in a typologically literal sense, which is as much as to say that flesh is ontologically an allegory for spirit. Milton thought so.[26] But this play draws attention to the problematics of marriage discourses only to invite us to laugh at how easily we ignore or deny them, not to propose dogmatic or ingenious solutions.

Antipholus of Syracuse sets out to find his long-lost brother because he feels somehow incomplete without him. He cannot be content. Because his quest for self-content has been long and unfruitful, he fears he has managed nothing more than self-loss. He expresses the depth and breadth of this loss using the image of an ocean:

> He that commends me to mine owne content,
> Commends me to the thing I cannot get:
> I to the world am like a drop of water
> That in the Ocean seekes another drop,
> Who falling there to finde his fellow forth,
> (Vnseene, inquisitiue) confounds himselfe.
> So I, to finde a Mother and a Brother,
> In quest of them (vnhappie a) loose my selfe.   (197–204)

Whether Antipholus recognizes it or not (probably not), his speech puns on the word "content." His merchant acquaintance has just taken leave with the polite valediction, "I commend you to your owne content" (195), but the man in search of his long-lost brother and mother not only feels discontented, but also worries that he literally does not know all the contents, the inward parts, of his being. But what has flesh to do with content or inwardness? Surely one can achieve self-knowledge without knowing one's brother, or even mother, in the flesh. In his essay on friendship, Montaigne cites Aristippus and Plutarch in support of his disdain for carnal kinship compared to soul-sharing friendship:

> There have Philosophers beene found disdaining this naturall conjunction, witnesse *Aristippus,* who being urged with the affection he ought his children, as proceeeding from his loynes, began to

speake and spit, saying, *That also that excrement proceeded from him, and that also we engendred wormes and lice.* And that other man, whom *Plutarke* would have perswaded to agree with his brother, answered, *I care not a strawe the more for him, though he came out of the same wombe I did.* (Florio, 90)

Only friendship, he claims, brings one another self one can share a soul with. Kinship remains hopelessly carnal. Montaigne thought much the same was true of all relations with women. Perhaps the emptiness Antipholus feels and the self-dissolution he fears come from regarding things too carnally. Perhaps bodies may be as like each other as one drop in the ocean to another, and one may be confounded trying to find either his self-drop or his brother-drop, but finding a similar soul must be another matter entirely, must it not? In this drama, the quest to find a brother will also turn up a mother whose body and testimony ground the two brothers as one flesh. She is also one who, along with the father, one must turn away from in marriage to become one flesh with someone else. Is the "one flesh" a metaphor from the start, or a new kind of literalism?

The play's humor turns on the cognitive dissonance produced by literalizing and exaggerating the rhetoric of similarity central to both classical friendship and marriage. Both Adriana and Antipholus of Syracuse apply the same metaphor — a drop of water in the sea — to the two different discourses, Adriana to marriage and Antipholus to kinship. Adriana speaks to that same Antipholus, mistaking him for her husband:

> For know my love: as easie maist thou fall
> A drop of water in the breaking gulfe,
> And take vnmingled thence that drop againe,
> Without addition or diminishing,
> As take from me thy selfe, and not me too.   (520–24)

Antipholus of Syracuse must find it uncanny to hear a similar, but significantly different, version of the metaphor he had used to describe himself only moments earlier. In Antipholus's metaphor, the ocean represents the great wide world outside his native

Syracuse and insular Sicily. Seeking for his long-lost brother and mother is like seeking individual drops of water in an ocean; spending much time wandering in the ocean of the world threatens, he feels, to dissolve his distinctness, his identity. Ironically enough, the biggest threat to his sense of self and place is not the great wide ocean of the world, but the proximity, in Ephesus, of his brother, the man who looks and sounds exactly like him, the man Adriana mistakes him for. If one's self were located merely in the body, to find his brother would be to risk losing his distinctive self, for identity would instantly give way to dual identity, or shared identity, or some other equally oxymoronic or ontologically threatening state of affairs. The equation of same body to same self would deny identical twins distinct selves of their own, except insofar as they live far apart from each other, thus allowing each to live under the illusion that he is unique. That is the situation the play invokes with Father Egeon's opening story (35–142).

Friendship doctrine, unlike marriage or brotherhood, insists that the most "complete" or "virtuous" friends locate their similarity on a spiritual plane. Aristotle defined "complete friendship" as opposed to friendship for pleasure and friendship for utility as "the friendship of good people similar in virtue" (*Nicomachean Ethics*, 1156b5). When such friends take pleasure in each other, they seek the same pleasures. Friendship, even more than loving, is essentially a matter of the soul, for one can love "soulless things," and we do not regard this as friendship. Friendship may be understood, taught Aristotle, by reference to self-love. A virtuous person loves himself for all the proper reasons; he wishes goods desired by his "thinking part," or "his understanding part" more than for his body, and he does good deeds for the sake of his thinking part (1166a15–25). He is at one mind with himself and enjoys his own company. Virtuous persons wish goods for, perform deeds for, enjoy the company of, and share pleasures with friends just as they do with themselves. "The decent person, then, has each of these features in relation to himself, and is related to his friend as he is to himself, since the friend is another himself" (1166a30). None of this is true, he alleges, of vicious persons, so they cannot be proper friends to themselves or to others. Virtuous men are precisely those men most successful at disciplining their body's requirements, so that they never threaten undue disturbance to their reason. That is to say, in Aristotelian terms the virtuous man is the temperate, not simply continent, man, and temperance, as opposed to continence, is the result of rational discipline of bodily appetites (1151b35–1152a9). Therefore, the virtuous, unlike the vicious, love themselves as souls rather than bodies, and they love their friends the same way.

When Adriana mistakes Antipholus of Syracuse for her husband, then, we may justly suspect that she does not really know her husband, is not really friends with him at all, that although they are one flesh, their souls are strangers. It has become fairly commonplace to point out how easily the Antipholus brothers may be distinguished by their character traits. I think that these differences do more than suggest Adriana is a shallow nag. They prompt all sorts of meditations about how selves come to consciousness, both falsely and truly, in relation to other selves. The Syracusan is restless at home and eager to find his brother; the Ephesian apparently never gives his long-lost brother a thought. The Syracusan relies on his Dromio to lighten his humor with "merry iests" and with affection calls him "trustie villaine" (184, 182); the Ephesian's Dromio apparently is accustomed to blows from his master and mistress (247–48). This leaves us with the impression that the Syracusan Antipholus remedies his loneliness by conversing with his slave, but the Ephesian Antipholus seeks companionship in marriage and never treats his Dromio as anything like a friend. Thus, we are prompted to compare two forms of amity that classical doctrine always insisted were very rare — master with slave and husband with wife.[27] And this means comparing sexual inequality to slavery. It also suggests that mistakes about other selves — wives, slaves, husbands, brothers — lead to mistakes about one's own self. Does one, indeed, *own* a self as a master owns a slave or a husband a wife?

Other symmetries prompt similar comparisons. While the Syracusan volunteers information to a merchant about his relationship with his slave, the Ephesian, with little prompting, lets the goldsmith know he thinks his wife is "shrewish" (620). The Syracusan has, it would seem, lived in a homosocial world until he arrives in Ephesus. He lived with his father, Egeon, and for companionship turns to his Dromio. But in Ephesus he is taken for a married man, and one result of this mistake is that his relationship to Dromio begins to look more like the Ephesian's with his Dromio — frequent basting. Failing to find companionship in his wife, the Ephesian turns for solace, not to his Dromio's merry jests, but to "a wench of excellent discourse, / Prettie and wittie; wilde and yet too gentle" (770–71). A homosocially oriented Antipholus finds himself dropped into the heterosocial world of the Ephesian Antipholus's marriage, while the Ephesian Antipholus is driven nearly to madness by the errors precipitated by his twin brother's proximity. The mission one brother undertook to find his other self threatens utterly to undo both selves. We cannot help recalling that at the end of Plautus's play the married twin plans to flee the heterosocial world, sell his wife and home in Epidamnum and return to Syracuse with his brother. Shakespeare's play "corrects" this trajectory in its resolution. The homosocially oriented Syracusan will stay in Ephesus and probably marry his brother's wife's sister, thus becoming successfully heterosocialized. But the path is not smooth; self-loss and madness threaten at almost every turn.

Adriana balks at the doctrines of wifely submission. She has not cultivated the habit of suiting her discourse and behavior to his moods, as marriage manuals recommended and as the Syracusan's Dromio does for his master. She does, however, subscribe to a very literal understanding of the one-flesh doctrine of Genesis. Husband and wife, she reminds the bewildered Syracusan Antipholus, are "vndiuidable, Incorporate" (517):

> How deerely would it touch thee to the quicke,
> Shouldst thou but heare I were licencious

And that this body consecrate to thee,
By Ruffian Lust should be contaminate?
Wouldst thou not spit at me and spurne at me,
And hurle the name of husband in my face,
And teare the stain'd skin of my Harlot brow
And from my false hand cut the wedding ring
And break it with a deepe-diuorcing vow?
I know thou canst, and therefore see thou doe it.
I am possest with an adulterate blot,
My bloud is mingled with the crime of lust:
For if we too be one and thou play false,
I doe digest the poison of thy flesh,
Being strumpeted by thy contagion.   (525–39)

Adriana's notion of married union is decidedly carnal, but its carnality might well be said to agree perfectly with what one gospel records as Jesus' teaching in Matthew 5:32 and 19:4–12. The first text is part of the Sermon on the Mount. Jesus tries to turn attention toward the inward aspects of sinful behavior: not only killing, but anger is a sin; not only adultery but the lust that prompts it. But Jesus' apparent concern with inwardness turns sharply outward when he recommends plucking out eyes that look with lust and cutting off hands that itch to kill or to touch another's wife. If he urges us to regard the heart and will as inward sites of sin, he also appears to recommend avoiding inward sin by disciplining the body. In Matthew 19:12, male genitals join eyes and hands on the index of potentially offensive bodily members one should consider cutting off to avoid sinning in one's heart. What's more, a woman unjustly put away — that is, divorced for any reason besides carnal fornication — Jesus says cannot marry another without committing adultery. Her inward innocence and righteousness count for nothing if she marries someone else; in doing so she and her new husband both commit adultery (Matt. 5:32, 19:9). The heart may be the site of sin, but avoiding sin is, according to this teaching, a very outward bodily discipline.

Adriana carries the Gospel's concern with the discipline ("pluck it out" "cut it off") of corporeal members and punishment ("cast into hell") of bodies to a satirical extreme. Being as indivisible from Antipholus as one drop of water from the next, being, as Genesis puts it and Jesus repeats, "one flesh" (Matt. 19:5), her husband's adultery poisons both their bodies at once. If he has looked with lust on another, he has committed adultery in his heart with the result that his flesh becomes infected, and his wife's as well due to the literalizing doctrine of "one flesh." Adriana's doctrine also agrees with Jesus in specifically indicting an otherwise innocent wife for a husband's injustice. Even where hearts have fallen apart, no man may "put asunder" bodies joined by God (Matt. 19:6).

Jesus and Adriana both present the state of matrimony as quite a bodily affair. The drop of water lost in the ocean represents the threat of being lost in the wide world; the drop of water in the breaking gulf represents the man threatened with a loss of self and identity in marriage. Aristotle says the self is the thinking or rational part, but marriage appears here as principally a worldly and carnal affair. In the case of Dromio of Ephesus, we are even invited to regard him as married to a personification of the world — his globular wife.

Dromio of Syracuse drives the letter of Paul's First Epistle to the Corinthians to a literalizing extreme. In 1 Corinthians 7:33, Paul says, "he that is married careth for the things that are of the world, how he may please his wife" and so tends to ignore "the things that belong to the Lord." In act 3, scene 2, Dromio tells his master he is running from a woman who claims to be his wife, a woman so large, "she is sphericall, like a globe: I could find out Countries in her" (905–6). The image evoked is Dromio running from the world and toward his master, escaping from the threat of being "a womans man, and besides my selfe" (868–69) to return to being a manservant, a man's man, his proper self. Perhaps because Dromio is a slave the play exaggerates the corporeality, even bestiality, of his marriage. Dromio fears that this woman "would haue me as a beast" (877). Not that Dromio is a beast, he explains, but that she, "being a verie beastly creature" claims him as one flesh with her (878–79). We cannot help also hearing, only a micron beneath the text's surface, the suggestion, common in Roman Catholic teaching on marriage, that even when sanctified by marriage there is always something beastly about sex. She is fat and greasy and gross, so filthily carnal that even "*Noahs* flood" could not cleanse her. If she is Dromio's second self, then to be married to her is to be beside himself in more than one way. Such a marriage threatens to unman him, dispossess him of a rational temperate self and transform him from a man's man "into a Curtull dog" turning a spit in the kitchen (935).

Marriage and sex in the Dromios' slave class is the most bestial sort of marriage and threatens to completely change a manservant into a kitchen drudge or to the lowest forms of earthliness. The relative dignity Dromio enjoyed by being Antipholus's man (despite a blow here and there) is lost in marriage to the greasy, globular woman whose carnality would survive both Noah's flood and a fiery doomsday (890–91). The things of her world would yank him brutally away from the cares of his master. Similarly, marriage for Antipholus, whether he accedes to playing the role with Adriana or contemplates marriage with Luciana, sidetracks him from his original quest to find his brother, his most originary other self and soulmate. Marriage means caring too much for worldly matters like regular sex, necklaces, dinners and the like. This is presumably why Antipholus of Syracuse, the bachelor, goes in quest of his brother instead of the other way around; Antipholus of Ephesus, the married man, is too concerned with worldly matters to undertake such a quest. The Syracusan's quest for a long-lost brother appears to have landed him in a marriage, and a sour marriage at that. Even worse, by falling in love with her sister, Luciana, he has almost become a traitor to himself:

> She that doth call me husband, euen my soule
> Doth for a wife abhorre. But her faire sister
> Possest with such a gentle soueraigne grace,
> Of such inchanting presence and discourse,
> Hath almost made me Traitor to my selfe:
> But least my selfe be guilty to selfe wrong,
> Ile stop mine eares against the Mermaids song.   (948–54)

When his homosocial quest for his other self takes these two unexpected heterosocial and heteroerotic turns, Antipholus fears he is losing his self, his soul, and may fall victim to the brutalizing charms of mermaids' songs or perhaps even Circe's cup: "There's none but Witches do inhabite heere, / And therefore 'tis hie time that I were hence" (946–47).

The Ephesian Antipholus knows all too well how threatening marriage can be to one's self-esteem and self-possession. The "venome clamors" of a jealous wife have prompted him almost to adultery, and if the abbess's words carry authority, have driven him out of his wits (1538–55). His "better half" has locked him out of the house and had him arrested and bound. When he comes before the duke to complain, the play has him echo the words of the newly fallen Adam complaining about the wife God gave him to be his helpmeet (Gen. 3:12):

> Iustice (sweet Prince) against y' Woman there:
> She whom thou gau'st to me to be my wife;
> That hath abused and dishonored me,
> Euen in the strength and height of iniurie:
> Beyond imagination is the wrong
> That she this day hath shamelesse throwne on me.   (1673–78)

The echo of Genesis calls attention to Antipholus's exaggeration; the shame Eve threw on Adam, most believed, was far worse. Still the echo repeats some of the most pedestrian misogyny of the day — that wives since Eve have been responsible for men's most profound loss of self and self-esteem. That said, though the play may get laughs by repeating such attitudes, it does not finally endorse them.

Two restored and one impending marriage dominate the end of the play. Egeon is restored to Emilia, but since she is now an abbess, what sort of marriage will they enjoy in their old age? Perhaps a friendship free of desire's burning? Nothing in the conclusion suggests that the two Antipholuses ever embrace. Indeed, the duke asks them to "stand apart" so that he and Adriana can tell "which is which" (1850). Restoring husband to wife appears more urgent than celebrating the reunion of long-lost brothers. This also allows the Syracusan brother to reprise his courtship to her sister. Marriage, not brotherhood, seems to bring resolution to "this sympathized one daies error" (1887).

Except for the Dromios. The Syracusan Dromio is relieved to confirm that the "fat friend" in the Phoenix's kitchen "shall be my sister, not my wife" (1906, 1908) and nothing suggests he wants to marry. And the two Dromios end the play by enacting between themselves an emblem of fraternal companionship and an equality that even brothers normally cannot enjoy: "We came into the world like brother and brother: And now let's go hand in hand, not one before another" (1917–18). They, rather than the Antipholuses, address themselves to the world after the drama, like Milton's Adam and Eve, hand in hand.

Two

The Sage and Serious Doctrine of Conversation

"Conversation" is a term and concept central to Milton's attacks on the canon laws regarding divorce and to his efforts to redefine marriage in the *Doctrine and Discipline of Divorce*. Despite its common use as a euphemism for sex, especially adulterous sex, Milton tries to use the word to redefine married conversation as something far more "rational" and dignified than sex. He regards sex for procreation as too undignified to be God's principal purpose in creating marriage because it was a necessity. Necessity, Milton believed, characterized beastly, not human behavior. God, in whose image man was allegedly made, was said to be utterly untouched by necessity. Human, or what Milton refers to as "manly," dignity was mitigated, limited, even polluted by necessity. According to Milton, when God said it was not good for man to be alone (Gen. 2:18), he did not, in the first sense at least, mean that man needed to procreate; rather, he meant that the first man, and every man thereafter, needed a soulmate, a conversation partner; in the language of classical friendship, he needed another self:

> God in the first ordaining of marriage, taught us to what end he did it, in words expresly implying the apt and cheerfull conversation of man with woman, to comfort and refresh him against the evil of solitary life, not mentioning the purpose of generation till afterwards, as being but a secondary end in dignity, though not in necessity. (*DDD*, YP 2:235)[1]

Milton challenges Roman Catholic marriage doctrine by relegating the "purpose of generation" to a secondary end, and, as I will explain at length below, he takes a step ahead of most Protestant thinkers when he defines married companionship as "a meet and happy conversation" quite apart from acts of "carnall knowledg" (2:246). Marriage, he thought, was far too dignified a relation to be concerned with "carnall lust" and "sensitive desire," things that could be managed just fine by temperate diet and exercise (2:251). Man's loneliness was principally intellectual and rational, so the conversational remedy must also be of that nature. Milton's first argument, then, is that if a wife fails to serve as a fit partner for such conversation, no matter how satisfactory she may be for sexual pleasure and procreation, the disappointed man should be allowed to divorce her and marry another. Canon law, he pointed out, privileged procreation and sensual pleasure over rational conversation because it allowed divorce only in cases of bodily impurity or incapacity.

No doubt Milton chose this word, *conversation*, carefully, weighing its ambiguities and range of both denotation and connotation. He must have known the word was liable to misunderstanding or even ignorant or willful misconstruction. Perhaps that is why he responded with such an unattractive display of self-righteous bile in *Colasterion* to the anonymous *Answer* that appeared in 1644 after his first edition of the *Doctrine and Discipline of Divorce*. None of Milton's polemical tracts is so addicted to insult and name-calling as *Colasterion*, a Greek word that may be translated as "the place of punishment." Milton complains that he expected the challenge he aimed at Parliament and the Westminster Divines in his first divorce tract would provoke a worthier opponent than this "Pork" of a "Serving-man" who, Milton alleges, never read any philosophy, has merely "puddered" in the law, and pretends to know Greek but cannot spell it correctly (YP 2:737, 726, 742, 724). Nevertheless, he undertakes to answer the *Answer* point for point.

By publicly responding to the *Answer* Milton enters, in a sense, into a conversation with his opponent, albeit a conversation in print with an anonymous opponent. And it almost becomes a conversation about the sage and serious doctrine of conversation, the proper mode, according to Milton, of wedded intercourse. I say "almost" because, although Milton takes pains at some points to represent his polemical attack on the answerer in the format of a reported conversation, he does so only to dramatize, in the end, the impossibility of carrying on a rational conversation about anything, especially something so serious as conversation theory, with an unfit partner. Milton casts the answerer as the epitome of an unfit partner for rational conversation. It is useful to think of *Colasterion* as a kind of violent divorce of an unfit conversation partner, kind of a rudely articulated bill of divorcement.

Though he normally refers to the anonymous answerer with insulting epithets, at one point Milton refers to him as his unexpected and unwelcome "Copes-mate" (YP 2:751). The Yale editor glosses "copes-mate" as "Adversary," but the context in which Milton uses it invites a richer reading. The term appears as Milton is concluding an allegorical interpretation of the Deuteronomic injunction against sowing a field with two different seeds or yoking an ox and ass together to a plow (Deut. 22:9–10):

> Against the sixth Argument, That to force the Continuance of Marriage between Minds found utterly unfit and disproportional, is against Nature, and seems forbid under that *allegorical* Precept of Moses, *Not to sow a Field with divers Seeds, lest both be defiled; not to plough with an Ox and an Ass together,* which I deduced by the pattern of St. *Paul's* reasoning what was meant *by not muzling the Ox;* he rambles over a long Narration, to tell us that by *the Oxen are meant the Preachers:* which is not doubted. Then he demands, *if this my reasoning be like St. Paul's:* And I answer him, Yes. He replies, that *sure St. Paul would be asham'd to reason thus.* And I

> tell him, No. He grants that place which I alledg'd, *2 Cor. 6.* of
> unequal yoking, may *allude to that of Moses,* but says, *I cannot prove
> it makes to my purpose,* and shews not first how he can disprove it.
> Weigh Gentlemen, and consider, whether my Affirmations, back'd
> with Reason, may hold balance against the bare Denials of this pon-
> derous Confuter, elected by his ghostly Patrons to be my Copes-mate.
> (YP 2:751)

Milton understands Paul's advice to Corinthian Christians not to
become "unequally yoked together with unbelievers" as a Christian
midrash on (interpretive application of) the Deuteronomic injunction (2 Cor. 6:14). In the case of his present conversation with the
answerer, Milton no doubt thinks of himself as the ox and his
unwanted "Copes-mate" as the unequal ass. He reports their debate
as if it were a conversation that begins to go awry: "he rambles . . . .
Then he demands. . . . And I answer. . . . He replies. . . . And I tell
him." It is as if Milton invites his readers — "Weigh Gentlemen"
— to witness, in the instance of this imagined unequal conversation, what violence and cruelty, what "divers evils and extremi-
ties . . . follow upon such a compulsion" as this he suffers in being
forced to discuss conversation with this "Pork" (*DDD,* YP 2:250).
Like Sophocles's hero Ajax, Milton represents himself as suffering
almost unimaginable shame in this "despicable encounter," but
he's willing to suffer it if only to dramatize in his own person the
wretchedness and shame so many men must suffer in a polity that
disallows divorce, forcing people to fadge together "only out of a
bestial necessitie . . . so that in some sense we may call them the
children of wrath" (2:260). He is forced to converse with this
answerer for a brief period, but in the end he divorces him.

In fact, it might be more accurate to call this interchange an anticonversation in which Milton punishes or scourges his interlocutor. The insults and name-calling mark this exchange as exactly
the sort of anticonversation one might expect from misyoked partners. And Milton appears to claim a certain justification for playing the role of an abusive partner. He has been driven to a righteous
madness by having been so unequally yoked to this "Copes-mate":

> Now therefore to your *Atturney,* since no worthier an adversary makes
> his appearance, nor this neither his appearance, but lurking under
> the safety of his nameless obscurity: such as yee turn him forth at
> the Postern, I must accept him; and in a better temper than *Ajax*
> doe mean to scourge this *Ramme* for yee, till I meet with his *Ulysses.*
> (YP 2:729)

Milton marks the answerer as an unfit conversation partner on more
than one score. He is unequal to Milton in terms of class ("Serving-
man"), education and temperament. Interestingly, however, Milton
does not consider him unfit by gender. Marriage, Milton insists,
was instituted by God to remedy the first man's loneliness by sup-
plying him with a fit partner for rational conversation. Why, according to Milton, this partner must be female is a matter we shall take
up later. Here I simply wish to note that Milton treats his conversation with the anonymous answerer as a kind of misfit marriage from which he should be allowed to extricate himself before
he is driven mad like Ajax or like a man driven by his wife's
"unhelpful and unfit society . . . through murmuring and despair
to thoughts of Atheism" (*DDD,* YP 2:260).

Throughout the *Doctrine and Discipline of Divorce* Milton frequently uses the term "conversation" to denote "the chiefest and
noblest end of marriage" as distinct from the accidental or secondary
ends of "carnal knowledge" and procreation (YP 2:246). Nothing
in the anonymous *Answer* calls forth a greater display of Miltonic
invective than his insinuation that Milton uses the term "conversation" equivocally, that however much Milton tries to drive
a wedge between carnal intercourse and intellectual or spiritual intercourse, despising the former and privileging the latter, the term "conversation" still bears a "nudge-nudge, wink-wink" sort of undertone
that secures an unspoken answer to a rhetorical "know-what-I-
mean?" The answerer raises the issue twice, both times implying
that Milton's arguments by example make no sense unless "conversation" is allowed to mean sexual as well as intellectual intercourse. When Milton complains that "the sobrest and best govern'd
men" are more apt to make mistaken marriage choices than men

"who have lived most loosely by reason of their bold accustoming" because "a discreet man" is all too likely to mistake "unliveliness and natural sloth" for "the bashfull muteness of a virgin" (YP 2:249), the answerer raises an eyebrow and responds:

> Some are bashfull and mute indeed: but what of that? you speak of triall of them whether they are fit for conversation or no: if you would once tell what you mean by conversation, I doubt there is none so modest but you may make tryall of that: If you mean fit for discourse, and flexible to your desire, to go abroad or stay at home, &c. I know nothing of any modesty to hinder you, the tryall of these things before marriage, if you have so much time.[2]

Milton also charges the canon law forbidding divorce with encouraging adultery and prostitution because a man whose wife is unfit to remove his "God-forbidden [and, as we shall see, God-installed] loneliness" with fit conversation is often tempted, beyond "humane strength," "to piece up his lost contentment by visiting the Stews, or stepping to his neighbours bed" (YP 2:247). Again the answerer quite shrewdly detects a crossing of the categories — carnal and intellectual — Milton has labored to keep distinct, and his response sneeringly belabors the Miltonic phrase "fit conversing soule" with all the glee of a debater who thinks he has caught his opponent in an equivocation:

> We answer you, what if he do look abroad, so long as it is but to meet with a fit conversing soule, provided he meddles not with her bodie, let him recreate himself, its lawfull enough: tis your own doctrine, A fit conversing soule is the noblest end of marriage: Therefore I think we may without danger, let a mans reines loose to accomodate himself so, if his Wife hath not so much a fit conversing soule as she should have, only let him remember to come home at night. . . . That desire which is not satisfied at home by a mans own Wife, will break out towards other mens Wives; but the desire which is to be satisfied by a mans own Wife is, that she be a fit conversing soule: *Ergo,* the not finding a mans Wife a fit conversing soule, will not endanger or stir up any other desires but to converse with the soules of other mens Wives; and this we allow you to do and keep your own still.

> But enough of this: only we desire the next time you write, to tell
> us the meaning of this fit conversing soule. (*Answer*, 32)

It would be easy enough, as I will argue below, for Milton to
explain that the confusion of carnal and intellectual desires betrayed
by his hypothetical discontented husband is precisely the social
pathology his polemic on divorce seeks to address and remedy, that
the laws forbidding divorce and remarriage share a major responsibility for perpetuating this confusion of categories, and that, in
any case, his argument doesn't require that one believe sexual and
spiritual desires are absolutely unconnected, merely that they be
better distinguished and ordered by priority than canon law has hitherto allowed. If they were better distinguished and better understood, Milton repeatedly argues in the *Doctrine and Discipline of
Divorce,* discreet and sober men would not be so likely to make such
terrible mistakes in choosing their mates, or, having made such a
mistake, they would not be so tempted to make the further mistake of thinking they could "piece up" their missed rational and
intellectual "contentment" in brothels or with their neighbors' wives.

Milton could have pointed to those other places in the *Doctrine
and Discipline of Divorce* where he makes at least a small effort
to explain how the blindnesses of canon law encourage exactly the
sort of category errors about marriage with which the answerer
charges him. For example, Milton explains that when canon law
"affirms adultery to be the highest breach" of marriage, it also
"affirms the bed to be the highest of mariage, which is in truth a
grosse and borish opinion, how common soever; as farre from the
countnance of Scripture, as from the light of all clean philosophy,
or civill nature" (YP 2:268). Because the Church has for so long taught
that carnal concerns — procreation and the avoidance of lust —
are the chief defining aspects of marriage, many men might almost
be excused for thinking that it is their carnal rather than their intellectual needs that have gone unfulfilled in a bad marriage.

Milton might also have cited another portion of his tract where
he explains how the two forms of masculine desire, rational and

carnal, actually interact with each other, crossing categories not simply out of confusion, but because these realms of desire, in this world at least, never can remain entirely distinct:

> And with all generous persons maried thus it is, that where the minde and person pleases aptly, there some unaccomplishment of the bodies delight may be better born with, then when the minde hangs off in an unclosing disproportion, though the body be as it ought; for there all corporall delight will soon become unsavoury and contemptible. (YP 2:246)

A man's chief desire, says Milton, is for rational conversation with a fit partner. If that desire is satisfied with his wife, some sensual "unaccomplishment," perhaps even outright frigidity, presents no true impediment to a happy marriage. One might have liked him to go even further and say that where minds and hearts meet, two people can manage to overcome any physical impediments and accomplish sensual delight, but he does not go so far. Milton, like his God, "does not principally take care for such cattell" (YP 2:251). But he does make something like the reverse argument when he observes in the revised version of the *Doctrine and Discipline of Divorce* that when a man's desire for rational delight in conversation with his partner is frustrated by his wife's unfit mind, sensual pleasure, even when "the body be as it ought," will dwindle away and even become a displeasure — a "grinding in the mill of an undelighted and servil copulation" (2:258). In this fallen world, implies Milton, irrational and rational desires are as closely bound up with each other as are good and evil in that famous image from *Areopagitica:*

> Good and evill we know in the field of this World grow up together almost inseparably; and the knowledge of good is so involv'd and interwoven with the knowledge of evill, and in so many cunning resemblances hardly to be discern'd, that those confused seeds which were impos'd on *Psyche* as an incessant labour to cull out, and sort asunder, were not more intermixt. (YP 2:514)

The traditional teaching on divorce and marriage, privileging according to Milton matters of carnal desire over matters of rational desire, has encouraged many otherwise sensible men to mistake one for the other, to suppose that rational desires can be satisfied by carnal means, even to ignore the existence in marriage of purely rational delights. Milton regards the answerer, a champion of canon law, as one of those responsible for promoting just such ignorance and confusion. So he refuses to carry on this conversation with an unfit partner any longer than necessary.

Up to this point Milton has tried to answer his unworthy "Copesmate" point for point with a combination of argument and insult. Now, however, when the doctrine of conversation becomes the focus of this anticonversation, Milton disdains to speak or argue any longer with this "Pork." At this point, Milton no longer represents the polemic as a conversation; now it is simply Milton scourging this man whose unfitness for conversation, it finally appears, is rooted precisely in his inability even to think about conversation as something distinct from sex:

> the Servitor would know what I mean by conversation, declaring his capacity nothing refin'd since his Law-puddering, but still the same as it was in the Pantry and at the Dresser. Shall I argue of conversation with this hoyd'n to goe and practice at his opportunities in the Larder? (YP 2:742)
>
> . . . .
>
> But this is not for an unbutton'd fellow to discuss in the Garret, at his tressle, and dimension of candle by the snuffe; which brought forth his cullionly paraphrase on St. Paul, whom he brings in, discoursing such idle stuff to the Maids, and Widdows, as his own servile inurbanity forbeares not to put into the Apostles mouth, of the soules conversing: and this hee presumes to doe being a bayard, who never had the soul to know, what conversing means, but as his provender, and the familiarity of the Kitchin school'd his conceptions. (YP 746–47)

Milton assumes here something like the role of the Lady in *A Mask Presented at Ludlow Castle,* and he casts the answerer as

Comus, saying to him in effect, "Thou hast nor ear, nor soul to appre-
hend / The sublime notion, and high mystery / That must be
uttered to unfold the sage and serious doctrine" of conversation;
"Thou art not fit to hear thyself convinced."[3]

To be sure, there is some catachresis in my substituting "conversation" for the Lady's "virginity" in the lines from *A Mask*
quoted above, but I believe there are good reasons, beyond the
apparently heuristic one of juxtaposing virginity and conversation, for doing so. A superficial reading of the *Doctrine and
Discipline of Divorce* might well leave one with the impression
that Milton deliberately deploys the term "conversation" to denote
every sort of marital intercourse except sex. This is the impression
gathered by the answerer and it prompts him to suspect that Milton
equivocates in his use of the term.[4] Indeed, much of the rhetoric
of the *Doctrine and Discipline of Divorce* seems intent on establishing what James Grantham Turner calls "a wide gulf between
sex and 'conversation,'" to make absolutely clear, in spite of the
term's well-established double-entendre, that when he speaks of
"a fit and matchable conversation," he is not speaking about "bodily conjunction" (YP 2:239–40).[5] "The apt and cheerful conversation of man with woman," which Milton argues is the chief end
intended by God in "ordaining" marriage — indeed in creating
woman at all — does not require, insists Milton, sexual intercourse. Grounding his argument in Genesis 2:18, Milton explicitly denies that the expression translated as *"help meet for him"*
necessarily implies "carnall knowledge":

> From which words so plain, lesse cannot be concluded, nor is by any
> learned Interpreter, then that in Gods intention a meet and happy
> conversation is the chiefest and the noblest end of marriage; for we
> find here no expression so necessarily implying carnall knowledg,
> as this prevention of loneliness to the mind and spirit of man.
> (YP 2:246)

The constitutive loneliness from which man suffers until he enters
into conversation with a woman is, Milton argues strenuously, a

strictly mental and spiritual loneliness: "that desire which God put into *Adam* in Paradise before he knew the sin of incontinence" (251). Against most of the received hermeneutic wisdom of his day, Milton insists that when Paul, in 1 Corinthians 7:9, says that *"It is better to marry then to burn,"* the burning he speaks of, "that trouble" marriage was given to remedy, is "certainly not the meer motion of carnall lust, not the meer goad of a sensitive desire; God does not principally take care for such cattell." Milton dubs this constitutively manly desire a "rational burning," to be carefully and strictly distinguished from "that other burning, which is but as it were the venom of a lusty and over-abounding concoction. . . . This is that rationall burning that marriage is to remedy" (250–51). It is one of the principal aims of his tract to make this distinction, as well as to point out that canon law perpetuates men's misery by failing to make precisely this distinction, or worse, by implicitly valuing the "satisfaction of an irrationall heat" or "the disappointing of an impetuous nerve" over "the soul's lawfull contentment" (249).

Throughout the divorce tracts Milton leaves the distinct impression that he deems sexual intercourse, even in the best of circumstances, a rather low and disgusting activity, barely "lawfull." Only "the fit union of their souls" can "make legitimate and good the carnal act, which els might seem to have something of pollution in it" (326). The "work of male and female" is a "poor consideration" (592) that occupies the minds of "grosse and vulgar apprehensions" (240) like those of the first century Pharisees and the law-puddering "Boar" of an answerer, "who never had the soul to know, what conversing means" (747).

Therefore, when the answerer snickers at Milton's use of the word "conversation" and appears incapable of understanding what Milton "could mean by this *Chimera* of a fit conversing Soul," Milton concludes that the man is no better than a beast, "like a Boar in a Vineyard, . . . champing and chewing over . . . notions and words never made for those chopps." Like a "generous Wine," the humane and subtle notion of conversation, well understood and properly concocted by "all persons of gentle breeding," serves only to make this bestial fellow "drunk, and disgorge his vileness the more openly. . . . But what should a man say more to a snout in this pickle, what language can be low and degenerate anough?" (747). The answerer is unfit to converse with the likes of Milton, especially on the topic of conversation about which "this Barrow" can do no more than "grunt" and snicker about sex. As with Comus, the answerer's rhetorical touch transforms the otherwise good wine of "conversation" into a "pleasing poison" that "The visage quite transforms of him that drinks, / And the inglorious likeness of a beast / Fixes instead, unmoulding reason's mintage" (*A Mask*, 526–29). And like the Lady, Milton thinks more than twice about unlocking his lips in such "unhallowed air," but that "this juggler" who, like Comus, obtrudes "false rules pranked in reason's garb" (756–59), went to print with the approbation of "a Divine of note" and "the commendations of a Licenser" (YP 2:727). The answerer, Milton believes, is more like a poor version of Comus, or perhaps one of his bestial followers, since unlike Comus he cannot even "feel the different pace / Of some chaste footing" or feel the "superior power" that sets off Milton's "words" about conversation (*A Mask*, 145–46).

I have claimed it is useful to read *Colasterion* as Milton's dramatization of how conversation with an unfit partner degenerates into abuse, and also as a kind of rhetorical divorce of his unfit "Copesmate." Now I also want to suggest that Milton rather enjoys this dramatization of what is supposed to represent the misery of unequal yoking. And he does not divorce his unfit "copes-mate" with the dignity befitting a generous but disappointed husband; rather, he scourges and punishes the answerer with undisguised relish. Milton prolongs his conversation with this unworthy and "ridiculous adversary" (YP 2:757) for dozens of pages. And few readers can fail to detect the gusto with which he abuses the answerer. Even though he describes his task as "this under-work of scowring and unrubbishing the low and sordid ignorance of such a presumptuous lozel" (756), he insists that it is work "meritoriously" (758) undertaken, not unlike the "labour" once "impos'd upon

[Hercules] to carry dung out of the *Augean* stable" (756). He even goes so far as to invite the "mongrel," if he "have the lustiness to think of fame," to reveal himself to Milton so that he may further exercise his "talent of sport" in public abuse, abuse of a sort even the most famous of ancient poets — Apuleius, Homer, Virgil, Boccaccio — did not consider beneath their dignity:

> let him but send me how he calls himself, and I may chance not fail to endorse him on the backside of posterity, not a golden, but a brazen Asse. Since my fate extorts from mee a talent of sport, which I had thought to hide in a napkin, hee shall bee my Batrachomuomachia, my Bavius, my Calandrino, the common adagy of ignorance and over-weening. Nay perhaps, as the provocation may bee, I may be driv'n to curle up this gliding prose into a rough Sotadic, that shall rime him into such a condition, as instead of judging good Books to bee burnt by the executioner, hee shall be readier to be his own hang-man. Thus much to this Nuisance. (757)[6]

On the one hand, Milton protests that he would be glad to be "ridd" (756) of this "bayard . . . who never had the soul to know, what conversing means, but as his provender, and the familiarity of the Kitchin school'd his conceptions" (747). He would rather not have "conversation" with such degenerate pests but would rather restrict his daily conversation to "such persons only, whose worth erects them and their actions to a grave and *tragic* deportment, and not to have to do with *Clowns and Vices*" (756–57). On the other hand, as long as the world is full of such "dorrs and horseflies, . . . bauling whippets, and shin-barkers," and as long as "Clergy men and Licensers" (757) commend and support them, Milton must defer his hopes for the day when his "conversation" is entirely "in heaven" (Phil. 3:20) and stoop now and then to beat the devil. Despite such protests, Milton's pleasure is evident in nearly every sentence of *Colasterion* and we must not forget that he deliberately courts further opportunities to revel in it.

This pleasure in abusive conversation with the answerer not infrequently assumes a sensually erotic flavor. At least Milton takes every opportunity he can find — and more that he invents — to allude to the answerer's genitalia and to draw conclusions about his sexual habits. These allusions are invariably coupled, of course, with rude slurs on the answerer's presumed social status — that is, subgentle, "a Servingman both by nature and by function," who pretends to the barely higher status (in Milton's estimation) of "Solliciter" (741). Since he cannot, reasons Milton, "ever come to know, or feel within himself, what is the meaning of gentle," he cannot ever understand "the gentlest ends of Mariage" (741). On such a subject, this "Boar" cannot possibly think of anything but sex; his "snout" is always in the "pickle" (747).

The answerer's paraphrase of Paul's advice to virgins and widows (*Answer*, 31–32; 1 Cor. 7:7–9), quite brilliantly designed to reduce Milton's case for "rational burning" to absurdity, Milton refers to as "his cullionly paraphrase" (746), as if there were some necessary connection between being born "base" and thinking with one's testicles. When Milton disdains to "argue of conversation with this hoyd'n to goe and practice at his opportunities in the Larder" (742), he implies — as he does with the "generous wine" image discussed above — that however carefully "men of quality" like Milton distinguish "conversation" from sex, degenerates like the answerer will always see and hear nothing but sex — "opportunities in the Larder." It is ridiculous to imagine that such low "unbutton'd" fellows could ever carry on a conversation free of erotic *frisson*. The "familiarity of the Kitchin," it seems, charges all intercourse among its denizens with the "noysom stench" of a "rude slot" (751), as if low birth and breeding inevitably endow such people with gaping orifices that drip an odorous trail of sex wherever they pass.

Milton invites us to imagine the answerer "unbutton'd" in his servant's "Garret, at his tressle, and dimension of candle by the snuffe" trying to "discuss" conversation (746). Not only does he find it impossible to imagine a servant discussing conversation without undressing, but he also imagines that his "candle" is too short — like the snuff-length bits cast off by the upstairs folk — to have much of a "conversation" with. This double insult links the answerer's wit to his penis, an equation that underlies Milton's entire attack upon him — that he "never had the soul to know, what conversing means." Such lowlifes, especially when they are pretending some accomplishment they lack, cannot so much as talk without their "conversation" degenerating into sensuality. They positively reek of sexuality and it infects everything they do, everything they touch, see and hear. We cannot imagine a partner less "fit" for conversation with any human being, let alone with Milton. Yet, in a way, Milton enjoys it.

Perhaps it should not surprise us that Milton so enjoys this conversation with the answerer and that his end of the conversation so often takes precisely the sensual turns and double-entendres he takes to be endemic to such degenerates as his unlooked-for "Copesmate." For Milton's own efforts in the divorce tracts to separate the "solace and satisfaction of the mind" (YP 2:246) in married conversation from "the solace of male and female" — the only solace in marriage the answerer can imagine — are far from entirely successful. And Milton is, perhaps somewhat dimly, aware of this.

Higher Love and Heavenly Conversation

Milton could hardly have chosen a less unambiguous term by which to denote the nonsexual — and therefore principal — ends of marriage than "conversation." In contemporary usage "conversation" appears to have done duty as an all-too-familiar euphemism for sexual intercourse. Shakespeare's Gloucester in *Richard III*, for example, describes Hastings's adultery — "his apparent open guilt" — as "conversation with Shore's wife" (3.5.30–31). When Enobarbus in *Antony and Cleopatra* takes the liberty of describing Octavia as "of a holy, cold, and still conversation" and Menas responds by asking rhetorically, "Who would not have his wife so?" (2.6.123–24), the joke depends on a double meaning familiar enough to be regarded as hackneyed. In some contexts, according to the *Oxford English Dictionary*, "conversation" behaves not just as a euphemism for sex, but as a common legal denotation for "sexual intercourse or intimacy." The *OED* cites Tomlin's *Law Dictionary*, where "criminal conversation" appears as a legal term for adultery.

Early modern usage in general, as the *OED* citations indicate, suggests that "conversation" served to denote the broadest possible range of human interactions — talking, gesturing, keeping company — in short, social behavior. When the social behavior in question involved interactions with women, sexual connotations were pretty much inevitable. In any case, there appears to be virtually nothing in the history of the word's usage before the eighteenth century to indicate it could be successfully used to denote the exclusively nonsensual or distinctly rational aspects of human interactions.

A cynical speculation about why Milton chose so ambiguous and unstable a term as "conversation" to denote "rational" as opposed to "carnal" desire and delight is that the word's very instability — its tendency to connote, include or pun toward sensuality — made it the perfect bait with which to trap the likes of the answerer into exposing his own "carnal" bent of mind.[7] This suggests a rhetorical, even a political strategy similar to the one Stanley Fish argues pervades *Paradise Lost:* repeatedly tempting a reader to hear the dirty sense of the word only to upbraid him or her for betraying a "fallen" "carnal" consciousness.[8] If this were part of Milton's plan, he certainly caught the anonymous answerer and wasted no time punishing him. Or perhaps Milton's choice of such a loaded word for unlikely duty is an early instance of the tendency James Grantham Turner detects in the epic poem — to try to "redeem" concepts and actions sullied by a fallen, this-worldly consciousness.[9] In this case it would mean reclaiming some kind of (impossibly) innocent sense of the word from the abuse it has suffered in the contaminated mouths and minds of men like the answerer, men Milton believes are not fit to hear themselves convinced, men who are insufficiently manly or even human to understand the sage and serious doctrine of conversation.

Another less speculative and less cynical line of inquiry leads to the Authorized Version of the Pauline and pastoral epistles, where "conversation" is a recurrent pastoral concern. In his use of the word "conversation," Milton tries to recover a Pauline distinction between earthly conversation and heavenly conversation, that is, between behavior characteristic of human beings in general and behavior measured by the higher standard of citizenship, especially the heavenly citizenship Paul says is held by Christians, those "born after the Spirit" (Gal. 4:29).

The 1611 Authorized Version uses "conversation" indiscriminately to translate three different Greek words: *anastrephe* (from the verb *anastrepho*), *politeuma* (verb form: *politeuomai*), and *tropos*.[10] The last of these, *tropos*, underlies only one instance of the word "conversation" in the Authorized Version (Heb. 13:5), and most modern translations render it as "conduct," or simply "life." That it could be rendered by the word "conversation" in 1611 indicates just how broadly the term was understood.

My concern here is with the other words, for Paul, unlike the other epistle writers, appears to distinguish between them in ways the seventeenth century translators failed to notice. The 1881 revisers of the Authorized Version (the Revised Standard Version) detected a significant difference between *anastrepho/anastrephe* and *politeuma/politeuomai* in Paul's usage, and their resulting translations reflect this distinction. I believe Milton also detected this distinction, but nevertheless retained the familiar word "conversation" in the *Doctrine and Discipline of Divorce* to speak of what Paul meant by *politeuma* in Philippians.

Both Greek words, *anastrepho/anastrophe* and *politeuma/politeuomai*, convey the sense of the word "conversation" as it was used in early modern English. The *OED* lists these senses under its first two definitions, both obsolete: "The action of living or having one's being *in* a place or *among* persons," and "The action of consorting or having dealings with others; living together, commerce, intercourse, society, intimacy," including sexual intimacy, as the *OED*'s citation from Caxton's *Eneydos* implies — "Dydo toke grete playsir in his [Aeneas's] conversacyon."[11] Among the New Testament epistle writers, Timothy, James and Peter all use *anastrophe* in exactly this broad sense to denote the exemplary conduct expected of Christians living "in the world" (1 Tim. 4:12; James 3:13; 1 Pet. 1:15, 2:12; and 2 Pet. 3:11), or the traditional modes of behavior from which Christians have been redeemed (1 Pet. 1:18). Peter also uses the term to describe both the "chaste" submissive behavior wives should show to their husbands (1 Pet. 3:1–2) and the "filthy" sexual practices of the ancient cities of Sodom and Gomorrah (2 Pet. 2:7). He also uses *anastrophe* when speaking of the false accusations about their conduct Christians must expect to suffer from unbelievers. Apart from Paul, then, the epistlers use *anastrophe* to refer to the whole range of human relational behaviors, sexual and nonsexual, holy or wicked, depending upon contexts and accompanying modifiers.

Unlike Peter and the others, Paul uses *anastrophe* and *anastrepho* with far more specificity. He reserves these terms to refer to behavior in this world, usually the worldly or fleshly behavior typical of the "old man" (Eph. 2:3, 4:22), but also exemplary behavior as measured by this world's standards (2 Cor. 1:12). In Galatians 1:13, he refers to his own "conversation [*anastrepho*] in time past" when as a zealously righteous Pharisee he persecuted what he later came to recognize as the "church of God." But when Paul wants specifically to refer to the behavior of spiritually reborn Christians as "citizens of heaven," living in the world but not of it, he uses the word *politeuma* or *politeuomai* (Phil. 1:27, 3:20). Paul is particularly sensitive in a way the others are not to the difference between conduct as a citizen, in this case a citizen of heaven, and all other human conduct, righteous, unrighteous or neutral. Both terms denote conduct in the world — "manner of life" as the Revised Standard Version sometimes translates *anastrophe* — but *politeuma* refers specifically to a citizen's behavior, conduct motivated and judged by a higher standard, the behavior of one who is quite conscious of enjoying, and being held answerable to, a higher status. In this case, the citizen of heaven has a being rooted in a place profoundly elsewhere. For Paul, then, *anastrophe* describes the conduct of one whose being and action is "in the world" but *politeuma* refers to the actions in the world of one whose being, thanks to spiritual rebirth, is "in heaven."

Citizenship and *politeuma* (citizen behavior) are concepts important to Paul in ways the other epistle writers probably could not share. None of the others were citizens of Rome as was Paul. In Acts 21–22, Luke tells the story of Paul's arrest in Jerusalem. When the centurion commands that Paul be interrogated by torture, Paul claims the rights of an "uncondemned" Roman citizen (22:25) and the centurion backs off. Earlier in this incident he had been granted permission to defend himself partly by pleading his citizenship as a "Jew of Tarsus, a city in Cilicia, a citizen of no mean city" (21:39). Finally, when he addresses the Sanhedrin, Paul defends his behavior in terms of citizenship, saying, "I have lived in all good conscience [*suneidesis agathe politeuomai*] before God until this day" (23:1). Citizenship plays a crucial role in Paul's understanding of identity. He defends his behavior according to who he is, and for him that is largely a matter of the polis to which he belongs — Tarsus, Rome, a fellow or "brother" of the council. For Paul, then, judgments about behavior are also matters of identity and citizenship. One's citizen behavior (*politeuma*) is quite a different matter from human behavior in general (*anastrophe*).

To put the matter back into the Authorized Version's early modern English, one's conversation as a citizen is a categorically different matter from one's conversation as simply a natural being. Citizen conversation answers to a higher authority and can only be judged by fellow citizens. More important, Paul thinks of it as behavior whose agent has his (citizenship was almost entirely gender-specific to men) being in another, privileged, community, regardless of where the behavior actually takes place. Being a Roman citizen living in Jerusalem is analogous, for Paul, to being a citizen of heaven living in the world. The citizen is in Jerusalem, but not of Jerusalem, as the spirit-born Christian is in the world but not of the world. Thus *politeuma*, a legal concept with roots in ancient Athens, offers itself to Paul as a perfect analogy for the spiritual citizenship of spirit-born Christians who, as Paul puts it in Philippians 3:20, have their "conversation [*politeuma*] in heaven."[12] Heavenly citizenship, according to Paul, transcends all worldly citizenships in that it takes no account of race, class or gender: "There is neither Jew or Greek, there is neither bond or free, there is neither male or female; for ye are all one in Jesus Christ" (Gal. 3:28).[13] As such, behavior as a citizen of heaven cannot be properly understood or judged by citizens of the world — Romans, Jews of Tarsus or Sanhedrin councilors. Citizens of the spiritual polis of heaven, Paul reminds the Corinthians, may be judged only by "the Lord" of that polis, not by the world (1 Cor. 11:31–32).

The anonymous answerer to the *Doctrine and Discipline of Divorce* is unfit to converse with Milton because, Milton implies, he lacks citizenship among the company of gentlemen. He is a "Serving-man" (YP 2:726), wears a "Livery cloak" (725), writes with "peasantly rudeness" (724) and, in general, has his conversation in the kitchen and the larder rather than among educated gentlemen, and certainly never "in heaven." He is, says Milton, unfit to converse on this topic and unfit to converse with him or any gentleman. When Milton condescends to converse with this "hoyd'n" (742), he runs two risks: one, the shame of an unequal "Copes-mate," and two, Milton's own conversation degenerates to the answerer's carnal level of sexual innuendo and abuse. Conversation, apparently, settles into a least common denominator. One should converse in the world as a citizen of heaven, not as a citizen of the world. If one must, from time to time, converse with the likes of this "Pork," one should be brief, scour and "unrubbish" the world's stage of such *"Clowns and Vices"* (756–57) and return as quickly as possible to conversation befitting a gentleman and a citizen of heaven.

But the answerer achieves something remarkable in his conversation with Milton. He demonstrates, not just by argument, but by the example of his own conversation with John Milton, just how impossible it is to draw a sharp distinction between intellectual and carnal desires, between conversation that satisfies one's rational desires and conversation that satisfies one's irrational desires. Milton allows himself to be goaded into punishing his "Copes-mate," not just with classist insults, but also with sexual innuendo. He implies that for people like the answerer there is no conversation free of sexual under- and overtones, and sensual *frisson*. And this is certainly true of the conversation Milton carries on with this man as he imagines endorsing him "on the backside of posterity, not a *golden*, but a brazen Asse" (757).

Conversation and Citizenship

Paul's notion that conversation is closely bound up with citizenship is adapted from classical theories of friendship. Aristotle's *philia*, in its broadest sense, describes all the bonds that unite human beings in relations with each other — family members, business partners, fellow citizens, soldiers, lovers, teachers, students and spouses. Different degrees of friendship answer different desires; some make friends for their usefulness, some for pleasure, but, says Aristotle, only good, virtuous and free men — what Milton calls "generous persons" — enjoy the most complete kinds of friendships. These friends regard each other as other selves because they want the same things for each other — the same pleasures, goods and virtues — that they desire for themselves. Vicious people, slaves and most women never make such friendships because their desires remain on the level of pleasure and utility. But a few rare, generous people forge relationships in which the most humane virtues may be cultivated through conversation with an other self in a kind of virtuous narcissism:

> We agreed that someone's own being is choiceworthy because he perceives that he is good, and this sort of perception is pleasant in itself. He must, then, perceive his friend's being [together with his own], and he will do this when they live together and share conversation and thought. For in the case of human beings what seems to count as living together is this sharing of conversation and thought, not sharing the same pasture, as in the case of grazing animals. (*Nicomachean Ethics*, 1170b8)

When Milton scoffingly observes that "God does not take care for such cattell," referring to carnal desires, he makes much the same distinction as Aristotle. Indeed, H. Rackham's translation comes closest to Milton's own reading of Aristotle: "Therefore a man ought also to share his friend's consciousness of his existence, and this is attained by their living together and by conversing and communicating their thoughts to each other [*koinônein logôn kai dianoias*]; for this is the meaning of living together as applied to human beings, it does not mean merely feeding in the same place, as it does when applied to cattle."[14] Virtuous friends may get pleasure from one another and they may also be useful to one another — "nothing," says Aristotle, "is as proper to friends as living together," which presumably includes sharing meals and physical pleasures (1157b20) — but that is not what defines the best or most human kind of friendship. Animals also form relationships, often very temporary ones, based on pleasure and utility, mutual or otherwise, but only the best sort of humans can be friends for virtue's sake. The conversation between virtuous persons whose pleasure in one another is comparable to the pleasure each takes in complacent self-regard identifies those people as the few, the rare and, according to classical tradition from Aristotle to Cicero, to Montaigne, the most manly.

Gregory Chaplin has argued that "the marital ideal Milton articulates in his divorce tracts . . . develops out of the Platonically inspired friendship that he shared with Charles Diodati" (Chaplin, "One Flesh, One Heart," 267). Chaplin suggests that Milton, steeped in humanist friendship theory and lore, experienced all the refined humanist delights of homoerotic friendship with Charles Diodati in a relationship that began at St. Paul's school in about 1620 and ended with Diodati's death in 1638. Then, following the sharp initial disappointment of his apparently disastrous marriage to Mary Powell in 1642, Milton set himself the task of redefining marriage not just along the lines of classical friendship doctrine, but also in a futile effort to reproduce in marriage the relationship he lost when Charles died (Chaplin, "One Flesh, One Heart," 279).

This makes for a wonderful, if painful, story, and there is enough truth to it to enrich our readings of not only the divorce tracts but also all the representations of marriage and friendship in the major poems. However, I would like to offer some important adjustments to this story.

First, as I have already pointed out in an earlier chapter, Milton was by no means the only person struggling to reconcile the "one flesh" rhetoric of biblical marriage to the classical and humanist "one soul in bodies twain" doctrines of friendship. Far from being Milton's own personal project, it might be regarded as one of the dominant obsessions of an age in which the intellectual and religious elite tried to meld Reformation biblicism with Renaissance classicism. Aristotle, Cicero, Plutarch and Montaigne regarded friendship as the quintessentially human, if not originary, relation. Though it was not difficult to find biblical examples of homosocial friendships, the Bible, beginning with Genesis, advanced marriage as the original and most fundamental form of human society. When God saw that it was not good for Adam to be alone (Gen. 2:18), he made a woman to remedy his solitude. If the classical humanism of the new learning was to survive and inform the scholastic biblicism of Calvinism, marriage would have to replace friendship at the center of any theory of human relations, and marriage would have to be redefined as a friendship. With or without the "spurre of self-concernment," Milton was fated to take part in this difficult intellectual and hermeneutic task because reconciling classical ethics and anthropology to biblical Christianity was simply the task on the table (YP 2:226).

Second, Milton's doctrine of "conversation" owes far more to classical friendship doctrine, both Plato's and Aristotle's, than to his experience of friendship with Charles Diodati. However much the two young men loved and admired each other, they never lived together, never managed to practice with each other that most characteristic aspect of virtuous friendship — daily conversation. They probably met when Milton began at St. Paul's in 1620 at the age of twelve. In 1622 Diodati left for Oxford, where he remained until receiving his M.A. in 1628. Milton went off to Cambridge in 1625 and was awarded an M.A. in 1632. Diodati spent 1630 and most of 1631 in Geneva, returning in September of that year to London to study medicine. Milton spent the years from 1632 until 1637 at his father's houses in Hammersmith and Horton, visiting London only occasionally. If Milton and Diodati had wished to live together as friends, their most convenient opportunity to do so would have been in the years 1637 and 1638 before Milton left England for an extended tour of Europe. There is no evidence, however, that the two great friends ever managed to share the daily conversation friendship doctrine prescribed.

The only letters that survive — two in Greek from Diodati to Milton, and two in Latin from Milton to Diodati — indicate that both men regarded their friendship in classical terms, and they frequently expressed their desire to spend time together, but it appears their relationship remained largely epistolary and elegiac. They may have met during university holidays; they could have enjoyed each other's company at least occasionally during the five years Milton spent supplementing his education in his father's homes, but there is no evidence in the surviving letters, records or poems that they ever spent any significant time together at all after Diodati left St. Paul's for Oxford in 1622 when both boys were only 14.

The surviving letters actually highlight the fact that the two friends lived perennially apart. The first from Diodati complains that severe weather has kept them out of conversation with each other: "so much do I desire your company that in my longing I dream of and all but prophesy fair weather and calm, and everything golden for tomorrow, so that we may enjoy our fill of philosophical and learned conversation [*logon philosophon*]" (YP 1:336).[15] In his second letter, Diodati voices a complaint destined to be echoed years later by Milton's Adam: "I have no fault to find with my present mode of life except that I am deprived of any mind fit to converse with. I long for such a person" (French, *Life Records*, 105). Perhaps this complaint from his first and most intimate friend helped to shape the complaint Milton imagines Adam brought to God in Paradise:

Thou hast provided all things: but with mee
I see not who partakes. In solitude
What happiness, who can enjoy alone,
Or all enjoying, what contentment find?   (*PL* 8.363–66)

In his Greek letter, Diodati articulates what classical friendship doctrine regarded as the basic human need for an other self, a person similar enough in age, rank, education, and especially virtue, to be one's friend.

Milton's first 1637 letter to Diodati (probably in November) complains that, although Diodati had promised to visit, he "did not keep his promises" (YP 1:324).[16] But Milton was probably just as much to blame for their infrequent meetings; he explains that although Diodati's mode of study permits him to pause frequently for social intercourse, Milton's "temperament allows no delay, no rest, no anxiety — or at least thought — about scarcely anything to distract me, until I attain my object and complete some great period, as it were, of my studies" (323). And then, just a few months after completing this "great period" of study, Milton left in April 1638 for an extended tour of the Continent. His second letter in 1637 tries to blame Diodati for their separation, alleging that his friend has been overly devoted to "domestic matters, forgetting urban companionships," and he urges him to come stay with him for the winter of 1637–1638, but there is no evidence that he did (Lewalski, *Life*, 327–28). Milton left for his European tour probably without even seeing Diodati again, and Diodati had been dead and buried for a year or more when he returned to England and wrote *Epitaphium Damonis*.

The surviving letters actually suggest not only that they managed very few, if any, visits, but even that they wrote to each other far less than either wished. In a 1637 letter, Milton acknowledges that his obsessive commitment to his studies has made him a tardy correspondent.[17] Then he follows this admission with a kind of insinuated accusation against Diodati for leaving letters unanswered:

> In returning them, however, my Diodati, I am not such a laggard;
> for I have never committed the crime of letting any letter of yours
> go unanswered by another of mine. How is it that you, as I hear, have
> written Letters to the Bookseller, even oftener to your Brother, either
> of whom could conveniently enough, because of nearness, have
> been responsible for passing letters on to me — had there been any?
> (YP 2:324)

If Milton was slow to answer letters, and Diodati left some of
Milton's entirely unanswered, maybe there are far fewer lost letters than is usually imagined, perhaps even none. I agree with the
critical consensus that regards this friendship as Milton's most intimate with anyone, but I also wish to observe that these two
achieved whatever intimacy they enjoyed across a distance.[18]
Indeed, much of their conversation is carried on in an elegiac tone
of separation, and in its most moving expression — *Epitaphium
Damonis* — of loss. Two elegies (1 and 6), a sonnet (4), and a brief
exchange of letters in Latin and Greek — this was a friendship not
so much enjoyed as performed on paper, probably in a very deliberate imitation of the most famous elegiac friendships: Achilles and
Patroclus, David and Jonathan, Cicero and Scipio, Montaigne and
Etienne le Boëtie, Tasso and Manso. Both boys probably read
Cicero's *De Amicitia* with Alexander Gill at St. Paul's and chose
each other as partners in the practice of classical friendship, a practice that marked them as cultivated humanist gentlemen, a cut or
more above the hoi polloi who, like the answerer, cannot understand the erotics of a higher love. But the lives they led after the
age of fourteen or so, perhaps even the emergent bourgeois culture
in which they lived, made the daily conversation of enlightened
friendship impossible.

Milton probably also had read Aristotle's warnings about the toll
absence takes on friendship: "distance does not dissolve the friendship unconditionally, but only its activity. But if the absence is long,
it also seems to cause the friendship to be forgotten; hence the
saying 'Lack of conversation has dissolved many a friendship'"
(1157b10–13). I believe Milton studied the literature of friendship

as intensely as he studied everything else toward which he turned his attention. He realized that performing friendship in letters and poems was not truly a remedy for solitude however much it was a requisite practice for a gentleman and aspiring poet. He excelled at literary friendship both at home and abroad among the admiring Florentine humanist intelligentsia. Milton may well have learned of Diodati's death while he was visiting in Naples enjoying the new and encouraging friendship of Giovanni Battista Manso.[19] After Naples, he spent another two months visiting Rome and a second two-month stay in Florence, a city that offered him many of the joys of friendly conversation, especially at the private academies he had enjoyed so much during his first visit to Florence. Milton praises these academies "not only for promoting humane studies but also for encouraging friendly intercourse." There he enjoyed what Edward Phillips aptly described as "a Correspondence and perpetual Friendship among Gentlemen fitly qualified for such an Institution."[20] In the Florentine and Neapolitan private academies, Milton could experience an institutionalized form of classical friendship among equals, conversing almost daily, sharing poems, trading praises and prizes and even earthy humor (Lewalski, *Life*, 93). We must conclude, then, that Milton did not abandon classical friendship for marriage; in Florence he began to experience what Aristotle taught was the most characteristic practice of the most virtuous kind of friendship — living together in conversation.

Back in England, however, no such academies existed; even in Italy they already had dwindled to shadows of their former Renaissance glory. In England the emerging Puritan world of republican virtues and radically reformed churches promised a society built around heterosexual marriage and extended households, not the homosocial and homoerotic institutions of courts, gentlemen's academies and a celibate clergy. When Milton left Italy, he also left the refined practices of homosocial friendship behind, and he missed them, bitterly. In 1647 he wrote to Carlo Dati in Florence, lamenting what he took to be his unbearable fate — that he was daily surrounded with wearisome people, while "those whom character, temperament, interests had so finely united are now nearly all grudged me by death or most hostile distance and are for the most part so quickly torn from my sight that I am forced to live in almost perpetual solitude" (YP 2:762–63). Milton convinced himself, against the teaching of men like Montaigne, that marriage could be elevated to such refined practices, that a man could find such friendship in a wife.

"Twice wretched is he who loves late": Damon's Epitaph

Milton articulates his grief at the loss of his friend in the classic Renaissance homoerotic code of Theocritean pastoral elegy — "Sicilian song."[21] He follows the format of pastoral elegy perfectly, singing in the persona of Thyrsis lamenting the loss of Damon, one shepherd for another. When Milton sang such a lament for his fellow Cantabridgean, Edward King, his readers knew that the "self-same hill" upon which Lycidas and the pastoral speaker tended the "same flock" was code for Christ's College (*Lycidas*, 23–24). Five years earlier, Milton and King had been classmates, but not, as far as we know, friends. Now, two years later, Milton uses similar imagery to project onto a pastoral screen a memory of two friends as intimate shepherds, even though Milton and Diodati had not shared a hillside or flock or school or campus since they were lads at St. Paul's.

If Milton composed this poem in the fall of 1639, a little more than a year after his friend's death, he exaggerates its belatedness, measuring it by two harvests: "Twice the stalk had risen with green ear, and as often had the garners told off the yellow crops, since his last day had borne Damon down to the shades, and Thyrsis was not there the while" (9–12).[22] He was not there when his friend died because, he says, the "sweet Muse" detained him in Tuscany. Miltonists generally imagine that Milton did not hear of his friend's death until late in his travels, when he was already returning to England and stopped in Geneva to visit Diodati's uncle, Giovanni. But the poem does not say this, though it could have. The poem says that Thyrsis did not really feel the loss of his friend until, his mind overflowing with excitement from his experiences with the poets of Florence, he returned to England, "sat once more beneath his accustomed elm," and "then, then at last he felt in truth the loss of his friend and began to vent his measureless sorrow" (12–17). He returned for reasons other than grief or shock at the death of his friend. Perhaps he even stayed some months after hearing of Diodati's death. He returned because his mind was full (*mens expleta*), and the care of his flock, his sense of obligation to his native country, called him home (*Cura vocat*). The sense of loss, like the friendship itself, emerges belatedly, a kind of doubled elegiac mode. Milton himself recognized fairly well how much his grief for the loss of Diodati was prompted by and confusedly intertwined with his grief over leaving Florence. Years later he wrote to Carlo Dati,

> That separation, I may not conceal from you, was also very painful for me; and it fixed those stings in my heart which even now rankle whenever I think that, reluctant and actually torn away, I left so many companions and at the same time such good friends, and such congenial ones in a single city — a city distant but to me most dear. I call to witness the tomb of Damon (which shall always be sacred and solemn to me) that when I was burdened with the task of adorning it with every tribute of grief, when I wanted to turn to what comforts I could and pause for breath, I could think of nothing pleasanter than to recall the memory of you all, of you, Dati, especially. (YP 2:763)

In Milton's mind, and in *Epitaphium Damonis*, the two losses mix and trade places, back and forth. Even Dati's name contributes to the exquisite commingling of the two losses, each of which owes its intensity, even its existence, to the other.

In this mode of lament for a loss that is felt as a loss only at the moment that the poet articulates it in Sicilian song, Milton imagines a life of shared pastoral conversation that he and Diodati never enjoyed and laments it as lost:

At mihi quid tandem fiet modò? quis mihi fidus
Hærebit lateri comes, ut tu sæpe solebas
Frigoribus duris, & per loca fœta pruinis,
Aut rapido sub sole, siti morientibus herbis?
Sive opus in magnos fuit eminùs ire leones
Aut avidos terrere lupos præsepibus altis;
Quis fando sopire diem, cantuque solebit?   (37–43)

[What faithful friend will stay close by my side as you were wont to
do in bitter cold through places rough with frost, or under the fierce
sun with the herbage dying from drought, whether the task were to
go within spear's throw of great lions or to frighten the ravenous
wolves from the high sheepfolds? Who will now lull my day to rest
with talk and song?] (MacKellar, *Latin Poems*, 161, 163)

In the refrain, Thyrsis sends his lambs away unfed and uncared for.
If the flock is pastoral code for the political and ecclesiastical tasks
for which Milton left Italy to return to an England on the brink of
civil war, then the emotional situation evoked by this poem
becomes even more complicated. Milton briefly puts off his duties
in the antiprelatical cause to lament a loss that he feels only after
his return to that cause. It is more a feeling of loss for what could
or should have been than for what was, and the pastoral mode is
perfect for such retrojected memories, for it also expresses a sense
of loss for an Arcadian moment that also never was, but some feel
should have been. When did Charles and John ever share a flock
or "cheat the long night with pleasant converse"; when did they
ever lie concealed while the farmer snored and enjoy each other's
"blandishments, laughter, and Cecropian wit" (56)? His friend has
died, and only many months later, more than a year, does he feel
the loss. This is because his loss takes the shape, not of a lost beloved,
but of a missed opportunity — "Twice wretched is he who loves
late" (*bis ille miser qui serus amavit*) (86).

Thyrsis envies the beasts of the field, the fish of the sea and the
birds of the air because they do not require, as does the stony race
of men — "*Nos durum genus*" — special friends, mates for life, a

partner to share in conversation life's joys and sorrows. Cattle and seals, even jackals whose voices closely resemble men's — they all enjoy the friendship of the herd, but they do not pick out one in particular to love and live with (95–105). Thyrsis appears at first to be ignoring gender, but when he talks of "shaggy wild asses" which "by turn are joined in pairs" (*vicem hirsute paribus iunguntur onagri*), and the domestic English sparrows who build nests together with their mates and together feed from heaps of horse feed, he evokes images of heterosexual pairs of animals (98–105). But even these mated pairs happily move on to another companion with change of season or loss by death. Only humans truly mate for life, and a "truly kindred spirit," a partner fit to share one's life, is one in a thousand, a friend not just for feeding and flying and sensual pleasures, but also for conversation. Diodati was fit to be such a friend to Milton, but they missed their chance.

They missed their chance not just for their own personal reasons — Milton was addicted to his studies, his Muse, and then later to the "Tuscan shepherds" who showered him with praise — but also because in the emergent culture of bourgeois capitalism, classical friendship was no longer a convenient model for the most human of human relations. Puritan culture looked increasingly to the Bible as an authority for how to live. As Milton joined the polemical fight against episcopacy, his persistent argument was that Scripture alone should prescribe church discipline. The Bible taught that marriage was the originary human relation. The family and the gathered congregation were, many Puritans thought, destined to replace the court and the bishop-ridden church as the fundamental structures of human relations. Puritan republicanism, unlike Roman republicanism, or Athenian democracy, would ground itself more in heterosocial cultural models — husband and wife, Christ and his church, the family hearth and the communion table. David Norbrook hints at the difficulties involved in adapting classical republicanism to a culture committed to heteroerotic models of both intimacy and the polis.[23] Special friendships, like those of Jonathan and David, Achilles and Patroclus, Titus and Gysippus,

Pyrocles and Musidorus, Spenser and Harvey, Montaigne and Boëtie, friendships of the battlefield, the academy, the court and the monastery did not belong to the godly Zion Puritans imagined England would become. I suspect that is why Milton and Diodati conducted their classical friendship largely on paper, in Greek and Latin letters and verses, and never managed to practice it the way Aristotle and Plato and Montaigne insisted true friendship must be practiced: by living together and sharing each other's life in daily conversation.

Thyrsis blames himself for parting with his "charming companion" just to visit Rome: "Surely had I stayed I might at the last have touched the hand, and closed the eyes, of him who was peacefully dying, might have said, 'Farewell, remember me when you go to the stars'" (123). But though he thinks going to Rome was a mistaken wandering (*vagus error*), he regards the time he spent in Florence quite differently. The verse paragraph (124–39) begins as if it means to follow the pattern of the one before it — had I not wandered mistakenly to Rome, I could have been here when you died; had I not been attracted by the Florentine poets and the favors they bestowed on me, I could have said farewell to you properly. But the second part of this pattern never actually emerges. Instead, we are reminded that Damon himself was a Tuscan, from Lucca, a city older than Florence and once Tuscany's capital:

> Even though I shall never weary of remembering you, O Tuscan shepherds, youths devoted to the Muses, yet here too were grace and charm; and you too, Damon, were a Tuscan tracing your lineage from the ancient city of Lucca. O how elated I was when, stretched by cool murmuring Arno and the poplar grove that softens the grass, I lay, now plucking violets, now sprays of myrtle, and listened to Menalcas contending with Lycidas in song! (125–32)

Rather than dismiss Tuscany as a wandering error, Thyrsis translates Damon from England to Tuscany, or almost does. Thyrsis starts to say something like, I had a wonderful Tuscan friend right at home under the English elm, why did I not stay with him? He was even from a Tuscan town more ancient, more Roman, than Florence. But Thyrsis abandons this expected line of comparison almost immediately and rather than bring himself and our attention back to England, his imagination takes him back to Florence *without* Damon. He lies under the poplars along the Arno, not the elm by the Thames or Dee or Colne. He even breaks the poem's dominant second-person address — "you" — to Damon, and addresses the "Tuscan shepherds," in gratitude for their attentions and gifts: "Even I myself dared enter the contest, nor do I think I greatly displeased you, for I still have with me your gifts, reed-baskets, bowls, and shepherd's pipes with waxen stops. Nay, both Dati and Francini, renowned for their eloquence and their learning, and both of Lydian blood, have taught my name to their beeches" (133–38).

Once his imagination has transported him, and us, back to Florence among the famous Tuscan poets, Thyrsis recalls how often he thought of Damon, back in England lying on the banks of the Colne, or "in the fields of Cassivellaunus" (149). The double, even triple, distancing devices signal the intensity of the nostalgic imagination. Milton, masked as Thyrsis, a shepherd from the golden age of Arcadian pastoral, imagines himself back by the banks of the Arno, dreaming of keeping company with his old friend Damon: "let us go and lie down a while in the murmuring shade. . . . You shall go over [with] me your healing herbs and juices . . . and tell me of the physician's art" (148–52). The weight of such ambivalence is almost staggering. And while he lies by the Arno, his friend already has turned to "dark ashes" (*cinis ater*). Thyrsis curses the herbs and "simples" that proved helpless to save his friend's life, and he is on the verge of cursing his own art for proving just as useless, for seducing him so far from his friend, but as before, the symmetry of blame and regret falls apart:

> Ah! Perish the herbs and the simples, perish the physician's art, since they have profited their master nothing! And I — for I know not what my pipe was grandly sounding — it is now eleven nights and a day — and then perhaps I had put my lips to new pipes, but they burst asunder, broken at the fastening, and could no more bear

the deep tones — I hesitate too lest I seem puffed up, yet I will tell
the tale — give place then, O forests. (153–60)

With this passage the poem finally turns its back on grief and
despair. The tones that had dominated the poem up to this point —
"nothing in the present moves me, nor have I any hope for the
future" (93) — are now utterly changed. On the verge of blaming
his art or his muse for keeping him from his dying friend, Thyrsis
turns instead to tell of his ambitious plans to write a British epic.
Imitating Virgil and Tasso before him, Milton insists that his pastoral pipes cannot contain his epic ambitions; he is, as it were, bursting out of this very poem, bursting out of this elegy for his friend,
and into epic song. He stumbles a bit, for the very form of this poem
in which he announces his ambitions is itself too fragile to contain the message of its own undoing, but even his stumbling — "ab
undecima iam lux est altera nocte" — imitates Virgil's own tran-
sition from singing in and of the woods to the singing of imperial
history and the cosmos.[24] And he imagines that just as he bursts
from pastoral lament into epic song, so the object of his lament,
his friend Damon, will cease to be a mere shepherd and join instead
the "blessed dances" and "joyous revels" that "rage under the
thyrsus of Zion" (218–19).

"*Amor*," says Thyrsis, is not in the end a god of pastoral elegy,
but a god of highest heaven and most noble deeds:

> He does not aim at little souls and the ignoble hearts of the rabble,
> but, rolling his flaming eyes about, unwearied he ever scatters his
> missiles on high through the spheres, and never aims his shots
> downward. Hence minds immortal and forms divine are inflamed
> with love.
>
> You too are among these, Damon . . . surely you are among these.
> (193–198)

The poem bids farewell to Ovid's *Amor* and to the pastoral love of
forests, rivers, shepherds and nymphs. It announces that Thyrsis
will no longer be Thyrsis, but Milton, and Damon no longer Damon,
but Diodatus. The epic Milton finally composed sang a greater theme

than ancient British kings and heroes, and Diodati's place in that poem is indeed one of highest heavenly distinction. Milton's great friend, elegiacally recomposed of equal parts Charles Diodati, Carlo Dati, Manso and Florence, returns in *Paradise Lost* as Raphael, the heavenly friend, given by God to converse with Adam and tell him, among other things, something of the intense purity of heavenly love. Milton surely did not know this in 1639, but his lines to Damon anticipate the friendship between Adam and Raphael depicted in *Paradise Lost:*

> But now that the rights of heaven are yours, stand by my side and gently befriend me, whatever be now your name, whether you would still be our Damon, or whether you prefer to be called Diodati, by which divine name all the dwellers in heaven will know you. . . . Because a rosy blush, and a youth without stain were dear to you, because you never tasted the pleasure of marriage, lo! For you are reserved a virgin's honors. (207–14)

When we hear, in *Paradise Lost,* book 5, the Father's commission to Raphael,

> Go therefore, half this day as friend with friend
> Converse with *Adam,* in what Bowre or shade
> Thou find'st him from the heat of Noon retir'd,
> To respit his day-labour with repast,
> Or with repose,   (*PL* 5.229–33)

we remember Milton's elegiac nostalgia, retrojected memories of intimate conversations on elevated topics beneath an elm, along the Colne. If Milton never actually enjoyed such conversations with Diodati, nevertheless they inspire his imagination of Adam and Raphael's extended conversation, which is so delightful that Adam says to Raphael something Milton probably never had the chance to say to Diodati:

> while I sit with thee, I seem in Heav'n,
> And sweeter thy discourse is to my eare
> Then Fruits of Palm-tree pleasantest to thirst

> And hunger both, from labour, at the houre
> Of sweet repast; they satiate, and soon fill,
> Though pleasant, but thy words with Grace Divine
> Imbu'd, bring to thir sweetness no satietie.   (*PL* 8.210–16)

But he also no doubt wished he had.

Conversation, then, is erotic, and it is characteristic of the manner of life one shares with one's friend, one's other self. It denotes the community of conversation to which one belongs. A gentleman does not properly have conversation with rabble, with hearts *"ignobile vulgi"* (*Epitaphium Damonis*, 193). And a Christian, stipulated Paul, should have his conversation in heaven, even as he goes about life on earth. Conversation with a friend can emulate heavenly conversation, perhaps serve even as an earnest of its divine delights. But marriage? Is marriage not bound to the body — two become "one flesh"? What kind of conversation is marriage? Is it low and earthly or may it also be, like classical friendship, an earnest of heavenly love? Does marriage denote one's citizenship on earth, or in heaven, or in Paradise? Can marriage be reimagined as conversation fit for one whose dignity and citizenship belong in heaven? Is citizenship better figured, as in classical republicanism, as rooted in the friendships between virtuous men as equals, or figured as a marriage, still an insistently unequal — and as Aristotle insisted, aristocratic — relationship? More simply put, is heavenly citizenship more like a friendship or a marriage? A republic of heaven or a kingdom of heaven?[25] Norbrook is correct, of course, to point out that the "relations between king and subject were often figured as a marriage," but when Milton suggests that a man suffering from an imprudent match suffers a kind of tyranny, he reverses the figure's gender roles. A tyrant has ceased being like a husband and has become an unfit wife to whom continued submission and obedience threaten the utter loss of manly liberty.[26] Norbrook is also correct to suggest that Milton's republicanism grew as he wrote his tracts on divorce and on prelates. Milton believed that prelates also represented a threat to manly liberty; like unfit wives and tyrannical kings, prelates seduced men with their various charms into forms of submission unbefitting true manliness.[27] Those were some of the questions Milton wrestled with throughout the divorce tracts, and they were also the questions he posed over and over again in his greatest epic and dramatic poems.

THREE

"Single Imperfection" and Adam's Manly Self

*In the case of human beings what seems to count as living
together is this sharing of conversation and thought, not sharing
the same pasture, as in the case of grazing animals.*
— Aristotle, *Nicomachean Ethics*, 1170b13–14

Milton announced on several occasions that he learned most
about true love from Plato and Xenophon, especially, as I
will later consider, from Plato's *Symposium* and its remarkable teaching on enlightened pederasty. Socrates wanted to bring mutuality
and equality to the Athenian pederastic practices and so encourage the higher love that builds communities and can bring forth
immortal progeny in the shape of great art, laws, poetry and civi-
lizations. But when it comes to ontological distinctions between
human beings and other beings, Milton appears to rely heavily
on Aristotle, especially the *Nicomachean Ethics*. Milton read the
Creation accounts of Genesis as if they told the story behind
Aristotle's ontological distinctions between humans and animals,
humans and gods, and even between men and women. Much as he

95

believed that Plato's story of the birth of Eros "sorted" perfectly with the story of the creation of Eve in Genesis 2, he seems also to have believed Aristotle's ontological categories sorted perfectly with those of the Bible, both its Hebrew and Christian parts.

Human conversation requires human beings. Generally the process of identifying beings as human involves a lot of talk about what beings are not human, or less human, or even more human, than others. Though men may have friendly relations with animals, slaves, and other less-than-excellent or less-than-virtuous, even less-than-fully-human people, the conversation dignified enough to be characteristic of virtuous friendship takes place only between people who are equals in the pursuit of human happiness, dignity and magnanimity. Human happiness, says Aristotle, "is a certain activity of the soul expressing virtue" (*Ethics*, 1099b25–26). Animals are not said to be happy "since none of them can share in this activity." Children gradually learn to do the sort of actions that constitute happiness, but they are not, as children, fully human (1100a1–4). Aristotle allows slaves to be sort of human, but also sort of inhuman. "There is," he states, "neither friendship nor justice toward soulless things" (1161b1), and that is why no one can be said to hold friendly conversation with a horse or a cow or a plant or a tool. Since a slave is properly thought of as "a tool with a soul," one can have friendly relations with a slave insofar as he is human, but cannot insofar as he is a soulless tool. Slaves, then, are only part human. And in the *Politics* Aristotle discusses the relative humanity of women in the same paragraphs along with slaves and children, concluding that there exists a hierarchy of relative humanity, based on the assumption that humanity may be measured by the degree to which the soul's "deliberative faculty" is present:

> The freeman rules over the slave after another manner from that in which the male rules over the female, or the man over the child; although the parts of the soul are present in all of them, they are present in different degrees. For the slave has no deliberative faculty at all; the woman has, but it is without authority, and the child has, but it is immature. (1260a9–15)[1]

Authority, then, is said to be directly proportional to the degree and kind of "deliberative faculty" one possesses, and though women have a full human deliberative faculty, and thus are superior to and should exercise authority over children and slaves, their reason and virtues are differently directed than men's. Men show courage in commanding; women in obeying, says Aristotle, and "this holds of all other virtues" (1260a20–24).

Women then, by virtue of being human, are capable of virtuous friendship with men; nevertheless, Aristotle taught that only quite rarely did marriage achieve the status of a proper friendship of virtue. In the discussion of the kinds and degrees of *philia* that lie at the center of the *Nicomachean Ethics,* Aristotle discusses the relations of husbands and wives under the category of unequal or proportional friendships, those that fall short of fully virtuous friendships because of the inequality of the partners:

> The friendship of man and woman also seems to be natural. For human beings naturally tend to form couples more than to form cities, to the extent that the household is prior to the city, and more necessary, and child-bearing is shared more widely among the animals. With the other animals this is the extent of their community. Human beings, however, share a household not only for child-bearing, but also for the benefits in their life. For from the start their functions are divided, with a different one for the man and the woman; hence each supplies the other's needs by contributing a special function to the common good. Hence their friendship seems to include both utility and pleasure. (1162a17–24)

One of Aristotle's chief tasks in the *Ethics* is to distinguish between friendships based on utility and pleasure, on the one hand, and those founded in virtue, on the other. He also is everywhere concerned with how one properly manages inequalities in friendship, for the best friendships, he says, are between equals. By this reckoning, it is worth noting that Aristotle does not consider the Athenian pederasty of his day, which many thought the most human and dignified sort of relationship, a proper friendship of virtue, for he regards it as an "incomplete friendship" in which each does not "take pleasure in the same things."[2]

> With these [incomplete friends] also, the friendships are most endur-
> ing when they get the same thing — e.g. pleasure — from each
> other, and, moreover, get it from the same source. . . . They must not
> be like the erotic lover and the boy he loves. For these do not take
> pleasure in the same things; the lover takes pleasure in seeing his
> beloved, while the beloved takes pleasure in being courted by his
> lover. (1157a3–10)

Aristotle's notion of lovers getting the same benefits from each other
and taking pleasure in the same things may have taken its cue from
Socrates's criticism of Athenian pederasty in the *Symposium*.
When Alcibiades tries to insinuate himself as Socrates's darling,
Socrates responds by saying,

> You must see in me a beauty that is extraordinary, and quite differ-
> ent from your own good looks. If, having detected this, you're try-
> ing to partake of it with me and to offer beauty for beauty, you
> shouldn't think you can obtain more from me in return for less. You're
> trying to obtain true beauty in exchange for apparent beauty, "gold
> for bronze." (*Symposium*, 218e)

Socrates's enlightened pederasty brings equality to the institution,
equality of gifts, of pleasures, and of inward beauty.

Those who engage in sex merely for the sake of utility rather
than pleasure, says Aristotle, are friends to an even lesser extent
(11–14). Plato's Socrates taught a kind of enlightened pederasty that
brought equality, mutuality and duration to homoerotic love. He
taught that the best sort of homoerotic friends also procreate, and
bring to birth on each other's souls progeny more immortal than
those that heteroerotic couples can produce. He also taught that
the best sort of male friendships were higher and more dignified
than the best marriages, but Aristotle allows that some marriages,
though probably few, can rise above mere utility and pleasure and
achieve the status of virtuous friendship: "And it [friendship
between married people] may also be a friendship for virtue, if they
are decent. For each has a proper virtue, and this will be a source
of enjoyment for them" (1162a25–26).

Milton, and eventually modern society, takes this allowance several steps further. First, Milton will not be content to allow that some married people may also be friends in virtue; that would leave marriage as one sort of relationship (for utility and perhaps pleasure) and friendship another, as Aristotle supposed they were. Milton wants marriage *itself* to be redefined as a friendship of virtue even though he elsewhere gives plenty of evidence that he believes there are few men and even fewer women sufficiently virtuous to be capable of virtuous friendship, in or outside of marriage. Second, he wants marriage to be advanced to the status of *the* principal human relation, replacing homosocial friendship. Genesis taught that Eve was created to be Adam's first friend, to remedy his constitutive loneliness. Thus, even though Milton takes many of his cues and much of his doctrine about human relations from Plato and Aristotle, he no longer wants to believe that men define humanity and manliness chiefly in relations with other men; they must define it instead in relations with a wife, and a wife who is fully human, but not equal in authority nor exactly similar to a man in her "deliberative faculty." Human conversation must be rethought on a heterosocial model, for which Aristotle, by allowing that married persons (albeit in rare instances) could also be friends of virtue, provided a small opening through which Milton proceeded to drive a very large, and sometimes clumsy, wagon.

For Milton, a Christian and a republican, Aristotle's sense of dignified human conversation required some adjustments, but surprisingly fewer than one might expect or wish. Paul had taught that a Christian's conversation should be spiritually in heaven (Phil. 3:20) and warned his followers to abjure "the former conversation" of the old man (Eph. 4:22). Peter likewise taught his followers to cultivate a reputation among the as yet unconverted for holy conversation (1 Pet. 1:15, 1 Pet. 2:12). Once one had been made a "new man" and won citizenship in heaven, one's conversation was expected to be "honest," "chaste" and "holy." For women, "chaste conversation coupled with fear" meant being "in subjection to your own husbands" (1 Pet. 3:1–2). For men, it meant honoring their wives just as one would take special care for a "weaker vessel" and behaving with compassion and courtesy toward one's brethren (7–8). For Paul, Christian conversation should be as free as possible from concerns of the body, the old man, the flesh. He even recommended that "it is good for a man not to touch a woman" (1 Cor. 7:1). Good Christian conversation, like the conversation of classical friendship, was principally a homosocial, not a heterosocial matter. Just as Aristotle details the manners by which excellent people should interact with children, slaves, women and other unequals, so the apostles stipulate how Christians should interact with wives, gentiles and the as yet unconverted. If one's conversation (*politeoumai*) is in heaven, then one must be especially careful how one interacts with those whose conversation is of a lower order. Similarly, Aristotle taught that the excellent or virtuous man, born to rule rather than to be ruled, and guided by magnanimity and its attendant level of self-esteem, will form strong friendships with fit partners in virtuous conversation, men like themselves, but they must also then understand how to manage interactions with unequals. A citizen will have to deal with children, wives and slaves, but he will not want to live with them in daily conversation, nor should he.

The anonymous author of the *Answer* is explicitly excluded from such happiness, but so also, it would seem, are those unfortunate gentlemen whom canon law refuses to set free from the inhuman bondage of marriage to an unfit wife:

> when he shall find himselfe bound fast to an uncomplying discord of nature, or, as it oft happens, to an image of earth and fleam, with whom he lookt to be the copartner of a sweet and gladsome society, and sees withall that his bondage is now inevitable, though he be almost the strongest Christian, he will be ready to dispair in vertue, and mutin against divine providence. (YP 2:254)

Men like the answerer, indeed most of the vulgar sort, are suited to the sort of "conversation" cattle enjoy, but what of proper, well-bred and educated manly men who have been unfitly yoked in marriage? According to Milton's arguments, they can actually lose that dignity of soul that is requisite to manly liberty. *Paradise Lost* sings in tragic and epic strains about Adam, the first man to submit his heavenly citizenship to the indignities of fallen conversation. *Samson Agonistes* sings in tragic strains about a hero who tried to reclaim his position as a heavenly conversant by divorcing his unfit wife. Finally, *Paradise Regain'd* celebrates in heroic verse the patience and heroic martyrdom of a man — the first man since Adam — for whom loneliness, man's "single imperfection," is no longer a tragic problem, but instead an opportunity to reestablish conversation with God.

Adam's First Conversation

Let us return for an extended look at how Milton imagines human conversation and heavenly conversation within the context of a hierarchical ontology. In *Paradise Lost*, Milton imagines Adam's first investigations into self-knowledge as conversational. He tries to talk to his maker, he tries to talk to the hills and valleys, he tries to talk to the animals. Milton invites us to watch Adam discover and define his humanity — his manliness — according to which partners he finds are fit for conversation with him.

I take as my starting point Linda Gregerson's observation that Milton's Adam "invents a self through discourse, by naming his likeness to and his difference from the rest of creation. In this invention God is his Socratic tutor."[3] Gregerson's Lacanian analysis of Adam's subject formation (like the one she also does for Milton's Eve) is brilliant and suggestive and has helped many readers think harder and more clearly about this topic. But I think it needs correction. Milton does not imagine an Adam who invents himself. The manly subjectivity Adam represents was prescribed, according to Milton, by metaphysics and ontology. Self-fashioning and self-invention are practices familiar to Milton but hardly win his approval; in his epic cosmos the great self-fashioner is Satan.

Lacanian theory teaches that subjectivity and the unconscious underlying it are structured like a language, and that identity is acquired along with language through an elaborate series of misrecognitions and misnamings of others.[4] Milton's Adam, however, comes into being with language and his subjectivity hard-wired. He does not acquire language; it comes preinstalled like a computer's motherboard. He finds it fully functional the first time he tries to speak:

> to speak I tri'd, and forthwith spake
> My tongue obey'd and readily could name
> What e'er I saw. Thou Sun, said I, faire Light,
> And thou enlight'nd Earth, so fresh and gay,
> Ye Hills and Dales, ye Rivers, Woods, and Plaines,
> And ye that live and move, fair Creatures, tell,
> Tell, if ye saw, how came I thus, how here?   (*PL* 8.271–77)

Adam already knows the sun is a being apart from him and is addressable by its own name. So also the earth, hills, dales, rivers and woods. "I" and "thou" are always-already distinct for the first man. Because his language is hard-wired rather than acquired, the landscape he sees around him already slots very nicely into the not-I category grammar prescribes, and Adam addresses it as such. For Milton, Adam's apostrophic address to the hills and dales is a poetic figure, but not, I think, for Milton's Adam. Before he articulates his aloneness, his need for a conversation partner, Adam already betrays it by inviting conversation with whatever he sees.

The end result of the elaborate process of misrecognitions and misnamings by which Lacan traces the precipitation of human subjectivity constitutes what Milton takes to be the ontic state of things as they were created by God. Milton does not want us to regard Adam as precipitating an identity as he acquires language, still less as forging a self-invented humanness or manliness, but simply as discovering one already pretty firmly in place. I say *pretty* firmly in place because although the process of self-recognition Milton dramatizes is not psychoanalytic, it does betray traces of an emerging sense of psychological development. Adam learns about himself more as a humanist student of Socrates than as a Scholastic student of Aristotle, and though his language and basic subjectivity come fully formed, he needs to discover many of the subtle details of humanness and manliness by trial and error. And these trials and errors take on some of the character of a psychological process; that is to say, they look sometimes a bit more like experiential installations than discoveries. Nevertheless, Adam's Socratic interlocutor is the creator God who always-already knows what Adam will discover about himself.

In Milton's Paradise, the only truly self-fashioning activity Adam may pursue is disobedience, and Milton portrays that as self-annihilation. What is more, it is a self-annihilation that Milton's God has already predicted, and for which he already has made special arrangements.

Adam knows by "sudden apprehension" the names and the nature of the beings he addresses, but he does not automatically know which, if any, of them is a proper partner for human conversation. That he learns by talking. Thus, conversation not only denotes Adam's ontological status, where his proper conversation lies, but also the process by which he discovers his *politeoumai*, his conversational place. If conversation with nature could satisfy Adam, he would be one sort of being. If conversation with the sun were proper to him, he would be another; the same goes for conversation with animals. Milton's Adam tries all of these in turn. He also tries holding a conversation with God and, partially or temporarily, he succeeds.

Before turning to that conversation in detail, however, it is worth noting that one of Milton's contemporaries, Andrew Marvell, took a great deal of pleasure in imagining an Adam for whom conversation with nature was not only satisfying, but preferable to conversation with anyone else, including Eve. If Milton read Marvell's "The Garden" (and I find it hard to believe he did not), he would have paid special attention to the phrase "without a mate" and the words "solitary" and "alone," for Marvell's poem actually proposes two mildly contradictory but intensely heterodox notions. The first is that solitude, far from being a problem, is actually what made Paradise before Eve a happy state. Marvell, no doubt with tongue in cheek, directly contradicts the normally accepted sense of Genesis 2:18 in which God is reported to have said, "It is not good that the man should be alone, I will make an help meet for him":

> Such was that happy Garden state,
> While Man there walk'd without a Mate:
> After a Place so pure, and sweet,
> What other Help could yet be meet!
> But 'twas beyond a Mortal's share
> To wander solitary there:
> Two Paradises 'twere in one
> To live in Paradise alone.[5]

In this fantasy, Eden itself was Adam's special friend, his meet help, his individual solace dear: "After a Place so pure, and sweet, / What other Help could yet be meet!" Marvell's reverie is a version of the familiar misogynist fantasy of a world without women, the masculine paradise so often celebrated in song and story. Milton's story of Adam and Eve in Paradise directly challenges this misogynist fantasy, even though his version of heaven, at least as a fallen Adam imagines it, relocates it. Heaven is the place where there are no females, alleges Adam, and neither the Archangel Raphael nor the narrator disputes that:

> O why did God,
> Creator wise, that peopl'd highest Heav'n
> With Spirits Masculine, create at last
> This noveltie on Earth, this fair defect
> Of Nature, and not fill the World at once
> With Men as Angels without Feminine,
> Or find some other way to generate
> Mankind?   (*PL* 10.888–95)

Marvell's fantasy does not concern itself in the least with generating mankind, but it does meditate at length upon what it regards as the particularly elevated or sophisticated erotics at the center of an Eve-less Paradise. The best erotic partners, the poem tries to suggest, are trees; even the pagan gods, as Ovid reports, knew that:

> The *Gods,* that mortal Beauty chase,
> Still in a Tree did end their race.
> *Apollo* hunted *Daphne* so,
> Only that She might Laurel grow.
> And *Pan* did after *Syrinx* speed,
> Not as a Nymph, but for a Reed.   ("The Garden," 27–32)

The phrase "end their race" resonates in many ways, generating both humor and a certain disingenuousness about the speaker's ostensible arguments in favor of sex with trees. Nowhere do Ovid's stories suggest that gods like Apollo pursued females like Daphne because they knew in advance they would end up making love to decorative shrubberies. We are meant to see the silliness of the argument, especially when we consider that such nonprocreative lovemaking would indeed end their race. We are invited to chuckle a bit at paganism, misrepresented here as silly gods trying to copulate with trees. Milton's Adam considers intimate conversation with his natural environment, and the sun and moon, for only a second or two. They do not answer, at least not with human language, so he moves on, confident that they never were meant to be fit partners for him.

Marvell's speaker, on the other hand, imagines nature in all her forms, especially fruit trees, as catering to the first man's every sensual desire:

> Ripe Apples drop about my head;
> The Luscious Clusters of the Vine
> Upon my Mouth do crush their Wine;
> The Nectaren, and curious Peach,
> Into my hands themselves do reach;
> Stumbling on Melons, as I pass,
> Insnar'd with Flow'rs, I fall on Grass.   ("The Garden," 34–40)

In this erotic daydream, the speaker does not so much imagine copulating with Nature as simply lying back and letting nature attend to his every appetite, even, as it turns out, the appetite for solitary withdrawal into one's own mind, for what amounts to conversation with one's self, a second self within rather than without, an inner narcissistic best friend.

> Mean while the Mind, from pleasure less,
> Withdraws into its happiness:
> The Mind, that Ocean where each kind
> Does streight its own resemblance find;
> Yet it creates, transcending these,
> Far other Worlds, and other Seas,
> Annihilating all that's made
> To a green Thought in a green Shade.   (41–48)

There the mind accomplishes the kind of procreative erotics Plato's Diotima regarded as the highest form of procreation — the imagination of other and new worlds that transcend those familiar to the body.

Milton appears familiar with the sort of fantasy Marvell's poem advances and he rejects all the candidates for human companionship it proposes — trees, nature, even the inner mental self. What's more, the Adam of Genesis is commanded to reproduce. Bodily reproduction may be too undignified to serve as a defining purpose of marriage, but it is, Milton acknowledges, a necessity (*DDD*, YP 2:235). Milton's more orthodox version of Adam differs from God in two important ways: his need for companionship, a distinctly human need, and his need to reproduce, a need he shares with the other creatures. Milton's Adam longs for a human partner, for "Collateral love and deerest amitie," which will also enable the reproduction, both in body and in spirit, of man's image. The pleasure in solitude or in the self Marvell's poem imagines is a pleasure Milton's Adam says only God — the one and only, always happy alone God — can enjoy:

> Thou in thy secresie although alone,
> Best with thy self accompanied, seek'st not
> Social communication, yet so pleas'd,
> Canst raise thy Creature to what highth thou wilt
> Of Union or Communion, deifi'd.   (*PL* 8.427–31)

And God is untouched by any necessity, not only the necessity to propagate, but also the necessity for conversation of any kind (*Christian Doctrine*, YP 6:209). The pleasure in nature Marvell's speaker celebrates as a "meeter" help to man than woman, Milton's Adam also enjoys, but then he notices such pleasures will fail to bring the happiness and contentment proper to human beings unless they are shared with a friend: "In solitude / What happiness, who can enjoy alone, / Or all enjoying, what contentment find?" (8.364–66). Marvell's first man imitates God in his preference for solitude, if not in his special love of nature. Another godlike feature is his desire to withdraw into his own mind for happiness, though the narcissism implied by "its own resemblance" may appear to some ungodlike. Milton's Adam knows from the start that he is a godlike being (much as he later knows immediately that Eve is a "Man-like" being), but he also knows from the start that what makes him not-God, or human, is that solitude is "not good" for him as it is for God. We are reminded that Aristotle believed that though virtuous friends will always wish good for each other, no man will wish his friend the "greatest good, e.g. to be a god," for if one's friend becomes a god, "he will no longer have friends" since gods do not need friendship (*Ethics*, 1159a6–8).[6]

Milton's Adam comes to his conclusions about his ungodlike desire for companionship and his need for procreation over the course of a series of innocent mistakes. Somewhat like Marvell's speaker, he attempts a conversation with Nature, addressing himself to the sun, earth, hills, dales, rivers, woods and plains, but they cannot answer him (*PL* 8.273–82). And like Marvell's persona, Adam passes into a trancelike state wherein he becomes aware of himself as a being almost separate from his own consciousness, thinking of himself as passing into a "former state" (290). We would be mistaken to think that the "former state" Milton's Adam imagines is equivalent to Marvell's "green Thought in a green shade," but both share a quality of self-consciousness in unconsciousness — that uncanny sense of watching one's self fall asleep, or dream, or die. This divided self, the watcher and the watched, introduces the possibility of self-communion, the mind withdrawing into itself, and therefore of necessity dividing into two selves, the quintessential image of friendship — one soul in two bodies or two persons.

Milton's Adam finds no human conversation with Nature, nor does he seem interested in making friends with himself; his narcissism will be much more complex, routed or detoured through the othering differences of gender and gendered ontologies. He spends hardly a moment in self-regard of this sort:

> My self I then perus'd, and Limb by Limb
> Survey'd, and sometimes went, and sometimes ran
> With supple joints, as lively vigour led:
> But who I was, or where, or from what cause,
> Knew not.   (*PL* 8.267–71)

This knowledge of his own body is not the knowledge he seeks. Knowing his body is not tantamount to knowing himself. As Bruce Smith reminds us, the words "self" and "person" in early modern English usually refer to one's body, not one's inner self.[7] Adam's knowledge of his outward self and the rest of creation comes hardwired, requiring nothing like the mirror-stage of recognition and misrecognition Lacan describes, but knowledge of his inward self does involve a kind of mirror process — a dream vision of the "shape divine" in whose likeness his inner self was made.

Likewise, Milton's Adam spends no more than a moment contemplating conversation with animals. Milton follows a fairly standard Calvinist interpretation of Genesis that holds that Adam named the animals brought before him, not haphazardly or "rashly but from certain knowledge"; "having closely inspected them," he gave them "appropriate names, agreeing with the nature of each"

(*Commentary on Genesis*, 131–32). Says Adam, "I nam'd them, as they pass'd, and understood / Thir Nature, with such knowledg God endu'd / My sudden apprehension" (*PL* 8.352–54). "Sudden apprehension" endowed by God is how Milton's Adam knows the world around him. Milton's God disingenuously suggests that Adam might find delightful conversation with animals,

> What call'st thou solitude, is not the Earth
> With various living creatures, and the Aire
> Replenisht, and all these at thy command
> To come and play before thee; know'st thou not
> Thir language and thir wayes? They also know,
> And reason not contemptibly; with these
> Find pastime, and beare rule; thy Realm is large. (*PL* 8.369–75)

Embedded in this suggestion are two clues to its disingenuousness: the first is an allusion to a passage from the book of Proverbs, and the second is the reminder that Adam is meant to "beare rule" over these creatures. One cannot be proper friends, or complete virtuous friends, with one's subjects, and Adam instinctively knows this. The allusion to Proverbs illustrates much the same point using a biblical image that requires a bit more unpacking.

When the Creator tells Adam that he may command the various living creatures to "come and play" before him, the poem echoes the words a personified Wisdom speaks in Proverbs 8:30: "I was daily his delight, rejoicing always before him." Wisdom uses the past tense, speaking of the delight she afforded God in those days when he created the universe. Milton also alludes to this passage in *Tetrachordon*'s exposition on Genesis 2:18 where he claims that everyone, even the Creator himself, needs to have a vacation now and then. This is part of his argument against Augustine's "crabbed" opinion that a man, rather than a woman, would have been a more suitable companion to remedy Adam's loneliness. Augustine argues that procreation must be the principal end of marriage and the chief reason God created Eve for Adam; if conversation and companionship were the chief reason, God would have given him a male friend instead, for "Austin contests," "manly friendship in all other regards had been a more becoming solace for *Adam,* than to spend so many secret years in an empty world with one woman" (YP 2:596). Milton scorns this as nonsense, but he fails to make the argument we might well have expected — that a woman is as fit a conversation partner as a man, and that men can enjoy with women the same higher form of procreation Plato had reserved to male lovers. Instead, Milton argues that men need a break now and then from the intensity of homosocial conversation. What goes on between men can sometimes, it seems, be a strain.

> There is a peculiar comfort in the married state beside the genial bed, which no other society affords. No mortal nature can endure either in the actions of Religion, or study of Wisdom, without sometime slackening the cords of intense thought and labour: which lest we should think faulty, God himself conceals us not his own recreations before the World was built: *I was,* saith the eternal Wisdom, *daily his delight, playing always before him.* And to him indeed Wisdom is as a high tower of pleasure, but to us a steep hill, and we toiling ever about the bottom: he executes with ease the exploits of his Omnipotence, as easy as with us it is to will: but no worthy enterprise can be done by us without continual plodding and wearisomeness to our faint and sensitive abilities. We cannot therfore always be contemplative, or pragmatical abroad, but have need of some delightful intermissions, wherin the enlarg'd soul may leave off a while her severe schooling; and like a glad youth in wandring vacancy, may keep her holidays to joy and harmless pastime: which as she cannot well do without company, so in no company so well as where the different sex in most resembling unlikeness, and most unlike resemblance, cannot but please best, and be pleas'd in the aptitude of that variety. (YP 2:596–97)

We are asked to agree that a man cannot find the relaxation, the slackening of the cords of intense thought and labor, he requires by enjoying the company of another man, at least not so effectively as he can in the company of a woman. And this peculiar comfort only women can provide has nothing to do with sex. We are invited to liken such delightful intermissions to the pleasure God once took in Wisdom's company before he created the world. She played before him, and this constituted for him a welcome "recreation." For man Wisdom is an unsuitable partner for vacations and intermissions; to mortals, she is "a steep hill, and we toiling ever about the bottom." Only to the Omnipotent is Wisdom a delightful recreation. The analogy becomes clear: just as the omnipotent God finds delight in Wisdom, a partner slightly inferior to him, so man requires a slightly inferior partner so that his soul may have a holiday now and then. Milton's God wants Adam to recognize, however, that the creatures Adam may call to play before him are too inferior to be fit partners for his conversation. What this argument leaves unsaid but firmly in place is the same hierarchy of conversation partners both Plato and Aristotle assumed — a man has his serious conversation with other men, pursuing Wisdom and performing the "actions of Religion" and being "pragmatical abroad"; he has his holiday conversation with his wife. This certainly upgrades marriage from simple animal procreation to human conversation; a wife is much more than an animal delighting a man, but it disallows the full human status Milton probably meant to confer upon it. Just as important, it leaves a man with two conversations, two *politeumai:* he has one conversation abroad and another at home, one for *pro*creation of the soul and another for *re*creation of the soul. In *Paradise Lost* Milton shows us an Adam forced to choose between having a conversation that is virtually "in heaven" and having continued conversation with his wife.

Milton imagines that before Eve was made Adam had a serious conversation with God. God would seem, on a number of scores, to be a fit partner for conversation with Adam. Like God, Adam was intended to rule. Adam does not miss God's cues — "Find pastime, and beare rule"; he knows that on earth he is God's "substitute" (*PL* 8.381). Like God's, his beauty is the invisible sort — "manly grace / And Wisdom, which alone is truly fair" (*PL* 4.490–91). Eve's beauty, we later discover, is more "in outward shew / Elaborate, of inward less exact" (8.538–39). But, of course, no one can be equal to God, for all are God's creatures, and therefore inferior by definition.

Milton's monistic ontology, however, holds that all things once came from God and they all, if not perverted, will eventually return to union with God. The *telos* of all created things, according to this logic, would be intimate conversation with God. Raphael articulates the ontology of the prelapsarian world in book 5:

> O *Adam,* one Almightie is, from whom
> All things proceed, and up to him return,
> If not deprav'd from good, created all
> Such to perfection, one first matter all,
> Indu'd with various forms, various degrees
> Of substance, and in things that live, of life;
> But more refin'd, more spiritous, and pure,
> As neerer to him plac't or neerer tending
> Each in thir several active Sphears assignd,
> Till body up to spirit work, in bounds
> Proportiond to each kind.   (*PL* 5.469–79)

Milton also believed that fallen people could gradually earn heavenly citizenship and heavenly conversation, or at least he makes the Elder Brother in *A Mask* assert this:

> So dear to Heav'n is Saintly chastity,
> That when a soul is found sincerely so,
> A thousand liveried Angels lacky her,
> Driving far off each thing of sin and guilt,
> And in cleer dream, and solemn vision
> Tell her of things that no gross ear can hear,
> Till oft convers with heav'nly habitants
> Begin to cast a beam on th' outward shape,
> The unpolluted temple of the mind,
> And turns it by degrees to the souls essence,
> Till all be made immortal.   (*A Mask,* 453–63)

As long as Adam remains obedient and chaste, conversation with "heav'nly habitants" can help him become immortal. Adam knows,

again instinctively, that God can, if he chooses, "raise thy Creature
to what highth thou wilt / Of Union or Communion, deifi'd" (*PL*
8.430–31). Conversation with God could make Adam even more
godlike, but in the end friendship with God the Father is out of the
question, even though Milton fancies that Adam conversed at
length with God and together they made a new being, a woman to
be Adam's proper friend. God does not need a friend, so the two
cannot get the same things from each other as friendship requires;
they are hopelessly unequal. Until Adam lives in heaven, he cannot live with God; besides, carrying on a conversation with God
appears to overwhelm Adam.

Until he begins his conversation with God, Adam has been the
subject in all his interactions with others; he apostrophizes the hills,
dales, rivers and other fair creatures, he names the sun, moon, earth
and beasts. They all turn out to be unresponsive to direct address.
Adam even tries to address God, though indirectly and impre-
cisely, as "some great maker" (*PL* 8.278). But now Adam shifts into
the unfamiliar role of the *object* of address. The being he seeks but
can neither name nor know the way he knows the creatures, now
addresses him and names him: "Adam rise, / First man . . . / First
Father" (*PL* 8.296–98). To borrow Althusser's famous terminology,
Adam is hailed by name into his predetermined identity of "First
man," "first Father" and domestic lord of creation: "Thy mansion
wants thee, Adam" (*PL* 8.296).[8] Adam was created to fill the "mansion" of the new world as its lord; Satan thinks man was created
to fill the space in God's affections left empty by his own apostasy.
Adam is very much a being intended to fill a void, to address a lack.
He is also a being, as we shall later see, defined not only by *where*
he is wanted, but also by *what* he wants or lacks. Adam is both
lacked and lacking, wanted and wanting.

Adam's next step toward full self-awareness looks more psychological and bears comparison to the processes of recognition and
misrecognition described by Lacanian theory. Adam must gradually work out how he is different from God, a being he cannot at
first see or hear, for he is a spiritual, not a physical, being. Manliness,

from Milton's puritan perspective, lies along the asymptotic limit that distinguishes a bodiless, uncreated God from his creaturely image. Essentialist notions of gender and identity have their beginnings in this puritan ontology. Perfect manliness is to be as much like God as possible without passing back into the state of pure spirit that is God. Thus, manly grace and beauty at their best are invisible, inward; the puritan male ego forms around the hard kernel of an invisible God rather than a narcissistic relation to a body-image.[9]

In Milton's version of the story of the first man, the constitutive gender binary is not masculine versus feminine, but Godhood versus manhood. Before Adam knows himself as not-woman, indeed before he even imagines such a thing as woman, he must wrap his head around the more fundamental category of being godlike but not God, just as Eve is later defined as "manlike, but different sex" (*PL* 8.471). Adam is godlike, but different. What do we call this difference?

In dramatic contrast to Adam's first waking moments of clarity, a ready tongue, and instinctive and perfect recognition of all things around him, Adam's first encounter with his nonphysical maker begins in a dreamlike state. God first appears to him, not as one distinctly other, but as a "shape divine," an inward apparition, a dream vision. The being Slavoj Žižek often refers to as the "Big Other" — God — first appears to Adam as he sleeps, as his own sense of being feels like it is slipping away:

> gentle sleep
> First found me, and with soft oppression seis'd
> My droused sense, untroubl'd, though I thought
> I then was passing to my former state
> Insensible, and forthwith to dissolve:
> When suddenly stood at my Head a dream,
> Whose inward apparition gently mov'd
> My Fancy to believe I yet had being,
> And livd.   (*PL* 8.287–95)

Adam is dreaming; he thinks he is passing into his former state, out of subjectivity altogether, or perhaps back into that great ur-subjectivity to which all things belonged before anything was created, that is, back into oneness with God himself. God first appears to him as a dream, an inward apparition, a "God within," as Quakers might have termed it. The first effect of this inward apparition is to move Adam's "fancy" to a renewed conviction of his own being, as if meeting God for the first time is an experience quite indistinguishable from meeting one's self, as if a conviction of God's being were deeply wound up both with doubts about one's own being and renewed assurance of that same being. God, in Adam's first experience of him, is not immediately Other, but is more like the (M)Other in Lacan's model of emergent subjectivity, not at first other enough to be distinct; one who gradually by a discursive process becomes sufficiently alien to be recognized (and misrecognized) as an other.

Adam understands without being told that he is a god on Earth, but also a creature of another God. Almost as soon as he meets that God, he says: "My Maker, . . . / Hast thou not made me here thy substitute" (*PL* 8.381–82). Milton's Adam gradually learns that manliness is a matter of being godlike but different, much as Adam later recognizes Eve as "manlike but different" (8.471). In Eve's case, Adam calls the difference "sex," but in the case of Adam and God, the "first Father" and the ur-Father, the difference is much harder to name. So hard that Adam (and perhaps Milton) seems unable to do much more than register the difference as an unfilled blank in that famous and difficult sentence,

> My earthly by his Heav'nly overpowerd,
> Which it had long stood under, streind to the highth
> In that celestial Colloquie sublime,
> As with an object that excels the sense,
> Dazl'd and spent, sunk down, and sought repair
> Of sleep, which instantly fell on me, call'd
> By Nature as in aide, and clos'd mine eyes.   (*PL* 8.453–59)

Adam describes here the effects of extended conversation with God. Adam is overwhelmed; he falls into semiconsciousness. From that semiconsciousness (but not, we are supposed to believe, the sleep of reason), Eve is conceived and born. Adam is earthly, whereas God is heavenly; the adjectives must do all the work, functioning as substantives, for it is hard to name that "it," that quality, that essence, that distinguishes God from man. We are tempted to fill in a word like "nature," but speaking about the "nature" of an uncreated, and thus supernatural, being involves a category error. To not name this says more, as in negative theology, than any word could manage.

I think it is useful to think of that unnamed "it" as an early modern form of gender. Eve is manlike, but a different sex, and Adam here discovers that he is godlike, but a different gender. In early modern usage, to gender means "to beget, engender, produce" (*OED*, 2). Thus, to be gendered is, in the first instance, to be begotten or made. In this sense, then, God is not gendered. Milton, like everyone else in his day, spoke of God as "him," but he takes care in his *Christian Doctrine* to define God as "a SPIRIT," "that most perfect essence," the source of all things, and therefore only gendered as a manner of speaking by analogy with created things, a "mental image . . . within the limits of our understandings" (YP 6:140–41, 133).

The first gender distinction, then, at least as far as humans are concerned, is not one between masculinity and femininity, but between godliness and manliness, or between being unengendered (God) and gendered.[10] And thus the ground of all later gender distinctions is the distinction between metaphysical and physical, disembodied and embodied, supernature and nature. Supernatural spirits like God can be gendered masculine and yet "Can either sex assume, or both" (*PL* 1.424). God can be both father and mother to Adam; Adam, when unconscious and overcome by God's heavenly Spirit, can be Eve's mother. Spirits need not be bound by the sex-gender system installed in Creation. Milton, it would seem, knows how to understand sex and gender as performance and play, but only among spirits. The distinction that underwrites the normative sex-gender system is the distinction between God and creature, spirits without bodies and creatures with bodies.

All the rest of the sex/gender system that Milton wants to portray as normative in Paradise, installed by God as natural, follows from this first metaphysical binary. Gender distinctions are mapped on a scale that ranges from uncreated spirit at the top to utterly spiritless bodies at the bottom.

Submitting to God does not mark Adam as having a feminine side; submission is the normal order of things for Milton. Submission to God marks Adam as manly; submission to Adam marks Eve as womanly, and so on. Effeminacy and sodomy and bestiality are simply the practices of misdirecting one's submission. Milton defines original sin as Adam's willful submission to his wife, summarized by the divine prosecutor's case in book 10:

> Was shee thy God, that her thou didst obey
> Before his voice, or was shee made thy guide,
> Superior, or but equal, that to her
> Thou did'st resigne thy Manhood, and the Place
> Wherein God set thee above her made of thee,
> And for thee, whose perfection farr excell'd
> Hers in all real dignitie: Adornd
> She was indeed, and lovely to attract
> Thy Love, not thy Subjection, and her Gifts
> Were such as under Government well seem'd,
> Unseemly to beare rule, which was thy part
> And person, hadst thou known thy self aright.   (*PL* 10.145–56)

Eve was made *for* Adam and made *from* his body. Submitting to her desire spells the end of his manliness; his original manly tendency toward God and Spirit gets perverted. His new tendency aims toward his body and the product of his body, Eve.

Raphael, like *A Mask*'s Elder Brother, also taught that if Adam and Eve remained obedient, eventually their "bodies may at last turn all to Spirit" (*PL* 5.497) and merge back into the godliness whence they came. This would mean that the fundamental distinction between godliness and manliness could gradually be erased, all else remaining the same, simply "by tract of time" (498). Presumably on the way to becoming godly, Eve would pass through a state of manliness? Milton does not speculate so far, because there is a second constituent feature to manliness. Not only is manliness the state of being godlike but not God, it is also the state of being lonely without a woman. "It is not good that the man should be alone," says Genesis 2:18, and Milton explains that in this passage, "*alone* is meant alone without woman; otherwise *Adam* had the company of God himself, and Angels to converse with; all creatures to delight him seriously, or to make him sport. God could have created him out of the same mould a thousand friends and brother *Adams* to have bin his consorts; yet for all this till *Eve* was giv'n him, God reckn'd him to be alone" (*Tetrachordon*, YP 2:595).

Ancient Athenian and Roman culture taught that the quintessentially human relationship was that between friends. Homosocial (and for Plato, homoerotic) friendship was where men learned morality, acquired virtue and practiced citizenship. Men became manly in relation to men. Well schooled in the classical doctrines of friendship, but devoted to a puritan reading of Genesis, Milton insists that the principal human relationship is marriage. In this way, he tries to promote what was long considered a bodily, domestic and procreative matter to the status long enjoyed by classical friendship. In doing so he runs the risk of promoting Eve to full humanity, for friends, according to Aristotle and Cicero, must be equals in order for the friendship to be virtuous (Aristotle, 1156b20; Cicero, 7.23). Perhaps this is why he takes care to be so explicit in defining Adam and Eve as "Not equal, as thir sex not equal seemd / . . . Hee for God only, shee for God in him" (*PL* 4.296, 299), even though this runs the risk of settling marriage into a kind of heteropederasty rather than the enlightened eros Milton claimed to have learned from Socrates.

The path back to pure Spirit is blocked by this feature of manliness, this "single imperfection," as Adam calls it (*PL* 8.423). Conversation with God would not present any problems. Nor would conversation with the archangel, Raphael. Adam loves conversing with Raphael, perhaps even prefers talking with him rather than with Eve. At one point, Eve having left and neither Adam nor Raphael having noticed, Adam tells Raphael in so many words that he could never get enough of conversation with him:

> For while I sit with thee, I seem in Heav'n,
> And sweeter thy discourse is to my eare
> Then Fruits of Palm-tree pleasantest to thirst
> And hunger both, from labour, at the houre
> Of sweet repast; they satiate, and soon fill,
> Though pleasant, but thy words with Grace Divine
> Imbu'd, bring to thir sweetness no satietie.   (*PL* 8.210–16)

But the partner defined as meet for him, designed to remedy the loneliness that distinguishes him from both God and Woman, that partner must draw his attention down the scale of perfection toward the body and away from the spirit. Eve was made from his body; Eve has been declared not equal, inferior, subordinate. And the narrator tells us that the kind of conversation she prefers is more bodily than that Adam enjoys with either God or the archangel. Eve leaves Adam and Raphael alone together because,

> Her Husband the Relater she preferr'd
> Before the Angel, and of him to ask
> Chose rather: hee, she knew would intermix
> Grateful digressions, and solve high dispute
> With conjugal Caresses, from his Lip
> Not Words alone pleas'd her.   (*PL* 8.52–57)

Manliness is like godliness that suffers a lack — men *need* social communication, and thus *need* to propagate, need to solace "single imperfection" with a partner. Classical friendship theory, which Milton borrows to help him redefine marriage, requires that the most virtuous sorts of friends be equals and desire the same pleasures from and for each other, that they be the most intimate sort of "other selves" or "second selves" (*Ethics*, 1166a30; Cicero, *De*

Amicitia, 19.69, and Montaigne in Florio, 92).[11] When he imagines Adam asking God for an "equal," Milton almost appears ready to upset the sex/gender system that locates Adam between God and Eve. Milton teaches that woman cannot be man's equal because she was made *for* him, to remedy his loneliness.

One feature that marks her as unlike Man is that she, unlike Adam, was not created lonely. Eve does not suffer this constitutive lack; she is the remedy for "single imperfection." Perhaps this is why Adam, such a brilliant and discursively rational man, almost mistook Eve for a higher being — "so absolute she seems / And in her self compleat" (*PL* 8.547–48). Because Eve is formed to remedy Adam's loneliness, it only makes sense that she will never appear (to him at least) as lonely; her desire is not companionship, but simply the desire to be needed and desired. This would make her appear to Adam as self-sufficient, not needy, not lonely, even though her state is entirely and radically dependent.

So, one of the chief features of manliness is to be godlike, but lonely. Man knows himself and becomes properly himself in "social communication" in "conversation with his like" (*PL* 8.429, 418). But in place of the equal and similar other self of homosocial friendship, Milton tries to establish the manlike but subordinate partner known as a companionate wife — not unlike a girl Friday or gentleman servant.

Milton stakes a great deal on the claim that the first and most paradigmatic human relationship, the relationship in which man comes to "know himself" most intimately as a man with proper self-esteem, is marriage rather than homosocial friendship. Without granting equality and thus full humanity to women, his new dogma of manliness will always appear inconsistent, even though it has served for several centuries to make marriage appear more natural than any other human relation, thus stigmatizing homosexuals, spinsters and (to a lesser degree) old bachelors as unnatural. Man cannot grow in two directions at once; to use Milton's own puritan terminology, manly "conversation" cannot be both "in heaven" and on earth simultaneously; he cannot serve simultaneously two masters or tend in two directions, toward the spirit and toward the body. And if he were to grant equality to woman, he would have to abandon the metaphysics that places everything on that scale stretching from pure spirit to pure body; he would have to give up the metaphysical difference between woman and man. Indeed, he would have to abandon much of what counts as Christian metaphysics. As we shall see in even more detail in the next chapter, Milton cannot do that, but I hope someday we can.

Four

Milton's Wedded Love

Haile wedded Love, mysterious Law, true source
Of human ofspring, sole proprietie,
In Paradise of all things common else.

— *Paradise Lost* 4.750–52

This chapter will try to correct a widely accepted misconception about what John Milton meant by "wedded Love." Some of the best recent commentaries on this topic too easily equate "wedded Love" with what we today call sexuality.[1] James Grantham Turner, one of the most learned and otherwise careful authorities on this topic, substitutes "sexuality" for "wedded Love" in a paraphrase of a key part of the passage from book 4 of *Paradise Lost*, which is quoted as the epigraph to this chapter.

> In both *Paradise Lost* and the divorce tracts sexuality is the "sole proprietie / In Paradise of all things common else" — the term connotes privacy, closeness, and exclusive mystery as well as ownership — but in the prose this served only to explain what an "intimate evil" it becomes when the marriage turns sour. Now [in *Paradise Lost*] this intimacy is a source of delight rather than horror.[2]

123

The word "sexuality" invariably leads modern readers to think of sexual dimorphism, reproduction, genital sensual pleasures, and all the attributes and activities that arouse and satisfy the physical desires associated with sexual intercourse of any kind. The main point of all Milton's voluminous writing on marriage and divorce, repeated with what sometimes seems hysterical frequency, is that marriage is essentially and principally a conjunction of minds, hearts and souls, and only very secondarily, as "an effect and fruit" of such conjunction, concerned with the reproduction and delight of bodies (*Tetrachordon*, YP 2:610). Even those authors whose opinions on marriage Milton most admired — Martin Bucer, Desiderius Erasmus and Nicolaus Hemming — stopped quite short of Milton's radical insistence that the proper purpose of marriage was single, not threefold. God made marriage to remedy the first man's loneliness (Gen. 2:18), a mental and spiritual loneliness that yearned for the rational rather than sensual delights of a fit partner in conversation. Physical procreation was a secondary (though admittedly necessary) purpose, and sensual delight an incidental effect:

> God in the first ordaining of marriage, taught us to what end he did it, in words expresly implying the apt and cheerfull conversation of man with woman, to comfort and refresh him against the evill of solitary life, not mentioning the purpose of generation till afterwards, as being but a secondary end in dignity, though not in necessitie. (*DDD*, YP 2:235)[3]

Most Protestant writers before Milton, established churchmen and puritans alike, cited much the same three ends of marriage and differed only about which was most important: procreation, the avoidance of vice or sin, or mutual society.[4] Milton's radical contributions to Protestant marriage theory (which earned him estrangement and abuse from his co-religionists) were to seriously degrade the end of physical procreation as a matter largely beneath the dignity of man and to redefine matters of physical pleasure or desire as not properly ends, but coincident effects of spiritual and mental conjugation. Milton knew that this required some hermeneutic agility, since according to Genesis, Adam's first exclamation at seeing the partner God created for him was: "This is now bone of my bones, and flesh of my flesh. . . . Therefore shall a man . . . cleave unto his wife: and they shall be one flesh" (Gen. 2:23–24). This sounds as if Adam's initial reactions to his wife and his marriage focus on the physical. Milton's strategy was first to claim that God's purpose, stated in verse 18 (to make "an help meet"), must take precedence over anything Adam says, and second to redefine the meaning of the expression "one flesh":

> For *one flesh* is not the formal essence of wedloc, but one end, or one effect of *a meet help;* The end oft-times beeing the effect and fruit of the form, as Logic teaches: Els many aged and holy matrimonies, and more eminently that of *Joseph* and *Mary,* would bee no true mariage. And that *maxim* generally receiv'd, would be fals, that *consent alone, though copulation never follow, makes the mariage.* Therefore to consent lawfully into one flesh, is not the formal cause of Matrimony, but only one of the effects. (*Tetrachordon,* YP 2:610–11)[5]

When the hymn to marriage in book 4 of *Paradise Lost* invites readers to celebrate "wedded Love" as the "sole proprietie, / In Paradise of all things common else," it points to a relationship defined as quintessentially human; marriage was instituted for Adam's manly, not his animal, nature. This was to be a kind of love altogether different from that practiced and enjoyed by other creatures in Paradise. Animals, the poem teaches, know nothing of wedded love. Adam notices that the beasts pair off for some sort of solace and conversation (8.392–94), but nowhere is it suggested that they marry each other. Milton's Adam says he seeks a mate that can offer "rational delight," a sort of pleasure beasts probably know little or nothing about and certainly cannot supply to Adam (8.391–92). The poem wants to distinguish clearly, right from the start, between sexuality and wedded love: sexuality belongs to both men and beasts, wedded love is "the sole proprietie" of what Milton called mankind.

Halkett appears to make the same mistake as Turner when he refers to the "Haile wedded Love" passage (4.750–70) as "a hymn in praise of matrimonial sexuality" (*Milton and the Idea of Matrimony,* 27–28). Halkett, Turner and most other modern Miltonists assume that in the time between writing the divorce tracts (1643–1645) and composing book 4 of *Paradise Lost,* Milton softened in his attitudes toward sexuality. The generally accepted story is that the Milton of the divorce tracts is still bitter over a marriage apparently gone sour and so cannot bring himself to speak of sexuality "without tension, violence, and open disgust" (Turner, *One Flesh,* 232). The Milton of *Paradise Lost,* however, is older and mellower. Mary Powell returned to him in 1645 (and in 1646 brought her entire royalist family to live with them), and Milton even married twice more (Katherine Woodcock in 1656 and Elizabeth Minshull — aged 24 — in 1663). This later Milton is now prepared not only to speak of sensual matters with a civil tongue, but even to praise and celebrate sexuality as an essential element, even a defining aspect, of "wedded Love." This Milton, in Stephen M. Fallon's words, wants very much "to debrutalize and redeem sexuality," to proclaim "the refining of the 'quintessence of an excrement' into a 'fountain' of peace and love."[6] I don't think this account, accepted for so long, will stand closer scrutiny.

First, Milton often speaks frankly and openly, without disgust, about copulation and sensuality in the divorce tracts, especially in *Tetrachordon.* When he does exhibit disgust, especially in *Colasterion,* it is usually directed toward those who cannot bring themselves properly to understand the expression "one flesh" from Genesis 2:24 or what Milton in the *Doctrine and Discipline of Divorce* called "conversation" as signifying anything more or other than sexual activity. Conversely, in *Paradise Lost,* Milton reserves words of praise and celebration, not for sex (married or otherwise), but for "wedded Love" — that form of human (Milton would call it "Manly") *Eros* that tends away from the body and toward heavenly love. According to Milton's tracts and poems, wedded love does not debrutalize or redeem sexuality. Both beasts and humans enjoy sensual pleasures, and both generate offspring. According to the archangel Raphael, there is nothing impure about either activity until the first disobedience permanently taints both. When he describes the angel erotics toward which wedded love eventually will lead Eden's blessed pair, Raphael indicates that sensuality is not impure and so needs no redemption:

> Whatever pure thou in the body enjoy'st
> (And pure thou wert created) we enjoy
> In eminence, and obstacle find none
> Of membrane, joynt, or limb, exclusive barrs:
> Easier then Air with Air, if Spirits embrace,
> Total they mix, Union of Pure with Pure
> Desiring; nor restrain'd conveyance need
> As Flesh to mix with Flesh, or Soul with Soul.   (8.622–29)

As for debrutalization, I have little to say, except to repeat that Milton clearly believed sexuality and reproduction are things common to both beasts and men, and therefore technically brutal, though originally not impure. Wedded love, on the other hand, is an activity peculiar to men and women, and made specifically *for* humans.

If in the Paradise Milton imagines, sexuality and reproduction need no redemption, neither do they merit special celebration. Milton's wedded love points the way and begins the journey to a higher love where all has turned to spirit and physical reproduction is no longer even a necessity.

When Milton's Adam, in conversation with God, argues that he needs a partner with whom to share Paradise, he does indeed talk of propagation and of begetting "Like of his like," but Milton's poem nowhere suggests that this Adam, who has not yet seen a woman, is thinking of sexual reproduction. He simply knows that he must somehow produce a partner like enough to himself to share "Collateral love, and deerest amitie." Adam says to God,

> No need that thou
> Shouldst propagat, already infinite;
> And through all numbers absolute, though One;
> But Man by number is to manifest
> His single imperfection, and beget

> Like of his like, his Image multipli'd,
> In unitie defective, which requires
> Collateral love, and deerest amitie.   (8.419–27)

The only begetting Adam has heard about so far is the story of how the Father begot the Son; that cannot be properly thought of as heterosexual reproduction. He may have seen animals copulate, but Milton's Adam is keen to distinguish between his desire for "deerest amitie" and the kind of conversation the animals around him share. God praises him for understanding, even against God's apparent suggestion, that animal "fellowship" is "unmeet" for a man.

The Jesus of the Gospels taught that there would be no marriage in heaven (Matt. 22:30, Mark 12:25, Luke 20:35), but Milton frequently imagined heavenly love in nuptial terms (*Epitaphium Damonis*, 215–19; *Lycidas*, 176; *A Mask*, 1005–12). The heavenly love Milton celebrates, like the wedded love he praises in book 4 of *Paradise Lost*, cannot properly be glossed as "sexuality," no matter how much intelligent modern sensibilities might wish to. Those of us who truly love the body and its delights would like to have Milton on our side, but most of the evidence makes it clear that he is not.

Milton denies that marriage was ever intended as a remedy for lust. He radically reinterprets Paul's dictum "it is better to marry than to burn" (1 Cor. 7:9) as referring not to mere lust but to a "rational burning" for human companionship: "but what might this burning mean? Certainly not the meer motion of carnall lust, not the meer goad of a sensitive desire; God does not principally take care for such cattell" (*DDD*, 1.4, YP 2:250–51). This is not to say that God, as Milton imagines him, has no care whatever for Adam's sensual pleasures; he does. But that is not God's principal concern for a creature as dignified as man; and the institution of marriage, believes Milton, must be understood as crucial to manly dignity. Otherwise, it undermines precisely that dignity. That is Milton's repeated complaint against canon law's understanding of marriage: it deprives men of their manly dignity. By putting matters of the body first, canon law has committed "a hainous barbarisme both against the honour of mariage, the dignitie of man and his soule, the goodnes of Christianitie, and all the humane respects of civilitie" (*DDD*, 1, YP 2:238). Men have other, more effective means for controlling their physical appetites, says Milton. Exercise and a "frugal diet without mariage would easily chast'n" the most insistent sexual desire (*DDD*, 1.9, YP 2:269).[7] Marriage was instituted to address altogether higher, more manly, desires. Throughout the divorce tracts, Milton's point is that bad marriages and the laws that refuse to dissolve them depress "the high and Heaven-born spirit of Man, farre beneath the condition wherein either God created him or sin hath sunke him" (*DDD*, "To the Parlament," YP 2:223).

I recommend a closer look at the "Haile wedded Love" passage from book 4 of *Paradise Lost* (750–70). What warrant is here for equating Milton's "wedded Love" with "sexuality"? The passage opens with a string of appositions, as if the narrator knows the term has often been misunderstood and is likely to be misunderstood again; he is anxious to be very clear about what counts as "wedded Love." Can any of these appositives — "mysterious Law, true source / Of human ofspring, sole proprietie, / in Paradise of all things common else" — legitimately be glossed as a euphemism for sexuality? In what follows I will argue that in each instance the answer is no. I find myself in basic agreement with Irene Samuel's contention that Milton declares Adam and Eve's married love to be "unlibidinous," utterly devoid of passion, and devoted to a mode of procreation largely unconcerned with matters of the body.[8] Milton's poem insists that in Paradise there was nothing impure about sexual reproduction. Like Augustine, Milton imagines prelapsarian copulation as entirely free of "any lust," an absolutely rational act of the will in obedience to God, not to passion or physical desire.[9] That is why the poem celebrates a bed "undefil'd and chaste" (4.761). The words allude to the advice offered in Hebrews 13:4 to early Christians eager for the apocalypse: do not abandon your marriages and families, says the anonymous elder, "whore

mongers and adulterers God will judge." Adam and Eve's first copulation is not undefiled and chaste because it excludes other partners; it is undefiled and chaste because it is free of the desires and
passions that transform partners into others, into objects of one's
physical desire. Were it not, their copulation with each other would
be adulterous, as the poem suggests it is shortly after the Fall
(9.1034–45). Book 4 reserves its praise for "wedded Love" rather
than copulation, however pure and chaste. And wedded love has
nothing whatever to do with the "amorous play" of book 9.

There is more at stake in these matters than simply offering to
correct three talented scholars from whom I have learned so much,
and to whom all Miltonists are indebted. If what follows is con-
vincing, we may have to abandon the widely held notion that
Milton gradually abandoned his youthful and almost cultish devotion to purity (as articulated in *A Mask, Epitaphium Damonis,* and
the *Apology*), and came to embrace a more broad-minded appreciation for the God-given pleasures of the human body. And since
Milton often serves as a representative for English puritanism, we
may wish either to relieve him of some aspects of that role or reconsider the merits of a once popular but lately frowned upon sense
of the word "puritanical."

My analysis also tends to support the contention that Milton
was more of a Platonist than a Neoplatonist.[10] Milton read Plato's
Symposium with the same energy and independence that he brought
to his interpretations of Scripture. He does not conflate all of the
symposiasts' erotic theories and hymns of praise into one teaching called Platonic. He explicitly rejects Aristophanes's fables and
Pausanius's detailed prescriptions about when it is proper and
dignified to gratify a lover, and he embraces Socrates's (or Diotima's)
teaching about the procreancy of the soul. Unlike Neoplatonists,
and much more like Plato's Diotima, Milton tends to regard the
differences between spirit and flesh as differences of degree on a continuum rather than as differences of kind or binary opposites. This
is part of what Miltonists refer to as his monism, though we should
also note that Milton's sense of a matter-spirit continuum assigns

a greater moral value to the spiritual than to the physical end of that continuum; thus, the opposite ends of the matter-spirit continuum remain effectively a moral binary. Even opposite vectors along that continuum count as moral opposites (5.475–76).[11]

Finally, some of what follows suggests that Milton's monism need not always have the effect most often ascribed to it — that of redeeming the body from the detestation it suffers at the hands of Neoplatonic dualism. Raphael teaches Adam that the *telos* of all bodies well exercised by obedience is to "turn all to Spirit, /. . . and wingd ascend / Ethereal" as angels (5.497–99). Persistence in the body, according to this teaching, must be evidence of stubborn disobedience. A body that does not improve by "tract of time" into "all Spirit" is a body of sin. On this score, Milton's monistic continuum supports an ethics no less dualistic than Paul's *kata sarx* and *kata pneuma* in Romans 7 and 8. We shall even find that Milton often resorts to the quasi-allegorical practice of regarding spiritual things as the *true,* or more truly real, or more fully realized, versions of bodily things.

Mysterious Law

Milton spent huge amounts of time and effort between 1643 and 1645 trying to redefine marriage for a reluctant, even reactionary, English Parliament. For his pains he earned the ridicule of his friends and Presbyterian allies, and his efforts, however impressive to us, appear to have had no effect on marriage law in England during his lifetime.[12] Milton's epic narrator, therefore, is careful about the way he deploys the phrase "wedded Love," which is why he tells readers right away that the practices of "connubial Love" (*PL* 4.743) are "Mysterious," and repeats the word again in his hymn to wedded love (750). "Mysterious" designates something that is not what it appears to be, not what the many, especially the rabble or uninitiated, suppose it to be. In *Colasterion,* Milton derides his anonymous answerer, calling him a boar and a bayard, because when Milton speaks of a "fit conversing Soul," the answerer still hears nothing but sex (*Colasterion*, YP 2:747). Milton probably expected him to hear nothing more elevated in book 4's hymn to wedded love.

"Mysterious" also appears in book 3 to describe the stairs to heaven like those Jacob dreamed of in a place called Luz (Gen. 28:12). "Each Stair mysteriously was meant," says the narrator, to make it clear that these are not literally stairs at all, but a representation of the stages along a soul's journey toward or away from heaven and spiritual being (*PL* 3.516). In book 10 God punishes the serpent "in mysterious terms" (10.173), which means, as we know, that the curse is not literally about heads, heels and bruises. The poem ridicules Satan's willful carnal-mindedness when he later boasts, "A World who would not purchase with a bruise" (10.498–500), and carefully explains the mysterious sense to its fit audience in lines 183–90. These examples suggest that "mysterious" in this poem means not literal, not what something appears superficially to be, not what unfit readers are likely to think it means.

"Mysterious" in this passage from book 4 also alludes directly to the Pauline midrash on Genesis and marriage in Ephesians 5. There Paul explains that when Adam proclaims Eve "bone of my bones and flesh of my flesh" (Gen. 2:23), we should understand such language as signifying a "great mystery."[13] However much the Adam of Genesis appears to speak about flesh and bones, marriage as instituted by God in Paradise is not about fleshly matters at all, but a *mega mysterion* signifying Christ's love for his church. The love Christ has for his church may be erotic, but it is not sexual. When Paul invokes such love as a model for husbands, his point is to promote something other than sexual love between husbands and wives, perhaps even something meant to replace sexual love in what he believed were the last days of life in this world (1 Thess. 4, esp. 3–8 and 16–18). Milton's Adam adopts this midrash in book 8 when, upon first seeing Eve up close, he exclaims:

> I now see
> Bone of my Bone, Flesh of my Flesh, my Self
> Before me; Woman is her Name, of Man
> Extracted; for this cause he shall forgoe
> Father and Mother, and to his Wife adhere;
> And they shall be one Flesh, one Heart, one Soule. (8.494–99)

This passage is more than 80 percent Genesis, but the language Milton's narrator adds, as a hermeneutic gloss on the passage, is important, for it is the language of classical friendship — "my Self . . . one Heart, one Soule."[14] The Adam of Genesis appears to speak of flesh and bone, but Milton's Adam gives such language the Pauline spin Milton believed it always already had. By "flesh" and "bone," heart, soul and self mysteriously are meant. Marriage is a law pronounced and a rite enacted not literally, but in figures.

Thus, with his first appositional definition of "wedded Love" Milton takes pains to remind readers that the "one flesh" of Genesis 2:24 should not be taken literally to mean marriage itself has anything to do with flesh. "One flesh" should be read mysteriously, allegorically, to signify those distinctly nonsensual aspects of marriage, aspects that might also be understood as similar to Christ's attentions to his church. Milton's invocation of "mysterious Law" here is all of a piece with his argument in *Tetrachordon* that we should no more take the words "one flesh" as a literal description of marriage than we should hear "Take eat, this is my body. . . . This is my blood" (Mark 14:22–24) as a literal description of the Lord's Supper:

> Why did *Moses* then set down thir uniting into one flesh? And I again ask, why the Gospel so oft repeats the eating of our Saviours flesh, the drinking of his blood? *That wee are one body with him, the members of his body, flesh of his flesh, and bone of his bone. Ephes.* 5. Yet lest wee should be Capernaitans, as wee are told there, that the flesh profiteth nothing, so wee are told heer, if wee be not deaf as adders, that this union of the flesh proceeds from the union of a

fit help and solace. Wee know that there was never a more spiritual mystery then this Gospel taught us under the terms of body and flesh; yet nothing less intended then that wee should stick there. What a stupidnes then is it, that in Mariage, which is the neerest resemblance of our union with Christ, wee should deject our selvs to such a sluggish and underfoot Philosophy, as to esteem the validity of Mariage meerly by the flesh; though never so brokn and disjoynted from love and peace, which only can give a human qualification to that act of the flesh, and distinguish it from the bestial.

(Tetrachordon, Gen. 2:24, YP 2:606)

The "act of the flesh" most of us value so dearly as sex Milton considered simply bestial; marriage, a partnership of "fit help and solace," qualifies that bestial act as fit for humans. Men and women may copulate and they may experience sensual pleasures, but that has nothing to do with marriage as God instituted it. Indeed, marriage is the mysterious conjunction of minds, hearts and souls that keeps such brutish activities and pleasures in their properly subordinated places.

Before moving on to the next appositive phrase defining wedded love, I want to draw attention to another use of the word "mysterious" in book 4: the narrator refers to Adam and Eve's genitals as "mysterious parts" (4.312). This may be nothing more than a rhetorically graceful way to say, "the parts we normally conceal were not then concealed." But if the rest of what I have said about the word "mysterious" is right, we are entitled to hear Milton's narrator here insisting that what we call sexual organs are not really about sex at all, but like the "Rites" of "connubial Love," mysterious. They are organs of generation in only the most shallowly literal sense; Milton would not have us "stick there" for they signify, mysteriously, another mode of procreation that is not of the body, but the soul, and thus peculiarly human. *Paradise Lost* teaches that the advent of shame followed closely on the heels of disobedience (9.1058–63). The body's shame focuses on the genitals, and most apparently the penis because it now obeys "upstart passions" more readily than reason, and so man is reduced from manly freedom to

brutal servitude (*PL* 12.88–90). Milton appears to have agreed with
Augustine about the prelapsarian penis. There was nothing shameful about it because it obeyed human will and human reason just
like most other members of the body. After the Fall, the penis appears
to have a will of its own, moving in response to "upstart passions," rather than to reason and choice.[15]

True Source of Human Offspring

Calling wedded love the "*true* source" of human offspring implies
that readers are apt to be mistaken in their notions of procreation
(my emphasis). The *true* source of offspring, human offspring, is not
what most people think. Milton shows us how difficult it was for
Eve to learn to distinguish between what is "fair" and what "truly
fair" in *Paradise Lost* 4.477–91. Adam has to resort to physical ped-
agogy to get her to yield, and thus to see that things "truly fair"
are invisible — the inward traits of "manly grace / And wisdom."[16]
Much the same is implied by calling wedded love the "true source /
Of human ofspring." "True" here means not what you expect, not
what you see, something invisible and mysterious as opposed to
visible and obvious.

If wedded love is, as the next appositional phrase insists, unique
to humans, something proper only to Adam and Eve and not "common" to the rest of creation, then it cannot refer to the physical
acts of sexual intercourse. Certainly the animals in Eden enjoy coital
relations with each other. Sensual pleasures are among the "all things
common else" from which wedded love is specifically excluded as
peculiar to the human pair. The wedded love this poem celebrates
is something distinctly unsensual, something utterly devoid of
"touch" and "passion." The archangel Raphael, sent by God the
Father to teach Adam all he needs to know to remain obedient,
specifically identifies "the sense of touch whereby mankind / Is
propagated" as common to beasts and therefore not proper to the
"true Love" Adam was meant to feel for Eve:

> But if the sense of touch whereby mankind
> Is propagated seem such dear delight
> Beyond all other, think the same voutsaf't
> To Cattel and each Beast; which would not be
> To them made common and divulg'd, if aught
> Therein enjoy'd were worthy to subdue
> The Soule of Man, or passion in him move.   (8.579–85)

Milton expected his fit audience to hear in this an echo of his claim in the *Doctrine and Discipline of Divorce* that "God does not principally take care for such cattell"; God did not provide an institution like marriage for the remedy of "carnal lust" (which Adam does not experience before the fall) or "sensitive desire" (the dangers of which Raphael carefully warns him about).[17] Adam confesses to Raphael he sometimes fears he might be inordinately moved by "touch" and "passion" when he beholds and touches Eve's outward fairness:

> transported I behold,
> Transported touch; here passion first I felt,
> Commotion strange, in all enjoyments else
> Superiour and unmov'd, here onely weake
> Against the charm of Beauties powerful glance.   (*PL* 8.529–33)

According to this poem, wedded love was meant to be the remedy against the very charm that subdues Adam in the Fall and renders him unmanly: "fondly overcome by Femal charm" (9.999). Marriage keeps sensuality in proper subordination and thus passion at bay. What, then, does the poem mean by saying wedded love is the "true source of human ofspring"? Are we mistaken in thinking that heterosexual coitus is what makes offspring?

Yes and no. Sensual arousal, touching and rubbing and orgasm and ejaculation are indeed necessary to propagate the flesh, but that is not, the poem implies, what makes offspring *human*. Furthermore, however "crabbed" Milton may have regarded Augustine's opinion about women as friends, he probably shared his conviction that before the Fall, coitus involved no arousal, no passion, nothing irrational or unwilled. Only wedded love can make offspring that are truly human, and that is Milton's point here. Animals and people both make young through the fleshly act of coitus, but Adam and Eve will make human offspring by a kind of love that is distinct from and higher than coitus, a love of which coitus is the mere earthly sign — wedded love.[18] Not only is this kind of love distinct from sensual erotics, but also, when properly practiced, it will discipline and eventually displace sensuality. After the string of appositions, the hymn continues in apostrophic address to wedded love itself:

> By thee adulterous lust was driv'n from men
> Among the bestial herds to raunge, by thee
> Founded in Reason, Loyal, Just, and Pure,
> Relations dear, and all the Charities
> Of Father, Son, and Brother first were known.   (*PL* 4.753–57)

Wedded love drives lust out of men, replacing it with something more godlike. "Adulterous" here does not specify a certain kind of lust; it designates lust as adulterous by definition.[19] Lust is unconcerned with the humanity of its object; indeed, it objectifies human subjects into something like mere flesh or remedies of fleshly desire. This is why most animals are not monogamous; they reproduce by lust and so range from partner to partner unconcerned with anything that makes one sexual partner unique. Humans, the poem insists, because they are flesh, can also love in this way, but truly human love and truly human reproduction is something else. When people reproduce, their bestial nature may bring forth young, but only human nature can reproduce human relations that are "Founded in Reason," relations that are "Loyal, Just, and Pure." Animal reproduction knows nothing of fatherhood, brotherhood, filial devotion. Animals reproduce flesh; humans reproduce human relations.[20] Heterosexual coitus can do the former, but only wedded love can do the latter. Thus, the poem distinguishes wedded love from anything we might recognize as sexuality.

Socrates, Plato and Heavenly Love

Being so quick to find in Milton's epic a celebration of the sort of sensual erotics we frankly and unashamedly enjoy, many Miltonists have mostly missed the poem's celebrations of nonsensual, and often nonhetero-, erotics. Milton says in the 1642 *Apology against a Pamphlet* that his primary teachers in the lore of love were "the divine volumes of *Plato,* and his equall *Xenophon*" (YP 1:891). From them, he says, he learned of both "chastity and love" together, by which he means something other than physical, or what Neoplatonists called "earthly," love. Plato and Xenophon teach a doctrine of manly love, or

> that which is truly so, whose charming cup is only vertue which she bears in her hand to those who are worthy. The rest are cheated with a thick intoxicating potion which a certaine Sorceresse the abuser of loves name carries about; and how the first and chiefest office of love, begins and ends in the soule, producing those happy twins of her divine generation knowledge and vertue.
>
> (*Apology*, YP 1:891–92)

In other words, he learned from reading Xenophon and Plato to distinguish between what Xenophon refers to as heavenly and vulgar love. The Socrates of Xenophon's *Symposium* largely echoes the Pausanias of Plato's in this matter. He is not convinced, as is Plato's Pausanias, that there are actually two Aphrodites, each with her own son, but he does affirm that there are two different temples, altars, and distinct rituals for the followers of earthly, carnal, vulgar love, on the one hand, and the noble, spiritual "love of friendship and noble conduct" on the other.[21] Xenophon's Socrates teaches not only that "spiritual love is far superior to carnal," but also that it is altogether distinct from carnal love. It is "less liable to satiety" (Xenophon, 8.16), noble rather than servile (8.23–27), and grows stronger with age rather than weaker because, unlike carnal love, it "progresses towards wisdom" (8.15).

Milton's Adam feels this sort of insatiable, wisdom-directed love in conversation with his heavenly guest, Raphael. He says to his angel guest:

> while I sit with thee, I seem in Heav'n,
> And sweeter thy discourse is to my eare
> Then Fruits of Palm-tree pleasantest to thirst
> And hunger both, from labour, at the houre
> Of sweet repast; they satiate, and soon fill,
> Though pleasant, but thy words with Grace Divine
> Imbu'd, bring to thir sweetness no satietie.   (8.210–16)

Thus, Adam's transparent delaying tactics are aimed at detaining his heavenly guest (206–8). Linda Gregerson correctly identifies these as hyperbolic compliments typical of fond love poets: she suggests that the sun itself may be charmed to a halt by Raphael's voice and "Sleep list'ning to thee will watch" (7.99–100, 106).[22] In Raphael's company, Adam finds that his "conversation is in heaven," as Paul says of his heaven-bound followers in Philippians 3:20–21.

The insatiable desire Adam feels for unending conversation with Raphael may be Milton's finest image of heavenly love; it reminds one of the love he felt for his friend Charles Diodati even, perhaps especially, after his death. In *Epitaphium Damonis*, we remember, Milton imagines his friend enjoying the ultimate erotic experience reserved for the pure in body when they finally reach heaven — the "immortal nuptials" and the Dionysiac "rage" only possible when the flesh has been turned "all to Spirit" (*Epitaphium Damonis*, 212–19; *PL* 5.497). He imagines Charles playing Raphael to his Adam. When Raphael admires Adam's graceful lips (*PL* 8.218) and smiles "Celestial rosie red" (8.619) as he describes "Union of Pure with Pure / Desiring," we witness Milton's idealized version of the love he shared with Charles — highly erotic conversation, intensely and exclusively masculine, intellectual and strictly nonsexual.[23] Gregerson is surely right to remark that Milton runs the risk of making Raphael seem more appropriate a lover, more fit a conversation partner, than Eve (171). And that entails the even more startling risk of suggesting that the pederasty of the soul Socrates recommended in Plato's *Symposium* might be more fitting than marriage as a means to lead Adam toward heaven.

But Milton staunchly rejected the notion that Adam might have been better off with a male partner, even though he was clearly attracted to the idea. In *Tetrachordon*, he explains that "alone" in Genesis 2:18 means specifically without a woman (YP 2:595). Milton strained to redefine marriage as the friendship Socrates recommended — an erotics beyond the sexual. As a result, his notion of marriage sometimes looks a lot like a heteroerotic pederasty, with Adam as the lover and Eve the philerast destined never to outgrow the role of student and beloved. However disappointing his own marriages may have been, Milton tried hard to imagine Adam and Eve before the Fall enjoying a heavenly erotics, free of earthly passion, perfectly free of lust.

Conventional wisdom would have us think that Milton abandoned his fantasy of chaste love, gave up his youthful and cultish devotion to the heavenly Aphrodite or the "Celestial Cupid" of the Attendant Spirit's closing song (*A Mask*, 1002–11).[24] Stephen Fallon argues that in *Paradise Lost* Milton manages to shrug off the "dualist drag" of the divorce tracts and, in imagining Adam and Eve's love life, comes close to a more monist blending of body with spirit that appears as "frank eroticism" (81). I agree that *Paradise Lost* frankly celebrates eros. I have already cited the erotics of Adam's conversation with Raphael, and could dwell for some time on the erotics of Adam's conversation with God, but the eros celebrated there and hailed as wedded love is not sensuality. In Milton's Paradise, as I have already said, sensuality needed no redemption, but it also was never meant to be mistaken for wedded love.

Many will object that Milton must somehow have mended the breach between body and spirit that yawns so largely in Neoplatonist erotics if only to make sense out of God's injunction to "Be fruitful, and multiply, and replenish the earth" (Gen. 1:28). Does not God command the practice of earthly love? Must there not be, then, some pure form of procreation, both in body and in soul? In pursuit of this question we should turn to Milton's other teacher, Plato's Socrates.

From Plato's *Symposium* Milton learned the love lore of Diotima or, according to Milton, the erotic doctrine Socrates "fain'd to have learnt from the Prophetesse *Diotima*" (*DDD*, 1.4, YP 2:252). This doctrine, somewhat at odds with those of the other symposiasts, teaches that love is centrally a matter of procreation: "it is giving birth in beauty both in body and in soul" (*Symposium*, 206b). The sharp distinction Neoplatonists routinely draw between earthly carnal love and heavenly spiritual love follows Pausanias's doctrine of carefully regulated pederasty, articulated in *Symposium*, 180d–185c.[25] Christian and Jewish Neoplatonists quietly adapted the symposiasts' explicit homoerotic assumptions and examples to the implicitly heteroerotic nature of the first pair of humans according to Genesis. Most Neoplatonists also merged the various doctrines articulated in the *Symposium* into one, despite the contradictions and inconsistencies among Pausanias, Aristophanes, Phaedrus, Eryximachus and Diotima. Milton, I believe, read Plato somewhat more critically than they. He dismisses Aristophanes's myth of originary hermaphrodites, one of the Neoplatonists' favorite parts, as "*Plato's* wit" and opposes it to Socrates's doctrine of love. He rejects the Neoplatonic conflation of Genesis 1:27 and Aristophanes's primeval androgyne, a reading the Jewish Neoplationist Leone Ebreo embraced. Milton regarded such conflation as typical of the way "the Jewes fable, and please themselvs with the accidentall concurrence of *Plato's* wit" (*Tetrachordon*, Gen. 1:27, YP 2:589).[26] Milton singles out Socrates's teaching, which he "fain'd to have learnt from the Prophetesse *Diotima*," as Plato's true teaching on love. This doctrine, and not Pausanias's meticulous rules of pederasty or Aristophanes's anthropological just-so stories, is the teaching that "divinely sorts" with what Moses teaches in Genesis (*DDD*, 1.4, YP 2:252).

Socrates teaches that love is principally about giving birth. Some people, so the doctrine goes, understand procreation as what Milton in the *Doctrine and Discipline of Divorce* derides as "the purpose of generation" or "the work of male and female," but for a more dignified sort of people — those Milton calls "all generous persons" — procreation is altogether a matter of the soul rather than the body

(*DDD*, YP 2:235, 240, 246). Here is how Socrates says he learned it from Diotima:

> Now those who are pregnant in body are more oriented toward women and are lovers in that way, providing immortality, remembrance, and happiness for themselves for all time, *as they believe,* by producing children. Those who are pregnant in soul however — for there are people who are even more pregnant in their souls than in their bodies, . . . these people are pregnant with and give birth to what is appropriate for the soul. . . . Good sense [*phronēsis*] and the rest of virtue, of which all poets are procreators, as well as artisans who are said to be inventors. But much the most important and most beautiful aspect of good sense . . . is that which deals with the regulation of cities and households, the name of which is judiciousness [*sōphronsunē*] and justice.
>
> (*Symposium,* 208e–209b; emphasis added)

Poets, lawgivers, artists, great men of virtue — these procreate in the soul and give birth to children more truly immortal than fleshly children. "Everyone," says Diotima, "would prefer to bring forth this sort of children rather than human offspring" (209d), which is why people envy Homer, Lycurgus and Solon. Milton certainly imagined he was one of that sort, and he could not have imagined any less for Adam. Indeed, Eve often calls Adam her "Author" (*PL* 4.635, 5.397), as virtually a synonym for parent (4.660). Some people must procreate in the body, and no doubt Adam and Eve will do this at some point, but Milton would hardly waste his efforts at celebrating the first nuptials in Paradise on "such cattell" as bodily procreation. Indeed, Milton quietly leaves intact the almost universal assumption that Adam and Eve do not procreate *in the body* until after the Fall. In *Paradise Lost* 9.270, the narrator refers to Eve's "Virgin Majestie" at a point chronologically posterior to the "Rites / Mysterious of connubial Love" celebrated in 4.742–43. After the Fall Eve implies that Adam has not yet begotten nor she conceived fleshly children (10.986–89), even though they have certainly experienced the "wedded Love" that is the "true source of human ofspring" (4.750–51). Why would Milton lead us to believe that Adam and Eve's first performance of the mysterious rites of wedded love produced no offspring? He doesn't. The procreation Milton celebrates as proceeding from wedded love in Paradise is the procreancy of the soul, the first purposes of the Author and Disposer of humankind. Only a reader like the anonymous answerer to the *Doctrine and Discipline of Divorce* would hear any note of sensuality in Milton's celebration of wedded love.[27]

With this in mind, let's take a fresh look at what critics have long understood as Milton's frank description of prelapsarian sex.[28] The poem tells us that the blessed pair finish their evening devotion to God and go to bed.

> This said unanimous, and other Rites
> Observing none, but adoration pure
> Which God likes best, into thir inmost bowre
> Handed they went; and eas'd the putting off
> These troublesom disguises which wee wear,
> Strait side by side were laid, nor turnd I weene
> *Adam* from his fair Spouse, nor *Eve* the Rites
> Mysterious of connubial Love refus'd.   (4.736–43)

Consistent with what we already have inferred from the poem's celebration of wedded love that follows this narration, there is nothing here about desires of the flesh.[29] Adam and Eve may indeed be "one flesh" in some mysterious sense, but their nuptial relations are not about bodily desire. We are told that Adam *did not turn away* from Eve, and that Eve *did not refuse* "the Rites / Mysterious of connubial Love." Everywhere is talk of spontaneous obedience and ritual; nowhere is there talk of desire, unless it is the desire to adore and obey God who "bids increase" (748). The repeated word "Rites" (736, 742) should, in any fit reader's mind, evoke images of spontaneous expressions of gratitude to and adoration of God both times it is used. Desire here, in both instances, is vertical toward God, not horizontal between Adam and Eve. They perform the spontaneous ritual of evening prayer unanimously; they also perform the mysterious rites of connubial love unanimously, that is to say their desire is unanimously directed toward God.[30] So far from any sort of earthly desire are these two, they seem put to bed by another hand: "Strait side by side were laid." The poet uses the word "Mysterious" here, as before, to guard against the possibility of mis-interpretation. To see this as a description of sensual copulation is to read the way the answerer reads, and so to earn the poet's con-demnation: "But what should a man say more to a snout in this pickle? What language can be low and degenerat anough?" (*Colas-terion*, YP 2:747). "Mysterious," as I have already argued, means that something is not what it appears to be at first glance, or not literally what you see, or not what the unlettered rabble mistake it for. Milton argued that Jesus' words about "body" and "blood" in Mark 14:22–24 are meant mysteriously; so also Adam's decla-ration of marriage as becoming "one flesh." Jacob thought at first that he saw a ladder, but the ladder "mysteriously" meant some-thing else. The mysterious rites of connubial love are meant to be understood this way. This may look like sex at first. Men like the answerer will always see this as sex, but the fit few see something else: utterly lust-free connubial rites undertaken without any pas-sion or compulsion, but in deliberate rational obedience to God by two perfectly free wills. No one and nothing is swept up or away; here reason does not sleep, or even nod.

Pure procreation is procreation without the least hint of fleshly desire, performed out of a desire to adore and gratify God, not each other or one's self, and to produce more human beings who will stand in proper "filial" relation to the God in whose image they were procreated (*PL* 4.294). Though Adam and Eve apparently do not conceive children on their wedding night, they do conceive, mentally and spiritually, the "Relations dear, and all the Charities / Of Father, Son, and Brother" that are "Founded in Reason, Loyal, Just, and Pure" (4.755–57). Those who complain that such activity is insufficiently pure for Paradise are called "Hypocrites" (4.744) not because they have an unjustly low opinion of sex — Milton also has a low opinion of sex — but because in such complaints they betray their carnal minds; apparently, like the answerer, they cannot read "wedded Love" without thinking it means sex. Thus the famous sex scene in book 4 turns out to be not about sex as we know it.

Adam, who confesses to Raphael that sometimes he feels passion and has much ado to keep it subjected to his reason, knows that the "genial Bed" is a place for procreation of quite a different sort than that "common to all kindes" and thus requires a "mysterious reverence" (*PL* 8.596–99). Indeed, when Raphael upbraids him for tending to overvalue passionate feelings and the object toward which they yearn, Adam corrects himself, "half abash't," by thinking about marriage and the special mysteries of the nuptial bed. These thoughts help him to drive off lust and carnal desire. Milton imagines Adam and Eve practicing the *true* procreation of human offspring; this does not exclude, but need not include, what we think of as sexual activity. And in either case, what we think of as heterosexual coitus is more an accidental aspect of their "true" intercourse — imagining into being the "Relations dear" that will be formed among their children. This truer form of intercourse *always* succeeds in conceiving.

Before concluding, at least one objection raised by Turner still needs to be answered. Turner makes much of the poem's description of Adam as "only 'half abasht'" at Raphael's condemnation of passion and his warnings about overvaluing "the sense of touch whereby mankind / Is propagated" (Turner, *One Flesh*, 277–78). Adam, he says, is only half-abashed because Raphael, though normally an "impeccably orthodox speaker," is on this score only half correct. Being an angel Raphael does not really understand, Turner suggests, human lovemaking. Turner argues that Adam successfully "challenges the archangel's estimation of sexual desire, and so redeems some of the rhapsodic 'Passion' that had inspired his high valuation of Eve and thus caused the [Raphael's] frowning interruption" (278). Turner plays masterfully on his reader's biases here, portraying Raphael as insensitively doctrinaire, a masculinist martinet of orthodoxy. Condemning passion, Raphael appears to condemn Adam's passion-inspired vision of Eve as an equal, even sometimes superior, being:

> yet when I approach
> Her loveliness, so absolute she seems
> And in her self compleat, so well to know
> Her own, that what she wills to do or say,
> Seems wisest, vertuousest, discreetest, best;
> All higher knowledge in her presence falls
> Degraded, Wisdom in discourse with her
> Looses discount'nanc't, and like folly shewes;
> Authority and Reason on her waite,
> As one intended first, not after made
> Occasionally; and to consummate all,
> Greatness of mind and nobleness thir seat
> Build in her loveliest, and create an awe
> About her, as a guard Angelic plac't.   (*PL* 8.546–59)

Truth be told, Raphael frowns at this speech because he is indeed a masculinist martinet of orthodoxy, but one whose position on this score the entire poem endorses. The sensations Adam here confesses to his heavenly teacher are not in themselves sinful sensations, any more than the fantastic images of Eve's dream (*PL* 5.35–93). But they are, just like her dream, mistaken sensations and notions that, if approved by Adam's reason, could lead to more than mistakenness. Everything we have heard so far about this heaven-blest pair, even from Eve's own mouth, indicates that Eve is neither "absolute" nor "in her self compleat," let alone "wisest, vertuousest, best." The very ugliness of the word, "vertuousest" suggests that what we are hearing from Adam strikes a sour note. When he is not on the verge of passionate sensual commotion, Adam knows that Eve was formed *for* him and *from* him, and without him she is pointless (*PL* 4.440–42). She sometimes may seem absolute and self-complete, especially to Adam, because unlike Adam she was not created lonely. She was created as the remedy for human loneliness. Her first experience of an apparent other — the "watry" shape in the lake — was not, as Turner supposes, desire for the other or the self but the excitement of being desired (*One Flesh*, 267). She thought the shape was "Bending to look on me" (*PL* 4.461); her primary desire is to be desired. That is the end for which she was created, and that is why in the divorce tracts Milton refers to the husband as "the wanting soul" and mutual pleasure in marriage as "the mutual enjoyment of that which the wanting soul needfully seeks" (*DDD*, 1.4, YP 2:252). He desires; she desires to be desired. Because of this asymmetric mutuality, Eve might well be mistaken as complete in herself, for unlike Adam she is not constitutively lonely. But this is a mistake born of passion, not the well-managed, rational self-esteem Raphael recommends (*PL* 8.572).

In the oncoming rush of passion prompted by Adam's inordinate attention to Eve's loveliness, he risks forgetting that only the inward qualities — "manly grace / And wisdom" — are "truly fair." As "Best Image" of himself and his "dearer half" (*PL* 5.95), Eve displays as "an outside" (*PL* 8.568) the inward virtues that count as truly human and truly fair, because truly in the image of the invisible God. But Adam, says the poet and Raphael, must take care not to let "an outside" dazzle him into forgetting that he, not she, properly possesses such beauties, and that such beauties, in their most proper godlike form, are invisible. Eve possesses them only insofar as she is part of Adam, his "Best Image." Apart from him, such loveliness deceives. This passage is Milton's frontal attack on those protofeminist pamphlets that asserted Eve's superiority; such notions, alleges Milton, are the mistakes passion makes when it slips reason's control.[31]

Adam's account of his first experience of sensual erotics complements that of Eve's dream in book 5; the two are companion pieces. Just as Adam reassured Eve that evil images and notions, unapproved by reason and not activated by consent, "leave / No spot or blame behind" (5.118–19), so Adam, prompted by Raphael's frown and disapproval, reassures himself that he has not been foiled by his experiences of passion and carnal delight because they have not won his approval or his following. Adam is only "half

abash't," because he has not sinned; he has merely left Raphael with
a mistaken, or incomplete, impression of his nuptial experience.
Actually, Raphael interrupted Adam before he could finish his
story, before he could reassure Raphael that he left "passion," "the
sense of touch," and "carnal pleasure" unapproved and followed
instead the delights he experienced in Eve's graceful acts of wedded conversation — what Milton in *Tetrachordon* calls "a thousand raptures . . . farre on the hither side of carnall enjoyment"
(*Tetrachordon*, Gen. 2:18, YP 2:597).[32] That is to say, Adam already
knew what Raphael was going to say, and he agrees completely with
Raphael's point.

> Neither her out-side formd so fair, nor aught
> In procreation common to all kindes
> (Though higher of the genial Bed by far,
> And with mysterious reverence I deem)
> So much delights me as those graceful acts,
> Those thousand decencies that daily flow
> From all her words and actions mixt with Love
> And sweet compliance, which declare unfeign'd
> Union of Mind, or in us both one Soule;
> Harmonie to behold in wedded pair
> More grateful then harmonious sound to the eare.
> Yet these subject not; I to thee disclose
> What inward thence I feel, not therefore foild,
> Who meet with various objects, from the sense
> Variously representing; yet still free
> Approve the best, and follow what I approve.
> To Love thou blam'st me not, for love thou saist
> Leads up to Heav'n, is both the way and guide.   (8.596–613)

Turner may not be wrong in endorsing a proper appreciation of sensuality in marriage. I agree that frank sensuality and physical
erotics deserve more praise than Christianity traditionally has
allowed. But Turner is wrong to try taking Adam's side against
Raphael, for in the end Adam fully agrees with Raphael on this score
as on all others. After all, God sent Raphael to help Adam get and
keep all the most important matters clear; Milton does not mean

us to regard him as misleading Adam on any matter, least of all this one. Milton, Raphael and Adam all share the same highly sophisticated misogynist convictions.

Milton's sage and serious doctrine of wedded love, I have argued, is not principally about sex. It does not embrace a "frank eroticism," if by erotic we mean anything lusty or passionate; it does not try to redeem sensuality or celebrate it as "wedded Love." Sensuality, the poem teaches, is always something low and brutal, though in Paradise it once was pure. Milton never retreated from the doctrine of "rational burning" he developed in the *Doctrine and Discipline of Divorce* (YP 2:251). We might even say that the mysterious rites of wedded love are not as different from the Lady's "sage / and Serious doctrine of Virginity," as many have supposed (*A Mask*, 786–87). Milton's sense of manly dignity, especially Father Adam's, requires that marriage and *true* procreation, like *true* beauty, be a matter of the soul rather than the body. Milton's monism, after all, does not erase dualism; it simply translates a binary opposition into a hierarchical scale, an important adjustment, certainly, but not a thorough departure from body-spirit dualism. "All Spirit" is still the desired country; all body is still the great fear.

Wedded Conversation in Paradise

Even though Milton worked so hard to redefine marriage as principally a conversation, he does not show us many conversations between Adam and Eve in *Paradise Lost*, at least not as much conversation as Adam enjoys with Raphael, and presumably Eve enjoys with her garden flowers. We listen to Adam and Raphael converse from 5.360 until the end of book 8. Included in this is Adam's relation of his conversation with God (8.357–452), and of his fascination with looking at and touching Eve (8.500–613). Milton represents Adam and Eve in extended conversation chiefly in two places: book 5's talk about Eve's disturbing dream (28–128) and book 9's intense argument about separation (205–375). Adam and Eve argue over many things in their last conversation before falling; some of the issues are explicit, but many remain unarticulated. Both Adam and Eve fail to say exactly what they are thinking in this argument. From the standpoint of friendship doctrine, however, the chief issue is clear: does their married friendship depend on physical proximity, or can they still share one heart and one soul when their bodies are quite literally twain, separated?

Aristotle taught that there is nothing more characteristic of virtuous friends than living together and sharing everything in common. Ciceronian doctrine, however, brings to friendship doctrine an elegiac tone that colors all discussions and performances of friendship through the early modern period. Cicero, like Aristotle, taught that virtuous friendship is grounded on similarity; a friend is a second self. But he also insisted that true friendship could survive the greatest of separations, even death. Indeed, the occasion that prompts Cicero's narrator, Laelius, to speak at such length on friendship is the grief he feels for the loss of his own dear friend, Scipio Africanus. Laelius says,

> he who looks upon a true friend, looks, as it were, upon a sort of image of himself. Wherefore friends, though absent, are at hand; though in need, yet abound; though weak, are strong; and — harder saying still — though dead, are yet alive; so great is the esteem on the part of their friends, the tender recollection and deep longing that still attends them.[33]

In book 9, Milton's Eve, whether intentionally or not, tests the spiritual depth and strength of their married friendship, their fit conversation. Can they still share one heart and one soul when their bodies are apart? Do they carry each other's strength and beauty and dedication with them when they can no longer literally see and touch each other?

The first four syllables of book 9 threaten to answer these questions in the negative: "No more of talk."

> No more of talk where God or Angel Guest
> With Man, as with his Friend, familiar us'd

> To sit indulgent, and with him partake
> Rural repast, permitting him the while
> Venial discourse unblam'd.   (*PL* 9.1–5)

These lines bring a full stop to the long conversation between Adam and the archangel that began in book 5. The conversation that follows between Adam and Eve will usher in an age when such conversations will be largely impossible. Friendly conversation between God and man or even angel and human is over; disobedience will render human beings unable to be either worthy hosts or worthy guests.

Milton represents the last prelapsarian connubial conversation as an argument. Eve, for reasons she keeps to herself, wants to try a short separation from Adam; Adam does not want her to go off alone, but for some reason (again unclear) finally allows it. Both Adam and Eve articulate reasons for their positions, but the reasons they offer, especially Eve's, sound disingenuous. Milton imagines this first married couple as talking to each other but failing truly to communicate.

Eve begins this anticonversation by observing that they could better keep up with Eden's wild growth if they worked apart from each other:

> Let us divide our labours, thou where choice
> Leads thee, or where most needs, whether to wind
> The Woodbine round this Arbour, or direct
> The clasping Ivie where to climb, while I
> In yonder Spring of Roses intermixt
> With Myrtle, find what to redress till Noon:
> For while so near each other thus all day
> Our taske we choose, what wonder if so near
> Looks intervene and smiles, or object new
> Casual discourse draw on, which intermits
> Our dayes work brought to little, though begun
> Early, and th' hour of Supper comes unearn'd.   (214–25)

Her ostensible concern is to keep ahead of the wild vegetable growth in Eden, which she says "derides" their efforts at control

(211) and may even grow wild faster as an unintended consequence of their efforts: "the work under our labour grows, / Luxurious by restraint" (208–9). It sounds as if Eve is accusing Nature, and perhaps by extension, God, for turning their "pleasant task" into an impossible labor (207). But we are led to suspect that none of this is the real reason Eve proposes a separation. Even though Adam praises Eve for studying "houshold good," he does not accept her premise: "These paths & Bowers doubt not but our joynt hands / Will keep from Wilderness with ease, as wide / As we need walk" (244–46).[34] Adam assumes that she is simply mistaken in her fears, but readers may suspect that Eve has another concern she does not share with Adam. The narrator told us in book 8 that Eve left Adam and Raphael to converse by themselves, not because she was incapable of understanding cosmic matters, nor because such topics bored her, but because she preferred to learn of such things in conversation alone with Adam, a conversation that would include sensual digressions:

> Yet went she not, as not with such discourse
> Delighted, or not capable her eare
> Of what was high: such pleasure she reserv'd,
> *Adam* relating, she sole Auditress;
> Her Husband the Relater she preferr'd
> Before the Angel, and of him to ask
> Chose rather: hee, she knew would intermix
> Grateful digressions, and solve high dispute
> With conjugal Caresses, from his Lip
> Not Words alone pleas'd her.   (8.48–57)

Now Raphael is gone; once again she is alone in Paradise with Adam. Inexplicably, Eve now seems anxious to avoid the pleasure she preferred before, the very pleasure she took pains to preserve for herself by leaving Adam and Raphael only a few days before.[35] Now looks, smiles and "Casual discourse" appear to count as interruptions of their work rather than "Grateful digressions," as if garden work took precedence over the very purpose for which she was created — to remedy Adam's solitude with fit conversation. Adam does not say so at this point, but later he admits that he regards Eve's proposal as prompted by some "strange / Desire" (9.1135–36).

Maybe Adam is fishing for a complimentary denial when he allows that perhaps Eve may be sated with his conversation: "But if much converse perhaps / Thee satiate, to short absence I could yield" (9.247–48). Adam told Raphael that he could never be sated with such heavenly conversation as they enjoyed together; simple symmetry should suggest that Eve cannot get enough of conversation with Adam. Moreover, there is something illogical, however debonair, about Adam's concern since her chief reason for being is to satisfy *his* need for conversation. Adam, it seems, is unable to account for the source of this "strange / Desire."

Eve, however, supplies us with a clue in her next speech. Adam reminds her of the "malicious Foe" lying in wait to work them woe and shame (253–55), and for some reason she takes this reminder amiss. She takes Adam to be implying, unkindly, that she lacks the "firmness" required to repel the foe. Her response betrays a possible source for such apparently unprovoked resentment:

> That such an Enemie we have, who seeks
> Our ruin, both by thee informd I learne,
> And from the parting Angel over-heard
> As in a shadie nook I stood behind,
> Just then returnd at shut of Evening Flours.
> But that thou shouldst my firmness therfore doubt
> To God or thee, because we have a foe
> May tempt it, I expected not to hear.   (9.274–81)

Eve, it seems, returned from her flowers before Adam and Raphael had finished their conversation. She overheard, she says, the angel talk about their enemy as she stood out of sight in a shady nook nearby. It is impossible to figure out, from Eve's report, exactly when she returned and what she overheard. In the book 8 conversation between Raphael and Adam, Raphael mentions the "enemy" explicitly only once (8.230–36), and that comes only a very short while after Eve left to tend her flowers (8.63). I cannot imagine that we are meant to believe that Eve returned almost immediately after leaving and eavesdropped on all of Adam's story. In his valediction to Adam, Raphael warns Adam to "stand fast" against "all "temptation to transgress," but the temptations at issue here concern passion's power to sway reason, and we hear no mention of the enemy (8.635–43).

Deliberately or not, Eve is not clear about when she started listening in to Adam and Raphael's conversation, and what she overheard. More than likely this is because Eve was, and still is, upset by what she heard, and she has had a week to dwell on her feelings. She probably overheard Adam and Raphael talking about her. She heard Adam confess that her beauty prompts passion in him, a "Commotion strange" that he fears signifies some weakness or failure in him (8.530–35). She heard Adam speak of her as if she were superior not only to himself but to Wisdom itself, an absolute goddess (8.547–59). This is Milton's misogyny at its most sophisticated. Eve is both hopelessly flattered by Adam's confession and devastated by the angel's response to that confession:

> For what admir'st thou, what transports thee so,
> An outside? fair no doubt, and worthy well
> Thy cherishing, thy honouring, and thy love,
> Not thy subjection: weigh with her thy self;
> Then value: Oft times nothing profits more
> Then self esteem, grounded on just and right
> Well manag'd; of that skill the more thou know'st,
> The more she will acknowledge thee her Head,
> And to realities yield all her shows.   (8.567–75)

And, of course, Adam agrees completely with Raphael's assessment of Adam's danger. He must keep passion in check by properly valuing his own inward virtue over Eve's stunning "outside." Eve must feel at once both flattered and utterly degraded. Her beauty is amazingly powerful, and that power may threaten Adam's manly firmness.

Hurt by what she has overheard, Eve shifts the issue away from Adam's manly firmness and tries to insist instead on her own. Raphael warned Adam to remain firm; Eve now accuses Adam of doubting her firmness.

> His violence thou fear'st not, being such,
> As wee, not capable of death or paine,
> Can either not receave, or can repell.
> His fraud is then thy fear, which plain inferrs
> Thy equal fear that my firm Faith and Love
> Can by his fraud be shak'n or seduc't;
> Thoughts, which how found they harbour in thy brest
> *Adam*, misthought of her to thee so dear?   (9.282–89)

Adam should respond that it is *his* business to be firm, not hers, and in effect he does, but he does so as a good humanist husband, using "healing words," not answering accusation with accusation or hurt with hurt (9.290). She knows perfectly well where such thoughts came from; they came from the archangel, though she has twisted their sense to make them sound like mean thoughts.

Or, more accurately, they are indeed mean, misogynist thoughts that Milton has dressed up to look like Nature and ontology and to which he has lent archangelic authority. Eve is Adam's friend in all ways except the most fundamental — equality. When it comes to depicting connubial conversation, Milton cannot help but betray the flawed kernel at the center of his effort to reimagine marriage as a friendship. Inequality will breed jealousy and distrust; Eve will want to be a true other self to Adam, not just an outward image of his inward manly firmness. The more she tries to be that other self, the more Milton depicts her as trying to be something she's not — a man.

Adam tries to explain, with some indirection, that having her nearby helps him stay firm. He echoes Phaedrus's claim in Plato's *Symposium* that an army of lovers would be the strongest, since such warriors "would abstain from everything shameful and would be jealous of their honor in front of each other" (178e–179a):

I from the influence of thy looks receave
Access in every Vertue, in thy sight
More wise, more watchful, stronger, if need were
Of outward strength; while shame, thou looking on,
Shame to be overcome or over-reacht
Would utmost vigor raise, and rais'd unite.   (9.309–14)

If they were equals, Eve would feel the same, and would want Adam always by her side to prompt her to remain firm and loyal. But they are not, and so Adam's question, "Why shouldst not thou like sense within thee feel / When I am present, and thy trial choose / With me, best witness of thy Vertue tri'd," requires no answer (315–17). And Eve does not even try to offer one.

Instead Eve complains that a world in which they are not both equally "endu'd / Single with like defence" would be a seriously imperfect world (9.324–25). How can such a world be? Eve's use of the word "Single" reminds us of Adam's conversation with God about man's "single imperfection," his need for a fit partner in conversation (8.423). Milton and Adam, no doubt, meant that man is imperfect when single — "it is not good for man to be alone" — but the other sense cannot be avoided or expunged. It is not entirely good for man to need company, especially when the partner may fall short of being what classical friendship defined as fundamental — an equal, other self. When Adam allows Eve to go, he puts equalist feminism to the test, and in doing so he finally fails in his proper role of humanist husband — to bear sway over the manifestly "weaker vessel" without force, violence or unkindness, to command her obedience as if it were her choice. And, of course, all hell breaks loose.

FIVE

Heroic Divorce and
Heroic Solitude

In the treatment of *Samson Agonistes* that follows, I want to focus on two things. Milton chose a Hebrew hero for this strictly neo-classical tragic poem, and, even though it required taking significant liberties with his biblical source, he made that hero a married man. Hebrew heroes were not unheard of in Renaissance literature, but they were usually dramatically Hellenized; married heroes were even rarer. It was commonplace, of course, for classical, even biblical, heroes to have a partner; David Halperin refers to such pairs as "Heroes and Their Pals."[1] Gilgamesh and Enkidu, Achilles and Patroclus, David and Jonathan are all familiar examples of heroic friendships. Clearly, friendship, not marriage, was regarded as the proper relationship for a hero. Marriages, like those of Heracles to Megara and, later, Deianeira, normally meant trouble for heroes. Though the two features under analysis here — Hebraic hero and married hero — are deeply interconnected, I will discuss them separately at first.

Jeffrey S. Shoulson quite properly reminds us of the long tradi-tion of Hellenizing Samson into a kind of Hebrew Heracles.[2] Josephus concludes his Samson story by urging his readers to admire the hero for his classical virtues, not his dedication to God or to Israel: "And it is but right to admire the man for his valour, his strength, and the grandeur of his end, as also for the wrath which he cherished to the last against his enemies. That he let himself be ensnared by a woman must be imputed to human nature, which succumbs to sins; but testimony is due to him for his surpassing excellence in all the rest."[3]

Courage, strength, magnanimity are the virtues hailed by classical culture, and even the failings Josephus lists — Achilles-style wrath and giving in to sexual temptations — are the failings typical of classical heroes.[4] Hellenizing biblical heroes was as important to Renaissance humanism as christening selected patriarchs and prophets was to medieval Christianity.[5] Perhaps the most graphic example of Hellenizing a Hebrew hero is Michelangelo's David — the king of Israel sporting a foreskin!

Milton's Samson receives no such treatment. Though the poem is insistently classical in form, it focuses on Samson as an Israelite, a promised deliverer, and, significantly, as circumcised. The poem pays persistent attention to his and his tribe's circumcision and the Philistines' lack thereof. The Chorus refers metonymically to Samson's Philistine victims as "A thousand foreskins" (144). Samson twice refers to Philistines as "the uncircumcis'd" (260, 640), which the Chorus further glosses as "Idolatrous, uncircumcis'd, unclean" (1364). Milton's Samson not only bears the outward sign of the covenant, he is also, unlike Josephus's Samson (or the Bible's for that matter), keenly concerned with details of the law. He married Dalila because he "thought it lawful from my former act" (231); he refuses to attend Dagon's festival because "Our law forbids" (1320); and he proves himself a skilled casuist, almost a proleptic Talmudist, throughout the play.[6]

Marriage or No Marriage

Milton was familiar with Hellenized Samsons, and he deliberately took another tack. His Samson stands midway between the first

Adam who resigned his manhood and the second Adam who restores fallen manhood by being (problematically enough) God. With Samson, Milton imagines a fallen man's best possible attempt at shedding the old Adam's "effeminate slackness" and reclaiming original manliness. For Samson to qualify for this role, he must do at least one thing Adam could not — divorce his unfit wife.[7] And since Milton based his arguments for divorce in large part upon ancient Hebrew law, his Samson must know the scriptures and the law.

Milton reimagines the Bible's Delilah as a perfect example of an unfit wife, unfit not because of adultery, the only sense of "uncleanness" allowed by canon law as grounds for divorce, but because she was no meet help to Samson. In *Paradise Lost,* the epic narrator likens both Adam and Eve, newly fallen and arising bleary-eyed from postcoital slumber, to "*Herculean Samson*" rising newly shorn from "the Harlot-lap / Of *Philistean Dalilah*" (9.1060–61), but there is nothing in *Samson Agonistes* to suggest that Dalila is a whore, or even sexually promiscuous. The Delilah of Judges might be called a harlot but not so the Dalila of Milton's *Samson Agonistes*.[8] Her sex with Samson, according to strict canon law, is married sex. Milton reimagines Dalila as Samson's wife in order that she may serve as a quasi-biblical and quasi-historical example of the unfit wife Milton discussed at such length in his divorce tracts from 1643 to 1645. Her unfitness makes their marriage "no mariage" in exactly the sense Milton imagines in the *Doctrine and Discipline of Divorce:*

> if the woman be naturally so of disposition, as will not help to remove, but help to increase that same God-forbidd'n lonelines which will in time draw on with it a generall discomfort and dejection of minde, not beseeming either Christian profession or morall conversation, unprofitable and dangerous to the Common-wealth, when the houshold estate, out of which must flourish forth the vigor and spirit of all publick enterprizes, is so ill contented and procur'd at home, and cannot be supported; such a mariage can be no mariage whereto the most honest end is wanting: and the agrieved person shall doe more manly, to be extraordinary and singular in

> claiming the due right whereof he is frustrated, then to piece up
> his lost contentment by visiting the Stews, or stepping to his neigh-
> bours bed, which is the common shift in this mis-fortune, or els by
> suffering his usefull life to wast away and be lost under a secret
> affliction of an unconscionable size to humane strength. Against
> all which evills, the mercy of this Mosaick Law was graciously
> exhibited. (YP 2:247)

Before he slaved in the grinding house for the Philistines, Samson
ground away in "the mill of an undelighted and servil copulation"
(YP 2:258). Samson can argue that the grinding work he performs
at the mill is "labour / Honest and lawful" (*SA*, 1365–66), compared
to the utterly unmanly grinding he performed in Dalila's embraces.
There he subordinated himself and his calling to what Milton
regarded as his most unmanly carnal desires, his specially conse-
crated body to a Philistine woman. Milton chose this story, and
adapted it significantly, because it so perfectly illustrates all his
earlier points about wifely unfitness. And because such a marriage
is, canon law notwithstanding, "no mariage," Milton may even claim
that he has not really altered the biblical tale — Dalila is not truly
Samson's wife in the only sense Milton regards as legitimate.

Deuteronomy 24:1 declares that a man may divorce his wife if
"she find no favour in his eyes because he hath found some *uncleanness* in her" (my emphasis). Milton preferred to translate the
Hebrew word, *'ervah* as "the nakedness of anything," which he further glossed as "any defect, annoyance, or ill quality in nature, which
to be joyn'd with, makes life tedious, and such company worse then
solitude" (*Tetrachordon*, YP 2:620). [9] Dalila, of course, did far more
than make Samson's life tedious; she betrayed his trust and threatened his life, but she is not, technically, an adulterer. This makes
her into exactly the example Milton needs to reinforce his case
against the canon law that, citing Jesus' words in Matthew 19:6–9,
forbids divorce for any cause other than sexual infidelity. Milton's
Samson divorces Dalila as unfit, using the very language of Jesus
from Matthew 19:6: "thou and I long since are twain," not by

adultery, but by her unfitness as a remedy for Samson's solitude (*SA*, 929). Milton's commentary on Matthew 19:6 emphasizes the word "twain": "For if they who were once undoubtedly one flesh, yet become twain by adultery, then sure they who were never one flesh rightly, never helps meete for each other according to the plain prescript of God, may with less adoe then a volume be concluded still twaine" (*Tetrachordon*, YP 2:650). In *Tetrachordon* Milton echoes the word "twain" as a counter to those insistently literal interpretations of Jesus' words against which he launches his arguments. In *Samson Agonistes* his Hebrew hero ventriloquizes Milton's echo of Jesus' word as if proleptically to prescribe what the word will mean when Jesus, to be born centuries later, comes to utter it (as if Jesus uttered the very word the 1611 translators chose to translate the Greek *duo*). "Twain" means unfit, not simply sexually unfaithful; it means never really married. Therefore, though Milton appears to have tampered with the Scripture story by making Dalila Samson's wife, in another even more significant sense he has not, because his point is, wedding or no, Dalila never was a fit help or partner in conversation, so never was truly a wife to Samson. A formal "bill of divorcement" appears unnecessary in such a case of egregious "wedlock treachery" and so Samson divorces her simply with words: "Out, out *Hyæna*," "Thou and I are long since twain" (748, 929).

Milton's Samson also echoes the author of the divorce tracts when he refers to those "wisest and best men full oft beguil'd" (759) by false women, tricked into trusting their repentance, or the "wisest men and best" (1034) who, "least practiz'd" in such affairs, mistake conversational unfitness for the "bashful muteness of a virgin" (*DDD*, YP 2:249, 312). Milton, who took pride in preserving his chastity until marriage and celebrated his friend Charles Diodati for having preserved his until death, understood himself as one of these "sobrest and best-govern'd men" who committed "an error above wisdom to prevent" in his first choice of a wife. The Bible's Samson is quite another sort of man, but Milton reimagines him as a Hebrew (Milton might have said Jewish) version of himself: a failed redeemer, held captive by his enemies, blind, misunderstood and unique among his contemporaries in his relationship to God.[10] Manoa's lament for Samson might serve equally as a lament for the post-Restoration Milton:

> Select, and Sacred, Glorious for a while,
> The miracle of men: then in an hour
> Ensnar'd, assaulted, overcome, led bound,
> Thy Foes derision, Captive, Poor, and Blind
> Into a Dungeon thrust, to work with Slaves?
> Alas methinks whom God hath chosen once
> To worthiest deeds, if he through frailty err,
> He should not so o'rewhelm, and as a thrall
> Subject him to so foul indignities,
> Be it but for honours sake of former deeds.   (363–72)

But Milton, like Samson, proves heroic partly by *not* uttering such laments himself. Milton puts them in another's mouth; Samson blames himself, not God or fate, for his failings as a man:

> But what avail'd this temperance, not compleat
> Against another object more enticing?
> What boots it at one gate to make defence,
> And at another to let in the foe
> Effeminatly vanquish't? by which means,
> Now blind, dishearten'd, sham'd, dishonour'd, quell'd,
> To what can I be useful, wherein serve
> My Nation, and the work from Heav'n impos'd.   (558–65)

Classical manliness prescribed modes of behavior that focused on a man's relations with friends, the polity and one's self. It was rooted in the doctrines of *amicitia*, homosocial relations between men. Milton was not alone in his efforts to redefine manliness around the heteroerotic center of marriage, but it may fairly be said that his efforts — five volumes on marriage and divorce, much of *Paradise Lost*, and *Samson Agonistes* — push the issues harder and so expose more clearly than most the problematic aspects of restructuring a classical homoerotic social imaginary into a bibliocentric heteroerotic social imaginary. According to Milton's version of originary manhood, Adam's best gift from God was a female partner. The way Milton imagines them in *Paradise Lost*, Adam's initial attempts at social conversation, first with the sun, earth, rivers, dales and creatures and second with God himself, turn out to be inappropriate. Those creatures are not fit partners for him, and he is not yet a fit partner for prolonged conversation with the noncreature, God. But the partner who is supposed to suit him — his "likeness," his "fit help," his "other self" (*PL* 8.450) — turns sour. God could not be his proper friend for, according to both Milton and classical doctrine, gods enjoy solitude and need no friends. Raphael might have been a perfect friend, much as Milton imagined Charles Diodati was a perfect friend, but both of those friends went back to heaven where neither Adam nor Milton could immediately follow.

Adam really had no choice; he had to stay with a fallen Eve. Nevertheless, Milton's God blames him for that choice and to that "effeminate slackness" Milton's archangel Michael traces all the failures of postlapsarian manliness (*PL* 12.634). When Samson divorces Dalila, declaring that they "long since are twain" (929), he takes the step toward redeemed manhood Adam could only imagine (*PL* 12.911–15), but not perform. The first marriage differs radically from all of those that follow: wives no longer are created out of their husband's own bone and flesh. "Bone of my bone and flesh of my flesh" is a literal statement only for Adam and Eve. Adam gave up his chance to remain fully manly when he chose "compliance bad" over divorce. Milton's narrator even refuses to dignify Adam's choice with the word "choice," calling it, rather, "compliance" by one "Fondly overcome with Femal charm" (*PL* 9.994, 999). The poem blames Adam and invites us to blame him for choosing bone and flesh over duty to God, even though it is impossible seriously to entertain for long the thought of Adam divorcing Eve. The poem dwells on this possibility of divorce for 220 lines (*PL* 9.780–999) and winds up condemning Adam for sinning with his eyes wide open, "Against his better knowledge, not deceav'd" (998).[11] The task of recovering true manliness from the stain of such "compliance bad" must fall to another, for the doctrine of the fortunate Fall, to which Milton's poem subscribes, requires that Adam grind for a while in a less than dignified bondage to a less than ideal partner. The world must be peopled for God to covenant with Israel, and the Messiah must be born. Before the Messiah's advent, Israel will recover some of mankind's lost manliness, but it rests with the Son of God to recover it completely.

This may be one reason why Milton twins these two poems in publication in 1671 — *Paradise Regain'd, . . . To which is added Samson Agonistes*. The story of Samson's recovery of lost manliness is closely related, but supplemental, to the Son's final victory. Samson does the work of divorce that the Son has no occasion for. Samson does as much as a man can do, short of being God as well. I shall have more to say about the Son's restoration of original manliness at the end of this chapter.

Samson does what Adam could not, but the result is not, of course, an opportunity for Samson to remarry a fitter spouse. Samson shifts his sense of a significant other from unfit female partners to God. Samson had been dedicated to God from before birth. His first marriage, normally unlawful like his suicidal and genocidal end, was God's idea, though the Timnan woman also "pleas'd" him (*SA*, 219). That marriage was, therefore, subordinated to his special relationship to God, a heteroerotic feature of a relationship between males, though God is not, strictly speaking, a man. Perhaps because he confused his pleasure with God's will, Samson made the mistake of thinking his subsequent choice of Dalila was "lawful from my former act" (231). Samson and God were fit partners; God's will and Samson's pleasure coincided so well as to make some issues of law look like "vain reasonings" (323). But no "intimate impulse" moved him to choose Dalila; there his desire and God's will became twain. Divorcing Dalila marks the beginning of Samson's return to intimacy with God and as the poem continues he sounds more genuinely heroic with almost every line.

As in *Paradise Lost,* Milton runs the risk of making marriage and godliness look like rivals in a zero-sum game. He wanted to redefine marriage as a friendship, and to the degree he succeeded, such friendship promised to refigure wives as men's equals. Friendship doctrine insisted true friends must be equals in virtue. But to the degree he failed, Milton clung to the Pauline preference for exclusive friendship with the risen Christ, a friendship whose highest form left no room for marriage, because marriage kept a man's mind focused on the "things of the world" (1 Cor. 7:32–33) at the expense of gradually being made one with God, man's more originary "other self." *Samson Agonistes* contains the least mitigated examples of Miltonic misogyny (1025–33) because it foregrounds this competition between friendship with a woman and friendship with God. The first relationship, if successful, would render women all but equal to men; the second promises to render a man all but equal to God, to make him God's friend. A husband's "despotic power / Over his female" should guarantee that his relation to God is not compromised by "female usurpation" (1054, 1060), but it is precisely that power that guarantees that marriage cannot be a friendship. This problematic structure means that every bid for female equality must appear as "female usurpation" and every grant of equality must appear as "effeminate slackness." Companionate marriage was always doomed to fail because the preferred puritan story tells men that their first and most significant other is God; a wife was God's gift to man. It was such a grand gift that man could never reciprocate, not only because man could not make or be a fit partner for God, but more significantly because God *needs* no partner. God is not lonely in solitude; he needs no friend. This also means that there can be no true friendship between the Creator and his creature, only a radical inequality that makes friendship impossible, even irrelevant. The Son of *Paradise Regain'd,* however much Milton depicts him as human, is a person content in solitude. He walks into the wilderness to seek solitude and he never complains that he lacks a fit partner. Like his Father, he in himself is perfect; in him is no deficiency found (*PL* 8.415–16), and he proves his perfection in the solitude of the wilderness where his only interlocutor is the most unfit conversation partner imaginable. When he finally stands, having recovered true manliness and inner Paradise, he does so alone.

At his end, Samson goes to live with God. Though he receives his reward, Israel has not been liberated or redeemed, nor is Paradise restored. Samson succeeds in divorcing the "specious Monster," his "accomplisht snare," but however necessary such a step, it is hardly sufficient to regain Paradise. That will require another sort of man. Milton's Samson, after all, is an Israelite, not a Christian. His intimacy is with God the Father, not God the incarnate Son, and that is an intimacy no creature can withstand for long. Even upright Adam found conversation with his maker life-threateningly intense:

> Hee ended, or I heard no more, for now
> My earthly by his Heav'nly overpowerd,
> Which it had long stood under, streind to the highth
> In that celestial Colloquie sublime,
> As with an object that excels the sense,
> Dazl'd and spent, sunk down, and sought repair
> Of sleep, which instantly fell on me, call'd
> By Nature as in aide, and clos'd mine eyes.   (*PL* 8.452–59)

So also do Samson's intimate impulses and rousing motions push him toward death. Does Samson, an Israelite, regain "to know God aright" and so help to "repair the ruines of our first parents" (*Of Education*, YP 2:366)? Or does he die still in the dark, well-meaning, perhaps, but still blind to God's Paradise-restoring plan? In the anti-Jewish argot of Milton's day, does Samson die a Jew? Approaching this question requires that we back up a step or two and have a brief look at the ambivalent structure of Christian images of Hebrew, Israelite and Jew.

Israelite or Jew

In 1975 Camille Slights noted in passing the general consensus among Miltonists that "Samson is a type of Christ" (Slights, "A Hero of Conscience," 395). She probably meant Milton's Samson, though she may also have meant both the Samson of Judges and Milton's Samson. Christian Miltonists have generally accepted and deployed notions of typology and fulfillment that closely resemble those of the early modern Protestants about whom they write. For many of those critics, "type of Christ" amounts to pretty much the same thing as "Christ figure," even though Anthony Low's 1974 *The Blaze of Noon: A Reading of Samson Agonistes* carefully corrects that mistaken conflation. He reminds critics that a type is not to be confused with its fulfillment. A type signifies something else, but lacks the substance of what it signifies: "Samson is not Jesus, or even Paul, because he can do no more than foreshadow and typify the new dispensation. He can only *partly understand* the implications of his own self-sacrifice."[12] Low reminds us that Milton's Samson is an Israelite, or in Low's own words, a Jew.[13] He does not live under the new covenant, he has not been baptized. He does not recognize the strange "rouzing motions" he feels as the promptings of the Holy Spirit, for the Holy Spirit has not yet been bestowed upon humankind. The poem deliberately uses terms like "intimate impulse" (*SA*, 223) and "rouzing motions" (1382) rather than "Spirit" to suggest Samson's limited "old covenant" relationship to God. Low judiciously retreats from interpreting Milton's Samson as a Christian hero for he acknowledges the poem's careful insistence that Samson belongs to and remains bound by what all Protestants regarded as an earlier dispensation of law, not spirit.[14] Samson's sacrificial death, however heroic, is not redemptive; Israel remains in bondage. As a judge in Israel he is a failure. Even as a type, he is really quite a sorry one, a type that emphasizes lack even more than similarity.

Some recent readings of *Samson* ignore Low's important cautions. David Loewenstein, for example, insists on regarding Milton's

Samson as "a militant Saint," even "a radical saint moved by the Spirit to enact the dreadful vengeance of the Lord."[15] Loewenstein never actually *argues* that Milton meant his Samson to represent the spirit-led divine vengeance of disappointed Quakers, Anabaptists, even Diggers and Fifth Monarchists; he just repeats the claim over and over: "*Samson* becomes a drama about the work of the Spirit and its conquering power that gives poetic vision to the notion voiced by the regicide and Anabaptist William Goffe during the famous Putney Debates of 1647" (164); "He [Samson] waits for the Spirit of the Lord to move him to commit one final, terrifying act of apocalyptic force" (163–64); "Milton . . . dramatizes at the end of *Samson Agonistes* the crucial activism of the vengeful godly saint whose destructive agency is interwoven with powerful divine forces" (175). Finally, Loewenstein calls Milton's Samson a "radical Old Testament saint" without considering the oxymoronic (and implicitly anti-Jewish) implications of such a sobriquet.

Such readings forget that Milton deliberately chose a failed Hebrew judge for this drama. They also forget the context of early modern anti-Jewish logic within which Milton writes. A type is a shadow, lacking the substance of what it points to. Low's explanation of the limited understanding displayed by Manoa and the Chorus is perfectly correct: they learn an Old Testament lesson from Samson's example, not a gospel lesson. The "new acquist" to which the Chorus refers at the play's end falls far short of the new covenant of the spirit. There is nothing apocalyptic about Samson's vengeance; the world does not end, nor is it even turned upside down. If Samson's end calls to mind Christ's sacrifice on the cross (as surely Milton meant it should), it does so in order to underscore the enormous differences, not the similarities. There is nothing redemptive about Samson's sacrifice, except perhaps personally; Israel remains in bondage. The redemption of Israel from Philistine bondage, as supersessionist logic insists, was never really the point anyway. Samson himself passes upon the Danites precisely the same judgment the Son of *Paradise Regain'd* passes upon all of Israel, calling it a people

> grown corrupt
> And by thir vices brought to servitude,
> Then to love Bondage more then Liberty,
> Bondage with ease then strenuous liberty;
> And to despise, or envy, or suspect
> Whom God hath of his special Favour rais'd
> As thir Deliverer.   (*SA*, 268–74)

In *Paradise Regain'd*, the Son even implies that Israel's impenitent apostasy has turned them into a race of people *deserving* enslavement:

> Nor in the land of their captivity
> Humbled themselves, or penitent besought
> The God of thir fore-fathers; but so dy'd
> Impenitent, and left a race behind
> Like to themselves, distinguishable scarce
> From Gentils but by Circumcision vain,
> And God with Idols in their worship joyn'd.
> Should I of these the liberty regard,
> Who freed, as to their antient Patrimony,
> Unhumbl'd, unrepentant, unreform'd,
> Headlong would follow; and to thir Gods perhaps
> Of *Bethel* and of *Dan?* No, let them serve
> Thir enemies, who serve Idols with God.   (*PR* 3.420–32)

The Son makes it clear to his tempter that he has no intention of liberating such a servile "race" from tyranny. The Father, he says, may at some future time turn them to repentance, but his messianic mission on this earth depends crucially on the persistence of exactly that stubborn Jewish apostasy. Milton's archangel Michael, we recall, levels the classic hateful charge against the Jews, prophesying that Jesus is to be "nail'd to the Cross / By his own Nation" (*PL* 413–14). According to this orthodox Protestant anti-Jewish logic, the Son's preordained act of redemptive sacrifice requires a race of self-enslaved, stiff-necked apostates.

Is Samson, then, a Jew like the bondage-loving Danites, or is he exceptional, like Abraham? Elisa Narin van Court detects in

medieval English literature an ambivalence about Jews that she takes
to be rooted in Pauline doctrine. Paul's teaching in Romans, she
argues, initiates "a division in Christian doctrine concerning the
Jews," a division persistently visible in English culture throughout the Middle Ages:

> This division is seen in its broadest and most simplistic form in those
> medieval representations of the Jews which are articulated through
> two paradigms of opposition: in the first, the Jew is the other (*inimici*)
> vis-à-vis the Christian; in the second, given the exigencies of Christian
> claims to a Hebraic heritage (*patres*), distinctions are made between
> Scriptural Jews, who are revered as the possessors of the Old Law
> (and prototypes of Christ), and historical Jews, who are reviled as the
> killers of Christ.[16]

Often, but by no means always, the two sides of the ambivalence
are marked by different names — "Israelite" for the scriptural
patriarchs, judges and prophets and "Jew" for the proverbially stubborn misbeliever. Abraham and the prophets, according to Paul's
logic of Romans 4, are heroes of faith, not works, and this makes
them virtual Christians. As I have pointed out in another context,
most Protestant commentators regarded the prophet Daniel as an
eyewitness to the glorified Christ, much as Paul claimed to be after
his Damascus road conversion.[17] But the Pharisees, scribes and rabbis of the Gospels and "the Jews" of John's gospel are the *inimici*,
the forefathers of those medieval Jews accused of poisoning wells,
murdering little Christian boys, and worshipping the devil, or at
least horribly misworshipping God.

The ambivalence could sometimes be even more complicated
than this. Even the stiff-necked, postadvent, misbelieving Jew,
according to Augustine's reasoning, is still a witness to God's original covenant with human beings. Though the old covenant may
be superseded, the existence of Jews who still believe themselves
bound by that covenant was thought to supply a visible historical
reminder that God makes covenants with humans, even though
that old covenant of laws was never anything more than a shad-

owy carnal type of the allegedly transcendent covenant of grace. Augustine rested his doctrinal ambivalence on a typological reading of Psalm 59:11 (58:12 in the Vulgate): "Slay them not, lest my people forget: scatter them by thy power; and bring them down, O Lord our shield." The psalmist ventriloquizes David's call to the Lord for deliverance from his enemies, but a deliverance that stops short of killing those enemies. Augustine interprets David's call as Christ's, and the enemies represent the Jews who are out to kill him, and later to kill Christians. Though such prowling dogs deserve no less than death for their sins, pride, curses and lies (Ps. 58:12–13), Christ wishes them preserved as an enduring witness to his death and resurrection by which their covenant of works was superseded. They must be kept alive because they *signify* redeemed humanity, though they themselves are considered less than human.

According to Jeremy Cohen, this Augustinian ambivalence, derived from Paul, "determined the basic stance of virtually all early medieval polemics against the Jews."[18] This is what Jeffrey Shoulson refers to as the "perpetual living proof" that is the meaning of Jewish bodies in the Pauline metaphysical imaginary (*Milton and the Rabbis*, 76–78). The "true" Christian self, according to Paul, has his "conversation in heaven" rather than among the vile bodies of this earth, but according to the binary logic of Christian metaphysics, that true self with a "glorious body" (Phil. 3:20) in heaven remains unimaginable unless some version of an earthly body and earthly conversation persists. That is why Christianity cannot afford, in the end, to do away with all the Jewish bodies, either by genocide or conversion.

Nor can Christianity do away with marriage, even though it teaches that marriage is an earthly conversation that will not follow men into heaven: "For in the resurrection they neither marry nor are given in marriage, but are as the angels of God in heaven" (Matt. 22:30, see also Mark 12:25 and Luke 20:35). Though he had plenty of opportunities to imagine heteroerotic relations in heaven, Milton never suggests that any female angels exist. When his archangel Raphael details angelic erotics for Adam, no mention is made of gender differences (*PL* 8.623–29). Sexual differences, of course, have no place in heavenly love since such love involves no flesh. Heavenly love, according to Raphael, involves such absolute union that even souls would involve too much "restrain'd conveyance" (628–29). When Milton's Adam later complains that females are a "noveltie" on earth that God wisely avoided when peopling heaven, no narrative, angelic, or godlike voice ever raises a challenge to his assumptions about the homogenous nature of heavenly beings:

> O why did God,
> Creator wise, that peopl'd highest Heav'n
> With Spirits Masculine, create at last
> This noveltie on Earth, this fair defect
> Of Nature, and not fill the World at once
> With Men as Angels without Feminine,
> Or find some other way to generate
> Mankind?   (*PL* 10.888–95)

The poem means us to regard Adam's complaint as a form of misogyny every bit as "crabbed" as Augustine's opinion about a male rather than a female companion for Adam, but it never gives the slightest indication that his assumptions are mistaken. Indeed, early modern orthodoxy is generally content to leave such assumptions quietly alone. Marriage has a persistently carnal aspect to it unsuitable to resurrection. In this it resembles the Christian imagination of the Jew who also has no place, as a Jew, in heaven. Heterosexual marriage shares some of the same status with the Jew as another of the impossible kernels of orthodox Christianity. Christianity wants to endorse marriage over friendship, and even redefine marriage as the first and only truly real friendship, but men who go to heaven become unmarried upon arrival, for they return to their originary significant other — God. Jews who go to heaven must arrive as converted Christians. Jewishness and marriage are treated as peculiarly carnal and temporary states, but homoerotic friendship is spiritual and eternal.

The virtually Christian patriarch or prophet from Scripture could also be made to stand for the as-yet imperfect faith of a contemporary Christian. As Barbara Lewalski describes it, the English Protestant version of this ambivalence is slightly different from its Catholic predecessors. Biblical Israel offered seventeenth century Protestants two typological versions of the Christian self:

> When the emphasis is on the great benefits and advantages the Christian enjoys in his religious life, the ease and comfort of the Gospel in comparison to the Law, the Christian may see himself (through Christ) as an antitype of the Israelite of old. But when on the other hand he concentrates upon his essential spiritual life and situation, his dependence upon faith and his imperfect spiritual vision in this life, he is more likely to view himself as a correlative type with the Old Testament Israelites, located on the same spiritual plane and waiting like them for the fulfillment of all the signs in Christ at the end of time.[19]

Here the ambivalence straddles the distinctions between antitype and correlative type, as well as between "the Israelite of old" and "the Old Testament Israelites," but both serve as meditational models for early modern Christians. In one meditation the Christian regards himself as a faithful Abraham or Moses, one of the special virtual Christians of the Scriptures. In the other meditation, an example of singular faith gives way to one of plural apostasy as the Christian compares the weakness of his faith and the incompleteness of his understanding and the inadequacies of his righteousness to the proverbially wayward Israelites of the Old Testament. Even the patriarchal Israelite is sometimes more like a misbelieving Jew; Noah has his nakedness and Moses his moments of doubt. And every Christian's ambivalence about himself finds articulation in this rhetoric of ambivalence about Jews. The unredeemed old self presents itself as the Jew and even after conversion it sticks around and requires attention of various sorts, some meditative and some violent, some contempt and some pity. The old self cannot be entirely shed, for it marks the place where "but for the grace of God" one belongs and so anchors the gratitude, love and devotion expected as the fruits, and therefore evidence, of redemption. And from a Derridean point of view, the persistence of the Jew-self is even more crucial, since without it the redeemed self cannot appear at all. Narin van Court speaks of the Jew in medieval culture as "socially marginal but culturally central"; in the Protestant imagination the Jew is also soteriologically central.

Is Milton's Samson a faithful Israelite or a carnal-minded, misbelieving Jew? Naturally he is both, and he is the perfect choice from among biblical characters for such an agonistic role. Like most puritans of his day, Milton was certain that Abraham, Moses, Elijah and Daniel wound up in a Christian heaven. The Israelite crowd around the golden calf, along with the Pharisees and scribes from the Gospels do not. The biblical Samson is not clearly among the sheep or the goats. The case for Samson as an exemplary "hero of faith" rests on Hebrews 11, a text that lays out a theory of supersessionist Christian typology, but the drama itself is our best evidence that Milton did not mean to portray Samson as a straightforward hero of spiritual faith.[20] Compared to Joshua, and even to the twelve other leaders mentioned in Judges, Samson appears a failure as a leader of Israel. Even Shamgar, whose only claim to fame is that he slew 600 Philistines with an oxgoad (Judg. 3:31), managed to deliver Israel from Canaanite rule; Samson slew thousands more Philistines, but Israel remained in bondage at his death. Recent biblical scholarship points out that the narrative of leadership in Judges moves from a focus on the offspring of the southern tribes, Judah and Benjamin, to the offspring of northern tribes, Ephraim and Dan, and the quality of the judges steadily worsens as leadership moves from south to north: "A clear pattern falls into place, which mirrors chapter 1: It is the Judean judges who are unambiguously good, and the northern leaders who are bad."[21] Brettler is right to point to a pattern, though it is neither as clear or unambiguous as he says. In general the southern leaders get better press in Judges, and Samson is indeed one of the northern leaders, a Danite. That does not mean that he is unambiguously "a negative role model" (Brettler, *The Book of Judges,* 112). He is certainly a figure of heroic strength and peculiarly divine election who squanders his gifts and, wallowing in uxoriousness, betrays his election, but still he is not unambiguously negative. Milton would have been especially impressed that Samson, unlike Adam, makes a comeback from his fall into "effeminate slackness," and executes revenge on his Philistine captors, divorces his unfaithful lover, and punishes his own rebellious flesh, all in one fell swoop.

Heroic Divorce: Samson Agonistes

Let us return now to Samson the married hero with a more detailed analysis than before, an analysis that looks at marriage as the carnal or Jewish version of a manliness that always lies elsewhere, in the world that is still to come.

Probably the simplest reason Milton modifies the biblical Samson story by making Dalila Samson's wife is to forge as clear a comparison as possible between Adam and Samson, and to set up a comparison between both of them and the Son of *Paradise Regain'd*. These comparisons get very complicated, and a detailed study of them will yield a fuller account of Milton's sense of what counts as true manliness and true marriage. For heuristic reasons, though, I will begin with a somewhat crude version of the comparison: Milton imagines an Adam who deliberately chose *not* to divorce Eve and a Samson who chose just as deliberately to divorce his unfit wife. The Son of God never married at all. Making Dalila Samson's wife, instead of just his mistress, appeared to be a necessary alteration to Milton if he wanted to line up precisely this sort of comparison. First Adam, second Adam, and a Hebrew Hercules in between — an opportunity imaginatively to analyze manliness, godliness and marriage across the three basic scenarios of what Christianity called salvation history.

Paradise Lost, prior to book 9, line 999, imagines marriage before the fall as a heterosocial conversation based upon "rational burning." Fallen marriage, tainted for the first time by carnal desire and "Lust" (9.1015), is epitomized in *Paradise Lost* by the figure of Samson rising from "the Harlot-lap / Of *Philistean Dalilah*" (9.1060–61). Milton treats Samson, "Shorn of his strength," as a metaphor for the newly fallen Adam and Eve, "bare / Of all thir vertue" (1062–63). Then in *Samson Agonistes* Milton asks readers to imagine the most a man can do, without benefit of Christian rebirth, to redeem himself from "effeminate slackness" (*PL* 11.634) and regain the firm stand against "the charm of beauties powerful glance" that Raphael once taught Adam to adopt (*PL* 8.530–84). Samson divorces Dalila.

Adam, insists Milton, walked into sin and disobedience with his eyes wide open. He had already seen that Eve was "Defac't, deflourd, and now to Death devote" (*PL* 9.901). He felt his joints relax, his hand go "slack," "speechless he stood and pale" (891–94). Before he even opens his mouth, he tells himself that he is resolved to choose death with Eve over obedience to God:

> Certain my resolution is to Die;
> How can I live without thee, how forgoe
> Thy sweet Converse and Love so dearly joyn'd,
> To live again in these wilde Woods forlorn?
> Should God create another *Eve*, and I
> Another Rib afford, yet loss of thee
> Would never from my heart; no no, I feel
> The Link of Nature draw me: Flesh of Flesh,
> Bone of my Bone thou art, and from thy State
> Mine never shall be parted, bliss or woe.   (9.907–16)

Milton imagines an Adam who deliberately chooses a relationship with Eve over one with God, who sets carnal desires ahead of rational. When the Son of God confronts Adam with his crime, he characterizes Adam's sin as a shameful resignation of the manhood he enjoyed as God's creation and Eve's superior:

> Was shee thy God, that her thou didst obey
> Before his voice, or was shee made thy guide,
> Superior, or but equal, that to her

> Thou did'st resigne thy Manhood, and the Place
> Wherein God set thee above her made of thee,
> And for thee, whose perfection farr excell'd
> Hers in all real dignitie.   (*PL* 10.145–51)

Adam chooses death over life, the same death the poem introduced at line 666 of book 2 as the only son of Sin and Satan:

> However I with thee have fixt my Lot,
> Certain to undergoe like doom, if Death
> Consort with thee, Death is to mee as Life;
> So forcible within my heart I feel
> The Bond of Nature draw me to my owne,
> My own in thee, for what thou art is mine;
> Our State cannot be severd, we are one,
> One Flesh; to loose thee were to loose my self.   (9.952–59)

Milton worked hard throughout his divorce tracts to argue that the biblical phrase "one flesh," attributed to Adam in Genesis 2:24, does not mean that marriage is principally about carnality or is even a "Bond of Nature." Eve was made from Adam's rib and so they had a "neerer alliance . . . then could be ever after between a man and wife," but that "neerer alliance" was something quite apart from marriage. Marriage, he declared, "is not a naturall, but a civill and ordain'd relation" (*Tetrachordon*, in YP 2:601). If it were a natural relation, like that of son to father, nothing could annul it; divorce would be simply unthinkable. He also argued repeatedly that marriage is about satisfying a "rational burning" for "fit conversation," not about fallen lusts or even procreation. With a hermeneutic effort running against the grains of logic and reason, Milton argued that in Genesis 2:24, "flesh" does not mean simply "flesh," and in 1 Corinthians 7:9 Paul does not mean to imply that marriage is a legitimate remedy for uncontrollable lust. Adam's first words to Eve, recorded in Genesis 2:24, says Milton, have always been misunderstood:

> This verse, as our common heed expounds it, is the great knot-tier, which hath undon by tying, and by tangling, millions of guiltles

consciences: this is that greisly Porter, who having drawn men and wisest men by suttle allurement within the train of an unhappy matrimony, claps the dungeon-gate upon them, as irrecoverable as the grave. But if we view him well, and hear him with not too hasty and prejudicant ears, we shall finde no such terror in him. (*Tetrachordon*, YP 2:603)

To "bind these words of *Adam* only to a corporall meaning" would be to suggest that there is little to marriage apart from a fleshly relation, "the meer anatomy of a rib" and to render Adam "as very an idiot as the Socinians make him" (YP 2:603–4). Such a reading would pit Adam's understanding of marriage against God's, as Milton derives it from Genesis 2:18 — marriage is a remedy for man's loneliness. Adam, says he, is not so stupid, nor so inattentive to God's words. "To all since Adam," marriage "is a relation much rather then a bone," and Milton's Adam well understood that souls and minds must knit themselves in fitness and likeness before bodies have any hope of becoming one. Men will leave fathers and mothers and cleave to their wives because it is a more specifically *human* relationship, that is to say, it is less carnal than kinship.

"Wee know," writes Milton in *Tetrachordon*, "that flesh can neither joyn, nor keep together two bodies of it self; what is it then that makes them one flesh, but likenes, but fitness of mind and disposition, which may breed the Spirit of concord, and of union between them" (YP 2:605). Likeness and fitness — Milton strains to make the terminology of classical friendship change the meaning of the word "flesh."

Milton's antiflesh rhetoric comes from Paul, but it also anticipates the republican rejection of human polities based on fleshly generation and bloodlines. Truly human marriage is a bonding of hearts and souls, not bodies, just as truly human civil relations are rooted in reason and agreement, not blood. When Adam tells Eve, "Our State cannot be severd, we are one, / One Flesh; to loose thee were to loose my self," Milton means us to hear Adam making not just the biggest personal, but also the most disastrous political, mistake ever made. Their married state is not and never was a fleshly matter; if it were to become a fundamentally fleshly "Bond of Nature," all the more reason to dissolve it. When he articulates this mistake, Adam has not yet disobeyed his God, but the mistaken logic enables that disobedience by making disobedience appear inevitable, natural, even "glorious," and "Illustrious," to borrow the words of an already fallen Eve (9.961–62). From this mistake, says Michael, comes the loss of all "true Libertie":

> Since thy original lapse, true Libertie
> Is lost, which alwayes with right Reason dwells
> Twinn'd, and from her hath no dividual being:
> Reason in man obscur'd, or not obeyd,
> Immediately inordinate desires
> And upstart Passions catch the Government
> From Reason, and to servitude reduce
> Man till then free. Therefore since hee permits
> Within himself unworthie Powers to reign
> Over free Reason, God in Judgement just
> Subjects him from without to violent Lords;
> Who oft as undeservedly enthrall
> His outward freedom: Tyrannie must be,
> Though to the Tyrant thereby no excuse.   (*PL* 12.83–96)

Adam chooses flesh over reason, resigns his manhood and his excellence and dignity of place to a subordinate, makes his wife his god, and so ushers two things into the life of men forever after: carnal lust and political injustice.

David Norbrook's discussion of the "language and politics of Eden" near the close of *Writing the Republic* frames the most important issues quite perfectly.[22] Milton could have figured the first human relationship, the first marriage, as the Hebrew Bible's version of Aristotle's perfect friendship between equals, the cornerstone or root of the republican *civis* originally intended by God. But Milton follows the story in Genesis 2, not Genesis 1, and so guarantees that his depiction of the first human polity is beset with tensions, precisely the tensions raised by the civil war and the failed attempts at establishing a godly republic. Norbrook writes,

> It is not at all surprising that there are some tensions. In *Paradise Lost,* the concord which God has drawn out of Chaos is always perilously close to collapse. That instability can be a source of excitement as well as of fear: in the sublimity of the unfallen universe there is an exhilarating openness and variety, which is matched in the spontaneous, unpremeditated prayers of Adam and Eve. But the structures of communication are not entirely open; as in the more oligarchical forms of republicanism, there is emphasis both on common interests and language and on the strong need for hierarchical distinctions. (489)

Milton, I believe, could not find a way past that need for hierarchies, that necessity, even though he recognized in other contexts that necessity is an enemy to liberty and often the "the tyrant's plea" (*PL* 4.394).

"To loose thee were to loose myself," says Adam, and the words, unmodernized, positively vibrate with irony. By not divorcing Eve, "loosing" her, man's "true Libertie" will be forever lost. To divorce her at this point would be to loose himself from that "Bond of Nature" that misleads him into "effeminate slackness," idolatry and sin. He mistakes their fleshly relation — a rib — for their rational relation — marriage — and so ushers in a Gordian knot of confusion that Raphael warned him about and Milton spent four divorce tracts trying to untie. In book 8, Milton shows Adam advancing rapidly in his understanding of marriage from notions of bone and flesh to notions of heart and soul:

> I now see
> Bone of my Bone, Flesh of my Flesh, my Self
> Before me; Woman is her Name, of Man
> Extracted; for this cause he shall forgoe
> Father and Mother, and to his Wife adhere;
> And they shall be one Flesh, one Heart, one Soule.   (*PL* 8.494–99)

Raphael also helped him recognize that touch, passion and the desire to procreate are traits men share with beasts, not specifically human traits — "attractive, human, rational" (8.586) — like those upon which human relations, love between mutual selves, may properly be built. And in book 4, Milton shows Adam teaching Eve to prefer the beauty of inward wisdom over the attractiveness of outward flesh (4.487–91). When Adam fixes his lot with a fallen Eve, he knows better; he chooses "the Bond of Nature" and flesh against his own reason, "not deceavd, / But fondly overcome with Femal charm" (9.998–99).

Milton's Samson, having allowed himself to fall under the sway of what the Chorus calls female beauty's "strange power," manfully resists it in the end, and divorces Dalila without hesitation or doubt:

> It fits not; thou and I long since are twain;
> Nor think me so unwary or accurst
> To bring my feet again into the snare
> Where once I have been caught; I know thy trains
> Though dearly to my cost, thy ginns, and toyls;
> Thy fair enchanted cup, and warbling charms
> No more on me have power, their force is null'd,
> So much of Adders wisdom I have learn't
> To fence my ear against thy sorceries.   (*SA* 929–37)

Samson does what Adam did not; he divorces his sinful, unfit wife. All wives, even those who manage the impossible pretense of friendship without appearing unsubmissive, must eventually prove unfit. That is why Milton makes Samson's story the pivotal episode in his multi-epic account of true manly liberty lost and regained.

Heroic Solitude: Paradise Regain'd

A more complete understanding of the Son's recovery of lost manliness in *Paradise Regain'd* requires that we return to a portion of Plato's *Symposium* Milton and most Renaissance humanists appear to have ignored — Pausanias's excruciatingly detailed apology for the Athenian institution of pederasty. I say "appear to have ignored" because I believe Milton, at least, does not ignore Pausanias's doctrine, but subtly demonizes it. As I argued in chapter 3, Milton subscribes to Socrates's teaching about love, and he claims that what Socrates "fain'd to have learnt from the Prophetesse *Diotima*" is virtually the same doctrine ("divinely sorts") taught by Moses in Genesis (YP 2:252). The Satan of *Paradise Regain'd*, however, appears to subscribe to Pausanias's doctrines of love, specifically that love Pausanias calls "heavenly" — homoerotic pederasty — and distinguishes from the always carnal and earthly attraction to women so characteristic of less manly men. In this way Milton revalues Pausanias's "heavenly love" as satanic.

Gregory W. Bredbeck traces out the discursive paths by which the Gibean "sons of Belial" from Judges 19:22 came to be equated in the early modern imaginary with the "men of Sodom" from Genesis 19:4, and how "Sodom" and sodomy gradually ceased to signify all manner of sexual transgressions and "progressed to a point where Sodom was specifically and only male sodomy."[23] The Belial of *Paradise Lost* belongs pretty much to this tradition; certainly the narrator identifies both the men of Gibeah and those of Sodom as "Sons / Of Belial" (*PL* 1.500–505), but he also names Eli's sons as Belialists for their liturgical transgressions, obtruding violence into the temple rituals of sacrifice. And though he identifies the sexual violence intended by both the Gibeans and the Sodomites against a male guest as "worse rape" (*PL* 1.505), the comparative implicitly acknowledges that the sons of Belial in both cases were not so exclusive in their sexual preferences as to forgo raping the hosts' daughters. It appears that Milton's Belial and sons of Belial stand slightly apart from the emergent sense of sodomy in the seventeenth century as exclusively homosexual lust.

In *Paradise Regain'd*, however, a fairly different Belial recommends a straightforwardly heterosexual sensualism as the preferred line of attack on the Son of God's virtue.

> Set women in his eye and in his walk,
> Among daughters of men the fairest found;
> Many are in each Region passing fair
> As the noon Skie; more like to Goddesses

Then Mortal Creatures, graceful and discreet,
Expert in amorous Arts, enchanting tongues
Perswasive, Virgin majesty with mild
And sweet allay'd, yet terrible to approach,
Skill'd to retire, and in retiring draw
Hearts after them tangl'd in Amorous Nets.
Such object hath the power to soft'n and tame
Severest temper, smooth the rugged'st brow,
Enerve, and with voluptuous hope dissolve,
Draw out with credulous desire, and lead
At will the manliest, resolutest brest,
As the Magnetic hardest Iron draws.
Women, when nothing else, beguil'd the heart
Of wisest *Solomon,* and made him build,
And made him bow to the Gods of his Wives.   (PR 2.153–71)

The narrator identifies this Belial as the "dissolutest" and "sensuallest" of all the devils, though not the "fleshliest"; in that arena he takes second place to Asmodeus, who killed seven men in an attempt to have a young maiden for his own pleasure (PR 2.150–51).[24] But both Belial and Asmodeus are presented here as decidedly heterosexual in their sinful proclivities. Satan accuses Belial of being so besotted by female charms that he cannot imagine anyone else resisting them or preferring other pleasures over those of heterosexual conversation:

Belial, in much uneven scale thou weigh'st
All others by thy self; because of old
Thou thy self doat'st on womankind, admiring
Thir shape, thir colour, and attractive grace,
None are, thou think'st, but taken with such toys.   (PR 2.173–77)

Satan goes on to identify these sons of Belial as those falsely called the sons of God in Genesis 6, supernatural beings who lusted after the "daughters of men" and sired upon them "men of renown" (Gen. 6:2–4). The narrator suggests that those unholy copulations are the true source of Ovid's fantastic stories of gods raping mortal women:

Before the Flood thou with thy lusty Crew,
False titl'd Sons of God, roaming the Earth
Cast wanton eyes on the daughters of men,
And coupl'd with them, and begot a race.
Have we not seen, or by relation heard,
In Courts and Regal Chambers how thou lurk'st,
In Wood or Grove by mossie Fountain side,
In Valley or Green Meadow, to way-lay
Some beauty rare, *Calisto, Clymene,*
Daphne, or *Semele, Antiopa,*
Or *Amymone, Syrinx,* many more
Too long, then lay'st thy scapes on names ador'd,
Apollo, Neptune, Jupiter, or *Pan,*
Satyr, or Faun, or Silvan?   (*PR* 2.178–91)

In short, in *Paradise Regain'd* Satan makes Belial stand for what the *Symposium*'s Pausanias identifies as a vulgar sort of erotics — the lusts and pleasures of the "common Aphrodite." Pausanias insists that there are two sorts of love, one for each of two Aphrodites. Heavenly love "is older, the motherless daughter of Uranus, whom we call the 'heavenly' Aphrodite" (*Symposium,* 180d–e). The other "is younger, the child of Zeus and Dione" (180e); those who practice the common sort of love "love women no less than boys." They love opportunistically and are focused on bodies rather than souls: "They love the most unintelligent people they can, because they are concerned only about achieving their goal" (181b). They care nothing for the manner in which they satisfy their lust, and even participate in "outrageous behavior" (181c). Heavenly love, on the other hand, "does not share in the female, but only in the male — this is love for young boys" (181c). Pausanias continues:

> Since this Aphrodite is older, she does not participate in outrageous behavior. Those who are inspired by this Love are oriented toward the male, cherishing what is by nature stronger and more intelligent. Anyone would recognize those who are motivated by this Love in a pure way, even in the case of loving young boys. They don't fall in love with boys until they begin to show some intelligence, which starts happening when their beards begin to grow. (181c–d)

Athenian pederasty, claims Pausanias, is higher love, though not all man-boy love is higher love. Some men pay insufficient attention to a boy's intellect and capacity for virtue, loving only a young body; they are actually common lovers who need to be kept away from "free-born women" as well as from boys (181e–182a). Some, like those in Boeotia and Elis, say it is always "noble to gratify one's lovers," regardless of their motives (182b). Pausanias does not agree. It is noble for a youth to submit to his lover only under very carefully specified circumstances. Both pederast (lover) and philerast (darling) must conform to a strict code of intentions and manners, otherwise the act of submission and the gratification it supplies are both utterly disgraceful and ignoble. No action, says Pausanias, "is noble and beautiful in itself"; "In actions, it is the manner of the doing that determines the quality" (181a). Much as Milton argued in the *Doctrine and Discipline of Divorce* that "the carnal act," which "might seem to have somthing of pollution in it," is made "legitimate and good" by the fit conversation of rational souls (YP 2:326), so Pausanias implies that for a young man to submit his body as an instrument of a pederast's pleasure is a noble and beautiful act *only* under very carefully specified circumstances:

> When a lover and his darling come together, each has a rule: The lover is justified in performing any services he can perform for the darling who gratifies him, and the beloved in turn is justified in providing whatever services he can for the one who is making him wise and good — assuming the former is able to introduce the other to prudence and other virtues, and the latter does want to acquire an education and other skills. When these two rules come together as a single principle, then and only then does it come about that a darling's gratifying a lover is a noble and beautiful thing. Otherwise, it is not noble at all. (184d–e)

Carnal acts in the service of virtue are "entirely noble," says Pausanias, and those who love boys in such a higher manner "are ready to be together with them for their entire lives and even live with them" (181d). This sort of eros covers an otherwise undignified act with dignity, a specifically manly dignity no heteroerotic relation can achieve.

Athenian pederasty, says Pausanias, cultivates the most manly, ambitious and virtuous men. It does this by being thoroughly and exclusively "oriented towards the male" (181c) in all desires and activities, remaining unpolluted by anything female. Pausanias believes that only in barbarian countries like Ionia do the rulers and their laws forbid pederastic relations between men and boys. "I suspect," he says, that "it does not suit the rulers to have strong ambitions develop in their subjects, nor powerful friendships and partnerships and all the other things Love so greatly enjoys engendering" (182c). Rulers who promulgate and enforce laws declaring it "shameful to gratify lovers" do so in order to keep other men submissive; they are tyrants, and those who submit to such rules suffer from a "lack of manliness" (182d). Pederasty cultivates manly liberty and virtuous ambition; heterosexual relations do not. They may even compromise manliness.

It is tempting to dwell at some length on how much Milton's fairly progressive notions of companionate marriage actually resemble Pausanias's pederastic doctrines, but I have dwelt on his doctrines of "heavenly Love" for other reasons. Satan in *Paradise Regain'd* might profitably be read as a disciple of Pausanias. When the Son walks away into the desert to seek "converse / With solitude" (*PR* 1.190–91), the very condition the God of Genesis 2:18 deemed "not good" for man, Satan, the bad son or evil brother, seeks him out for conversation of another sort. Satan first presents himself to the Son as a potential philerast, a darling. He acknowledges that he is not, like a young boy, fair to look upon, but still he casts himself as one who desires no more than to keep company with one so virtuous, excellent, and destined for "Godlike deeds":

> though I have lost
> Much lustre of my native brightness, lost
> To be belov'd of God, I have not lost
> To love, at least contemplate and admire
> What I see excellent in good, or fair,

> Or vertuous, I should so have lost all sense.
> What can be then less in me then desire
> To see thee and approach thee, whom I know
> Declar'd the Son of God, to hear attent
> Thy wisdom, and behold thy God-like deeds?   (*PR* 1.377–86)

No longer God's darling, Satan tries to pose as a worthy darling for the Son, but readers of *Paradise Lost* know as well as the Son that Satan is no proper philerast. When he first viewed Eve alone, according to the narrator of book 9, Satan was smitten, almost utterly disarmed, by Eve's charms:

> Her graceful Innocence, her every Aire
> Of gesture or lest action overawd
> His Malice, and with rapine sweet bereav'd
> His fierceness of the fierce intent it brought:
> That space the Evil one abstracted stood
> From his own evil, and for the time remaind
> Stupidly good, of enmitie disarm'd,
> Of guile, of hate, of envie, of revenge.   (*PL* 9.459–66)

Like a devotee of the earthly, common Aphrodite, Satan is unmanned by his desire for female charms. Just as men who are chiefly or exclusively attracted to women are said to lose their manly vigor, virtue and ambition, Satan finds himself disarmed, temporarily, of his adversarial weapons.

Satan's qualifications as philerastic partner to the Son of God appear poor in other regards as well. Even as he offers himself as a submissive pupil, eager to hear truth's dictates from his master, the Son, and eager even to endure reproof, Satan implies that he will not embrace those dictates, will not follow truth, and despairs from the outset of ever attaining virtue. He openly admits that he has no desire to become wise and good or to acquire an education in virtue; according to Pausanias's doctrine, then, he is as unfit to be the Son's beloved as he was for the Father. The conversation he proposes will be a matter of talking the talk, but avoiding the difficult walk of the "ways of truth":

> thou art plac't above me, thou art Lord;
> From thee I can and must submiss endure
> Check or reproof, and glad to scape so quit.
> Hard are the ways of truth, and rough to walk,
> Smooth on the tongue discourst, pleasing to th' ear,
> And tuneable as Silvan Pipe or Song;
> What wonder then if I delight to hear
> Her dictates from thy mouth? most men admire
> Vertue, who follow not her lore: permit me
> To hear thee when I come (since no man comes)
> And talk at least, though I despair to attain.   (*PR* 1.475–85)

Satan even betrays a remarkable similarity to the "Atheist" sons of Eli, whom the narrator of *Paradise Lost* identified with both the sons of Belial and the sons of Sodom (*PL* 1.494–505), when he claims that even God the Father "Suffers the Hypocrite or Atheous Priest / To tread his Sacred Courts, and minister / About his Altar, handling holy things, / Praying or vowing" (*PR* 1.486–89). On this precedent, he argues, the Son should not refuse him "access" (491). By offering himself to the Son in the role of a philerastic darling Satan is made to appear doubly shameful; first, because Milton means us to regard Pausanias's erotic doctrine as illegitimate, superseded by Socrates's teaching of higher love between equals who transcend bodily desires, sharing the same pleasures of intellectual and spiritual procreation, and second, because even by Pausanias's standards, Satan is a fraud and a shame to himself. He belongs to the followers of the "common Aphrodite."

The Son, though he feels real hunger for human food, apparently has no desire for human company. He has come to the desert to walk "alone," to seek "converse / With solitude," "far from the track of men" (*PR* 1.189–91). There may even be some question about whether, walking alone and led by the Spirit, the Son leaves a track of human steps behind him (1.298). In any case, Milton depicts the Son of God as lacking the constitutive loneliness by which Adam chiefly distinguished himself from God — he is just fine alone; he needs no partner in conversation, not a woman, not a man, and certainly not Satan. He does not have Adam's "single imperfection."

When, in book 2 of *Paradise Regain'd*, Satan reproves Belial for thinking that the Son of God could be unnerved, unmanned and thus undone by the fairest of the daughters of men (2.153–71), he recommends that the Son be tempted to inconstancy by "manlier objects":

> Therefore with manlier objects we must try
> His constancy, with such as have more shew
> Of worth, of honour, glory, and popular praise;
> Rocks whereon greatest men have oftest wreck'd;
> Or that which only seems to satisfie
> Lawful desires of Nature, not beyond.   (*PR* 2.225–30)

Readers usually have understood such "manlier objects" as the temptations to wealth, empire and glory that Satan rolls out later, but more recently, Gregory Bredbeck and Claude J. Summers have pointed out that the first temptation, the banquet described in lines 340–65, is hardly a temptation to glory and ambitious deeds. It is a temptation, on at least one level, to satisfy bodily desire. Bredbeck and Summers see the banquet temptation as a kind of code or allegory for homoerotic desire, specifically the "manlier objects" of desire represented by the "Tall stripling youths rich clad, of fairer hue / Than *Ganymede* or *Hylas*," who attend the offered banquet.[25] But I suggest we also regard the banquet as an appeal to the Son's real human hunger for human food.

Satan means to tempt the Son with "that which only seems to satisfy / Lawful desires of Nature, not beyond" (230–31). The adverb "only" squints in two directions here, implying first a modification of the infinitive "to satisfy," as if to say, "we will present him with objects that appear to satisfy lawful natural desires *and no more*." As the appearance is meant to deceive, of course, "only" also modifies "seems," implying that the banquet and all its attendant objects only seem to address legitimate bodily desires in a temperate manner, but really they threaten the Son with surfeit and thus intemperance.

It is difficult, even impossible, however, to see how anyone, much less the Son of God, would be fooled by the tempting banquet Satan presents. It is the last word in surfeit.

> A Table richly spred, in regal mode,
> With dishes pil'd, and meats of noblest sort
> And savour, Beasts of chase, or Fowl of game,
> In pastry built, or from the spit, or boyl'd,
> Gris-amber-steam'd; all Fish from Sea or Shore,
> Freshet, or purling Brook, of shell or fin,
> And exquisitest name, for which was drain'd
> *Pontus* and *Lucrine Bay,* and *Afric Coast.*   (*PR* 2.340–47)

The Son had just finished dreaming of satisfying his hunger with something like Elijah's fire-baked cake of bread and jug of water (1 Kings 19:6) or Daniel's "pulse" (2.270–78). Such meals promise no more than to satisfy "Lawful desires of Nature, not beyond." Satan had promised that he would offer no trafe (2.327–28), but the feast he presents includes shellfish (345).[26] Whole bays were drained to provide every sort of fish imaginable. It is difficult to imagine a meal better calculated to tempt one well beyond the legitimate needs of nature. The banquet is not, we must conclude, one of the "manlier objects" by which Satan means to tempt the Son's constancy.

Bredbeck and Summers suggest that the real, "manlier objects" of temptation here are not the viands but the stripling youths lined up all in a row. If so, then Satan has also hedged his bet by including some nymphs, naiads and ladies of the Hesperides as well. I think they are partly right and partly wrong. The real temptation here is for the Son to form a relationship with Satan, to allow Satan the privilege of satisfying any one of his bodily desires — food, drink, sex, ease, the pleasures of human touch and companionship. Even if the Son ate just a small bit of the food Satan offers, just enough to satisfy his hunger and no more, or looked with pleasure for even a moment at one of the youths or nymphs, he would be admitting Satan as his philerast, one who gratifies his mentor's bodily desires in return for instruction in wisdom and virtue. He would admit Satan to a relationship with him like that Hephaestion enjoyed with Alexander, or Laelius with Scipio — the very relationships Satan referred to as he tried to explain to Belial that there are men who are too manly to be trapped by the "bait of Women":

> . How many have with a smile made small account
> Of beauty and her lures, easily scorn'd
> All her assaults, on worthier things intent?
> Remember that *Pellean* Conquerour,
> A youth, how all the Beauties of the East
> He slightly view'd, and slightly over-pass'd;
> How hee sirnam'd of *Africa* dismiss'd
> In his prime youth the fair *Iberian* maid.   (2.193–200)

Summers reads these allusions to ancient friendships as code for a nonstigmatized version of homosexual love presented as a legitimate temptation, one for which a truly manly man might fall. Pausanias would, I think, have agreed with Summers, but Milton would not. Milton did not approve of Pausanias's sort of pederasty; he subscribed, rather, to a heteroerotic version of Socrates's enlightened Eros. The Son rejects Satan as an unfit partner with the rhetorical question, "with my hunger what hast thou to do?" (2.389).

Satan meets with no more success when he tries to play the role of pederast and enlist the Son as his beloved. In book 4 he offers the Son all the kingdoms of the world in return for "falling down" and gratifying him with "worship" as a "superior Lord" (4.166–67). He even tries to offer himself as a teacher of wisdom, Gentile wisdom, all the wisdom of the Academy, the Lyceum, and the Stoa, but the Son rejects both the gift and the giver. He needs no instruction in wisdom; still less does he need any companion with whom to share mutual benefits and conversation. He rejects all such relations because he does not need them. When Satan alleges that "The Wilderness / For thee is fittest place" (4.372–73), the lines say more than he intends. The Son eventually feels hunger and fatigue and cold but he never feels lonely without human companionship. He needs no philerast, no pederast, no wife, no fit partner other than the Spirit. He refuses to allow Satan to gratify him; he refuses to gratify Satan by falling down. Finally, he refuses even to cast himself down from the highest place in his Father's house (4.551–61). Announcing himself as "the Lord thy God," he stands. Unlike Adam, he needs no fit partner for conversation. He redeems mankind by being God. The only man capable of redeeming mankind from its effeminate slackness and shame turns out to be God. Real manliness, it seems, is not human, for it lacks that "single imperfection" that marked Adam as a man.

Milton's efforts to rethink and reimagine marriage as a friendship bore greater fruits than he imagined or even desired. He never intended to import into marriage the equality between friends classical doctrines required, but gradually equality in marriage appeared to be a logical thing. When he tried to define marriage as being no more about sex and childbearing than friendship is, he never intended to clear a path for same-sex marriage, but now that path appears to many as inevitable.

My account runs the risk of painting Milton's project as a failure, since at the end we find not friendship, but solitude, and the only way to perfectly imagine manly liberty is to see it in the king of heaven, the Son of God. A king, much less a god, needs no one. That is why classical friendship doctrine always reminds us that it is extremely difficult, even impossible, for kings to have friends. Of all the goods one might wish a friend, that he become a god or a king should not be one of them, since then he would no longer need friends. Milton the classicist and Hebraist knew that the desire for companionship is constitutive of humanness, but the Milton who desired citizenship in the kingdom of heaven wound up imagining his perfect man as solitary.

NOTES

Notes to Preface

1. Laurie Shannon, *Sovereign Amity: Figures of Friendship in Shakespearean Contexts* (Chicago: University of Chicago Press, 2002).

2. See the Vermont Secretary of State web site: http://www.sec.state.vt.us/otherprg/civilunions/civilunionlaw.html (accessed March 6, 2004).

3. Alan Bray, *The Friend* (Chicago: University of Chicago Press, 2003), argues that between the eleventh and sixteenth centuries in England, friends did "marry" each other and seal their vows in church and memorialize them on funereal monuments. Bray traces a different, parallel story of friendship that flourished in medieval English culture and went underground following the Renaissance and Reformation. The story of friendship and marriage I follow here has its roots in the "new learning" and emerged in the seventeenth century just as the practices Bray traces began to fade from view.

Notes to Introduction

1. The quoted phrase is from *Paradise Lost* 8.424. All quotations from John Milton's poetry are from *The John Milton Reading Room*, ed. Thomas H. Luxon (Hanover, NH: The Trustees of Dartmouth College, 1997–2005); available at http://www.dartmouth.edu/~milton (accessed May 21, 2005). Raphael's account of Creation in book 7 also endorses a homonormative logic: "conglob'd / Like things to like" (see *PL* 7.235–40). The useful terms "homonormativity" and "heteronormativity" I adopt from Laurie Shannon, "Nature's Bias: Renaissance Homonormativity and Elizabethan Comic Likeness," *Modern Philology* 98 (2000): 183–210. Also very influential to my thinking on marriage and friendship is Shannon's *Sovereign Amity: Figures of Friendship in Shakespearean Contexts* (Chicago: University of Chicago Press, 2002).

2. *One Soul in Bodies Twain* is a book on friendship in Tudor literature and Stuart drama by Laurens J. Mills (Bloomington, Ind: The Principia
Press, 1937). The phrase translates Montaigne's famous definition of
friendship in his essay "On Friendship." John Florio's 1603 translation of
the phrase is "one soule in two bodies," which Montaigne believes follows "the fit definition of *Aristotle*" — *The Essayes Or Morall, Politike
and Millitarie Discourses of Lo: Michaell de Montaigne* (London, 1603),
94. "One flesh," of course, comes from the King James Version of Genesis
2:24: "Therefore shall a man leave his father and his mother, and shall cleave
unto his wife: and they shall be one flesh."

3. Plato, *The Symposium*, in *The Symposium and the Phaedrus: Plato's
Erotic Dialogues*, trans. William S. Cobb (Albany: State University of
New York Press, 1993); hereafter cited in the text.

4. Aristotle, *Nicomachean Ethics*, translated by Terence Irwin
(Indianapolis: Hackett Publishing, 1985), 1157b20–22. Unless otherwise
noted, all quotations from the *Nicomachean Ethics* are from this translation and cited by Bekker line references.

5. Louise Schleiner, "Pastoral Male Friendship and Miltonic Marriage:
Textual Systems Transposed," *Lit: Literature Interpretation Theory* 2
(1990): 41.

6. Janet Halley, "Female Autonomy in Milton's Sexual Poetics," in
Milton and the Idea of Woman, edited by Julia Walker (Urbana: University
of Illinois Press, 1988), 230–45.

7. Gregory Chaplin, "'One Flesh, One Heart, One Soul': Renaissance
Friendship and Miltonic Marriage," *Modern Philology* 99 (2001): 267.

8. Essays on the Milton and Diodati relationship include John
Shawcross, "Milton and Diodati: An Essay in Psychodynamic Meaning,"
in *Milton Studies*, vol. 7, edited by James D. Simmonds, guest edited by
Albert C. Labriola and Michael Lieb (Pittsburgh: University of Pittsburgh
Press, 1975), 127–63; James Holly Hanford, "The Youth of Milton," in *John
Milton, Poet and Humanist: Essays by James Holly Hanford* (Cleveland:
Press of Case Western Reserve University, 1966), 57; John Rumrich, "The
Milton-Diodati Correspondence," *Hellas: A Journal of Poetry and the
Humanities* 3 (1992): 76–85; and Rumrich, "The Erotic Milton," *Texas
Studies in Literature and Language* 41 (1999): 128–41; Christopher Hill,
Milton and the English Revolution (Harmondsworth: Penguin, 1977), 31.

9. Edmund Spenser, *The Faerie Queene*, vol. 2, books 4–7, ed. J. C.
Smith (Oxford: Clarendon Press, 1909), 4.10.26–27.

10. Laurie Shannon, *Sovereign Amity*, 55.

11. *An Apology Against a Pamphlet Call'd A Modest Confutation of
the Animadversions upon the Remonstrant against Smectymnuus*, in
Complete Prose Works of John Milton, ed. Don M. Wolfe et al., vol. 1 (New
Haven, Conn.: Yale University Press, 1953), 890. All further quotations
from Milton's prose works come from this edition and will be cited as YP
by volume and page numbers.

12. My colleague Jonathan Crewe prompted me to look into the quality of the texts of Plato's *Symposium* that were available to Milton. Jackson Campbell Boswell, in *Milton's Library: A Catalogue of the Remains of John Milton's Library and an Annotated Reconstruction of Milton's Library and Ancillary Readings* (New York: Garland, 1975) is not much help, but does suggest that Milton probably owned a copy of the *Symposium* (196). Irene Samuel, *Plato and Milton* (Ithaca, N.Y.: Cornell University Press, 1947), writes: "No one, to my knowledge, has ever doubted that Milton knew the Dialogues and Epistles of Plato — along with everything else a man of his time might read" (vii). She never raises the issue of bowdlerized or expurgated editions of Plato. A very sound humanist edition of Plato's dialogues in Greek and Latin columns was published in 3 volumes by Henri Estienne in 1578 and dedicated to Queen Elizabeth: *Platonis opera quae extant omnis. Ex nova Ioannis Serrani interpretatione, perpetuis eiusdē notis illustrata . . . Henr. Stephani de quorundum locorum interpretatione iudicium.* The University Library at Cambridge and Dartmouth College each have a copy of this edition. I have compared portions of the Greek text in this edition to a modern standard — *Plato in Twelve Volumes,* vol. 4, trans. Harold North Fowler (Cambridge, Mass.: Harvard University Press, 1977), portions one might expect to find bowdlerized or expurgated (like Pausanias's specification of the circumstances under which a philerast might gratify his pederastic lover without risk of shame), and I found the Greek matches in all cases.

13. See Mary Nyquist, "The Genesis of Gendered Subjectivity in the Divorce Tracts and in *Paradise Lost,*" in *Re-membering Milton: Essays on the Texts and Traditions,* edited by Mary Nyquist and Margaret W. Ferguson (New York: Methuen, 1987), 99–127, for a discussion of efforts, early modern and modern, to reconcile the two Creation accounts in Genesis.

Notes to Chapter One

1. A very useful account of marriage law and doctrine in Reformation Europe and England is Eric Josef Carlson, *Marriage and the English Reformation* (Oxford: Blackwell, 1994).

2. Wallace MacCaffrey, *Elizabeth I* (London: Arnold, 1993), calls the proposal "A final bizarre touch" (85).

3. The proposal is recorded in the October 7, 1564, "Instructions for Bedford and Randolph" in *Calendar of State Papers, Foreign Series, of the Reign of Elizabeth, 1564–5,* ed. Joseph Stevenson (London: Longman, 1870), 219. This episode and these references came to me by way of one of my honors students, Rhiannon Lockwood, in "A Union in Partition: Revisiting Elizabeth I and Mary, Queen of Scots" (unpublished honors thesis, Dartmouth College, 2002).

4. Stephen Orgel, *Impersonations: The Performance of Gender in Shakespeare's England* (Cambridge: Cambridge University Press, 1996), 17.

5. Erasmus was fond of announcing and even playing a bit with homonormative doctrine in his *Adagia:* "Simile gaudet simile" (121) and "Semper similiem ducit Deus ad similem" (122). In almost every edition of the adages, the first was "Amicorum communium omnia." See Desiderius Erasmus, *Opera Omnia,* 2nd ser., book 1, ed. M. L. van Poll-van de Lisdonk, M. Mann Phillips and Christian Robinson (Amsterdam: North Holland, 1993); Margaret Mann Phillips, *The Adages of Erasmus: A Study with Translations* (Cambridge: Cambridge University Press, 1964); and William Barker, ed., *The Adages of Erasmus* (Toronto: University of Toronto Press, 2001).

6. Shannon writes, "Running athwart of the heterosexual organization of love and marriage, the powerfully homo-normative bias in Renaissance thought favors both self-likeness (constancy) and same-sex affects. Insofar as diverse logics rendering disparate phenomena 'normal' can coincide, given cultural moments contain competing 'normativities'" (*Sovereign Amity,* 55).

7. For a useful collection of classical and Renaissance "places" that articulate friendship theory, see Charles G. Smith, *Spenser's Theory of Friendship* (Baltimore: The Johns Hopkins University Press, 1935).

8. Margot Todd, *Christian Humanism and the Puritan Social Order* (Cambridge: Cambridge University Press, 1987), 100, argues that the promotion of companionate marriage was a humanist rather than a puritan innovation, and insofar as it is useful to distinguish reformers and puritans from humanists, I suppose that is fair. Todd points out that Erasmus and Vives, as well as Luther and Calvin, spent lots of energy trying to recover marriage from late medieval disdain. Milton, both a humanist and a puritan, probably regarded himself as continuing the work they had begun. On the medieval misogyny to which these humanists responded, see R. Howard Bloch, "Medieval Misogyny" *Representations* 20 (1987): 1–24.

9. Matthew 22:30 reports Jesus as saying: "For in the resurrection they neither marry, nor are given in marriage, but are as the angels of God in heaven."

10. John Calvin, *Commentaries on the First Book of Moses Called Genesis,* 2 vols., trans. John King (Edinburgh: Calvin Translation Society, 1847–1850), 1:135; my emphasis. Cited hereafter as *Commentaries.*

11. For Cicero, see *Laelius de Amicitia* on the Web in "a conflation of two texts": *M. Tulli Ciceronis: Laelius de Amicitia,* ed. Clifton Price (1902); and *M. Tulli Ciceronis: Scripta Quae Manserunt Omnia,* part 4, vol. 3, ed. C. F. W. Mueller (1890), paragraph 80; available at http://www.utexas.edu/depts/classics/documents/amicitia.html (accessed May 21, 2005).

12. Augustine, *The Literal Meaning of Genesis*, trans. John Hammond Taylor, S. J. 2 vols., *Ancient Christian Writers: The Works of the Fathers in Translation*, no. 42 (New York: Newman Press, 1982), 9:5.

13. I allude here to John Guillory, "Milton, Narcissism, Gender: On the Genealogy of Male Self-Esteem," in *Critical Essays on John Milton*, ed. Christopher Kendrick (New York, 1995), 194–223, esp. 209–15.

14. Calvin appears to ignore or fails to notice Socrates's express preference for homoerotic procreation over heteroerotic procreation. See Plato, *Symposium*, trans. Michael Joyce, ed. Edith Hamilton and Huntington Cairns, *The Collected Dialogues of Plato*, Bollingen Series 71 (New York: Pantheon Books, 1961), 209b–e.

15. Leonard Tennenhouse believes that the shift toward overvaluing heterosexual marriage as the default human relationship was actually relatively abrupt, accomplished "during the latter three decades of the seventeenth-century" (personal communication, October 15, 2002).

16. Martin Luther, *Lectures on Genesis Chapters 1–5*, in *Luther's Works*, ed. Jaroslav Pelikan, vol. 1 (Saint Louis: Concordia, 1958) 137–38; hereafter cited as *Works* in the text.

17. See Barbara F. McManus's and Katherine Usher Henderson's selections from these authors in *Half Humankind: Contexts and Texts of the Controversy about Women in England, 1540–1640* (Urbana: University of Illinois Press, 1985).

18. Letters to Katherine Luther from 1546 appear in *Martin Luther*, ed. E. G. Rupp and Benjamin Drewery (New York: St. Martin's Press, 1970), 169–73.

19. Edmund Tilney, *The Flower of Friendshippe*, ed. Valerie Wayne (Ithaca, N.Y.: Cornell University Press, 1992), 133.

20. *Homilie on Marriage*, in Church of England, *The Seconde Tome of Homelyes* (London, 1563), fol. 255v.

21. Church of England, *The Seconde Tome of Homilies* (London, 1623), 239. Cited hereafter as Homily 1623. In establishing the first instance of this change, I also consulted the 1587, 1595 and 1640 editions of *The Seconde Tome of Homilies* (London).

22. William Shakespeare and John Fletcher, *Two Noble Kinsmen*, 1634 ed., Electronic Text Center, University of Virginia Library at http://etext.lib.virginia.edu/toc/modeng/public/ShaTNKQ.html, April 24, 2003. For Plato's version of homoerotic love and procreation as higher and more noble than heteroerotic love and procreation, see *Symposium*, 208a–209e.

23. René Girard, "Comedies of Errors: Plautus-Shakespeare-Molière," in *American Criticism in the Poststructuralist Age*, edited by Ira Konigsberg (Ann Arbor: University of Michigan Press, 1981), 74–75.

24. William Shakespeare, *A Comedy of Errors*, in *The Norton Facsimile: The First Folio of Shakespeare*, prepared by Charlton Hinman (New York: W. W. Norton, 1968); hereafter cited in the text by line numbers.

25. *Twelfth Night* dances even closer to this image of brother and sister incest, and retreats from it in much the same manner.

26. *Tetrachordon,* YP 2:606, 610–11; see also my discussion of these in chapter 4 below.

27. For a great deal of information about contemporary attitudes toward violent treatment of servants in England, see Maurice Hunt, "Slavery, English Servitude and *The Comedy of Errors,*" *ELR* 27 (1997): 31–56. Hunt's essay brings up, but does not pursue, the apparently close connection most people made between wife beating and servant beating. Also see the essays excerpted in Frances Dolan's casebook, *The Taming of the Shrew: Texts and Contexts* (Boston: St. Martin's Press, 1996).

Notes to Chapter Two

1. The fullest, and for my purposes most useful, discussions to date of Milton's theories of marriage are John Halkett, *Milton and the Idea of Matrimony: A Study of the Divorce Tracts and "Paradise Lost"* (New Haven, Conn.: Yale University Press, 1970); James Grantham Turner, *One Flesh: Paradisal Marriage and Sexual Relations in the Age of Milton* (Oxford: Oxford University Press, 1987); Gregory Chaplin, "'One Flesh, One Heart, One Soul': Renaissance Friendship and Miltonic Marriage," *Modern Philology* 99 (2001): 266–92; Mary Nyquist, "The Genesis of Gendered Subjectivity in *Paradise Lost,*" in *Paradise Lost: Contemporary Critical Essays,* edited by William Zunder, 88–101 (New York: St. Martin's Press, 1999); and David Aers, "'Rational Burning': Milton on Sex and Marriage," in *Milton Studies,* vol. 13, edited by James D. Simmonds (Pittsburgh: University of Pittsburgh Press, 1979), 3–33.

2. Anon., *An Answer to a book intituled, The doctrine and discipline of divorce, or, A plea for ladies and gentlewomen, and all other maried women against divorce wherein both sexes are vindicated from all bonadge of canon law, and other mistakes whatsoever. . . .* (London, 1644), 15; available at *Early English Books Online,* http://gateway.proquest.com/ openurl?ctx_ver=Z39.88–2003&res_id=xri:eebo&rft_id=xri:eebo:image:4797 7:9 (accessed May 22, 2005).

3. *A Mask Presented at Ludlow* Castle (1645), in Tomas H. Luxon, ed., *The John Milton Reading Room* (Hanover, N.H.: The Trustees of Dartmouth College, 1998–2004), lines 784–87, 792; available at http://www.dartmouth.edu/~milton/reading_room/comus/index.shtml.

4. This is also the impression left by the *Oxford English Dictionary,* which cites Milton's use of the word under "*obs.* 2. The action of consorting or having dealings with others; living together; commerce, intercourse, society, intimacy Obs." rather than under "3. Sexual intercourse or intimacy."

5. Turner, *One Flesh,* 204. Other places where Milton insists on the

distinction are YP 2.235, 246, 248, 249, 250, 273, 275, 331, 355, 591, 609, 611, to cite only a few.

6. Milton refers here to the *Metamorphoses* of Lucius Apuleius, translated into English by William Adlington in 1566 as *The XI Bookes of the Golden Asse* and to the mock epic poem, the *Battle of the Frogs and Mice*, once ascribed to Homer, but known to Milton as spurious and probably regarded by him as ridiculous. Bavius was a poet lampooned quite savagely by Virgil in *Eclogue* 3.90: "Who hates not Bavius?" Calandrino, a character in Boccaccio's *Decameron*, is described as a "rude simpleton" ("uom semplice e di nuovi costumi"); see Brown University's *Decameron Web*, available at http://www.brown.edu/Departments/Italian_Studies/dweb/. A "sotadic" is a satire imitating Sotades, a third century BCE poet.

7. Juliet Fleming, "The Ladies' Man and the Age of Elizabeth," in *Sexuality and Gender in Early Modern Europe*, edited by James Grantham Turner, chapter 7 (Cambridge: Cambridge University Press, 1993), offers a fine example of how well established the punning "sexual freight" of "conversation" was in the late sixteenth century: in George Pettie's 1579 translation of Stefano Guazzo's *Civile Conversation*, "the mysoginist persona of Guazzo deliberately misunderstands the phrase that Pettie translates as the 'conversation' of women and offers an apology designed only to administer a further insult: 'Pardon mee, I pray you, I mistooke you then, for as soone as you began to speake of the Conversation of women: I thought you had ment of those with whom men trie their manhood withall in amoorous encounters'" (quoted in Fleming, "Ladies' Man," 160).

8. Stanley Fish, *Surprised by Sin: The Reader in "Paradise Lost"* (Cambridge: Harvard University Press, 1967).

9. Turner, *One Flesh*; see also William Kerrigan, *The Sacred Complex: On the Psychogenesis of "Paradise Lost"* (Cambridge: Harvard University Press, 1983), 157–58.

10. The *Blue Letter Bible*, an online resource that incorporates *Strong's Exhaustive Concordance* makes locating all the instances of "conversation" and their underlying Greek words quite simple; available at http://www.khouse.org/blueletter/index.html. *Anastrepho:* 2 Cor. 1:12; Eph. 2:3. *Anastrephe:* Gal. 1:13; Eph. 4:22; 1 Tim. 4:12; Heb. 13:7; James 3:13; 1 Pet. 1:15, 18; 1 Pet. 2:12; 1 Pet. 3:1, 2, 16; 2 Pet. 2:7; 2 Pet. 3:11. *Politeuma:* Phil. 3:20. *Politeuomai:* Phil. 1:27. *Tropos:* Heb. 13:5.

11. Among the citations for quotations under definition 1 in the *OED* is the incorrect one to "Philem. iii. 20"; it should refer to Philippians 3:20.

12. On the complicated relations between sexual pleasure, citizenship and prostitution in ancient Athens, see David Halperin, "The Democratic Body: Prostitution and Citizenship in Classical Athens," *One Hundred Years of Homosexuality and Other Essays on Greek Love* (New York: Routledge, 1990), chapter 5.

13. The best discussion of Paul's version of universalism is Daniel Boyarin, *A Radical Jew: Paul and the Politics of Identity* (Berkeley and Los Angeles: University of California Press, 1994), passim.

14. *Nicomachean Ethics*, vol. 19 of *Aristotle*, 23 vols., trans. H. Rackham (Cambridge, Mass.: Harvard University Press, 1934); available at the Perseus project Web site, http://www.perseus.tufts.edu/cgi-bin/ ptext?lookup=Aristot.+Nic.+Eth.+1170b+1 (accessed August 8, 2003).

15. I have transliterated the Greek in brackets from J. Milton French, *The Life Records of John Milton*, vol. 1 (New Brunswick, N.J.: Rutgers University Press, 1949), 98. French translates the same phrase as "philosophical and scholarly talk" (99). These two letters in Greek from Diodati to Milton bear no dates. Though they are often supposed to be from 1625 and 1626, there is little to prohibit later dates.

16. On the dating of the two 1637 letters, see Barbara Lewalski, *The Life of John Milton* (Oxford: Blackwell's, 2000), 69, 567 n. 69.

17. See ibid., 110.

18. Besides Chaplin, "One Flesh, One Heart," there have been relatively few studies of the Milton-Diodati friendship. Others include: John Rumrich, "The Milton-Diodati Correspondence," *Hellas: A Journal of Poetry and the Humanities* 3 (1992): 76–85; later revised as "The Erotic Milton," *Texas Studies in Literature and Language* 41 (1999): 128–40; and John Shawcross, "Milton and Diodati: An Essay in Psychodynamic Meaning," in *Milton Studies*, vol. 7, guest ed. Albert C. Labriola and Michael Lieb (Pittsburgh: University of Pittsburgh Press, 1975), 127–63. See also Donald Clayton Dorian, *The English Diodatis* (New Brunswick, N.J.: Rutgers University Press, 1950).

19. See Lewalski, *Life*, 98. Lewalski also appears to sense a connection between the pleasure Milton took in his Italian friends and that he wished to take with Charles Diodati; she imagines Milton substituting one for the loss of the other. It is possible, however, that Milton did not really know how to practice friendship this way *until* he traveled in Italy.

20. From *The Early Lives of Milton*, ed. Helen Darbishire (London: Constable, 1932), 57.

21. *The Latin Poems of John Milton*, trans. Walter MacKellar, Cornell Studies in English 15 (New Haven, Conn.: Yale University Press, 1930), 159. All citations in the text to *Epitaphium Damonis* are from this volume and cited by line number.

22. Merritt Y. Hughes, *John Milton: Complete Poems and Major Prose* (New York: The Odyssey Press, 1957), 132n, dates the poem's composition in 1640; MacKellar appears ambivalent, for although he dates the poem in late summer or fall of 1640 (*Latin Poems*, 22, 333), he still prefers to think of Milton as composing it only a "few months after his return from Italy, when still suffering the first pain of bereavement" (61). John Shawcross's ingenious suggestion in "*Epitaphium Damonis* Lines 9–13 and

the Date of Composition," *Modern Language Notes* 71 (1956): 322–34, about two harvests per summer in Tuscany has not survived Sergio Baldi's objections in "The Date of Composition of *Epitaphium Damonis*," *Notes and Queries* 25 (1978): 508–9. Either way, Milton returned from Italy late and wrote the poem late. If we opt for the earlier date, we are obliged to hear the poet exaggerating his lateness; if we opt for the later date, we still hear him calling attention to it.

23. David Norbrook, *Writing the English Republic: Poetry, Rhetoric and Politics, 1627–1660* (Cambridge: Cambridge University Press, 1999), 109–18.

24. Line 160, "vos cedite, silvae" echoes Virgil's *Eclogue* 10.63: "ipsae rursus concedite silvae." See *The Perseus Project*, available at http://www.perseus.tufts.edu/cgi-bin/ptext?lookup=Verg.+Ecl.+10.1.

25. I must recommend here Phillip Pullman's brilliant children's novel, *The Amber Spyglass* (New York Ballantine, 2001), an intensely Miltonic novel that tries to imagine the overthrow and execution of God, which paves the way for the advent of the republic of heaven. Pullman, I think, recognizes that Milton stopped short of such a radical vision. But see Michael Bryson, *The Tyranny of Heaven: Milton's Rejection of God as King* (Newark: University of Delaware Press, 2004), passim.

26. Norbrook, *Writing the English Republic*, 114.

27. On these themes, see also Ann Baynes Coiro, "'A ball of strife': Caroline Poetry and Royal Marriage," in *The Royal Image: Representations of Charles I*, ed. Thomas N. Corns (Cambridge: Cambridge University Press, 1999), 26–46, esp. 43.

Notes to Chapter Three

1. Aristotle, *Politics*, trans. Benjamin Jowett, *The Basic Works of Aristotle*, ed. Richard McKeon (New York: Random House, 1941).

2. Juha Sihvola, "Aristotle on Sex and Love," in *The Sleep of Reason: Erotic Experience and Sexual Ethics in Ancient Greece and Rome*, ed. Martha C. Nussbaum and Juha Sihvola (Chicago: University of Chicago Press, 2002), writes that "the aristocratic culture of fourth-century Athens" was "an erotic culture which favored relationships that included sexual conduct between older and younger males" (203). I am indebted to her careful discussion of the marriage passages in the *Ethics* (214–19).

3. Linda Gregerson, *The Reformation of the Subject: Spenser, Milton, and the English Protestant Epic* (Cambridge: Cambridge University Press, 1995), 164.

4. Jacques Lacan, "The Mirror Stage as Formative of the Function of the I," in *Ecrits: A Selection*, trans. Alan Sheridan (New York: W. W. Norton, 1977), 5–6.

5. Andrew Marvell, "The Garden," in *The Poems and Letters of Andrew*

Marvell, vol. 1, ed. H. M. Margoliouth, revised by Pierre Legouis and E. E. Duncan-Jones (Oxford: Oxford University Press, 1971), 51–53.

6. Monarchs present a similar problem with regard to friendship, as Shannon, *Sovereign Amity,* explains.

7. Bruce Smith, *Shakespeare and Masculinity* (Oxford: Oxford University Press, 2000), 7–9.

8. Louis Althusser, "Ideology and Ideological State Apparatuses," in *Literary Theory: An Anthology,* edited by Julie Rivkin and Michael Ryan (Oxford: Blackwells, 1998), 301–2.

9. On self-image and manly beauty in Milton's epic, see John Guillory, "Milton, Narcissism, Gender: On the Genealogy of Male Self-Esteem," in *Critical Essays on John Milton,* ed. Christopher Kendrick (New York: G. K. Hall, 1995), 194–233.

10. Of course, God is always, in orthodoxy, gendered male, but Milton loved to try to think of God as above gender, unengendered, as when he uses the image of a brooding dove in *PL* 1.20–22 to defy gender categories by invoking both masculine and feminine images for the Spirit of God.

11. Cicero, *De Amicitia,* trans. William Armistead Falconer (London: William Heinemann, 1927).

Notes to Chapter Four

1. Kent R. Lehnhof, "'Nor turnd I weene': *Paradise Lost* and Pre-Lapsarian Sexuality," in *Milton Quarterly* 34 (2000): 67–83, performs a thorough and judicious corrective to this critical consensus. He concludes that "Milton frustrates our desire to find irrefutable sexuality in the Edenic relationship because the presence of such indubitable evidence would degrade the pre-lapsarian integrity of Adam and Eve out of which their very acts of intimacy arise." I regret that I had not seen Lehnhof's valuable article when I first published this chapter as an article; I am pleased now to see that someone else recognizes this critical problem.

2. James Grantham Turner, *One Flesh: Paradisal Marriage and Sexual Relations in the Age of Milton* (Oxford: Clarendon Press, 1987), 233.

3. Richard Strier, "Milton's Fetters, or, Why Eden Is Better than Heaven," in *Milton Studies,* vol. 38, *John Milton: The Writer in His Works,* ed. Albert C. Labriola and Michael Lieb (Pittsburgh: University of Pittsburgh Press, 2000), 182–84, discusses the unresolved tension in Milton's poetry between positive and negative conceptions of necessity. The God described in *Christian Doctrine* carries out the first act of begetting, "'not from any natural necessity but of his own free will' — a method, Milton assures us, 'more excellent and more in keeping with paternal dignity' (*CD,* YP 6.209)" (173–74). For Adam, unlike God, procreation may be necessary (indeed, it is commanded by God) but the manly dignity of begetting has to do with an act of free will, not necessity.

4. John Halkett, *Milton and the Idea of Matrimony: A Study of the Divorce Tracts and "Paradise Lost"* (New Haven: Yale University Press, 1970), surveys Protestant authors on marriage (5–30).

5. Compare Milton's examples of marriage here with those of Massachusetts Supreme Judicial Court Justice C. J. Marshall, quoted as the epigraph to chapter 1 above.

6. Stephen M. Fallon, "The Metaphysics of Milton's Divorce Tracts," in *Politics, Poetics, and Hermeneutics in Milton's Prose*, ed. David Loewenstein and James Grantham Turner (Cambridge: Cambridge University Press, 1990), 80–81. Like Turner and Halkett, Fallon is a careful and extremely helpful scholar, and one of Milton's most attentive readers.

7. See also *DDD* 1.4: "strict life and labour, with the abatement of a full diet may keep that low and obedient anough" (YP 2:251).

8. Irene Samuel, *Plato and Milton* (Ithaca, N.Y.: Cornell University Press, 1947), 162. Samuel quotes from and refers to *PL* 5.499.

9. See Augustine, *The City of God against the Pagans*, 7 vols., trans. Philip Levine (Cambridge, Mass.: Harvard University Press, 1988), book 14, chap. 23–24. Unlike Milton, Augustine believed that Adam fell by disobedience before there was time to try rational, nonpassionate copulation. Milton performs the additional move of detaching the rational procreation between souls that results in human society from the more lowly "purpose of generation." Milton devotes only a rather short (for him) paragraph to explication in *Tetrachordon* of Genesis 1:28, the injunction to "be fruitful and multiply." Even here he cites Plato to help define what he calls an "honest and pious" desire for children that is not for children merely as offspring, but as "continuall servants of God" (YP 2.593), implying that raising and teaching children — reproducing regenerate souls — is as much or more a matter of true reproduction as the making of another body.

10. Samuel, *Plato and Milton*, 27–43, measures quite carefully and sensibly Milton's relation to his Neoplatonist predecessors.

11. Fallon, "Metaphysics of Milton's Divorce Tracts," makes a similar point (81). I thoroughly agree with Jason P. Rosenblatt, *Torah and Law in "Paradise Lost"* (Princeton: Princeton University Press, 1994), 71–137, who claims that Milton grounds his understanding of divorce on John Selden's nearly rabbinical study of the Torah, but I do not assume from that that he understands either marriage or human sexuality in a distinctly Hebraic way, nor is Milton's monism as "Hebraic" as Rosenblatt would like us to believe.

12. On the reception of the divorce tracts, see Ernest Sirluck, introduction to *DDD*, YP 2:137–41. Also consider the vituperative bile of *Colasterion* (YP 2:719–58) as Milton's response to their reception.

13. See the entry for *mysterion* in William F. Arndt and F. Wilbur Gingrich, *A Greek-English Lexicon of the New Testament*, 4th ed. (Chicago: University of Chicago Press, 1952), 532. The Roman Catholic Erasmus points

out in his *Institution of Christian Matrimony,* in *The Collected Works of Erasmus,* vol. 69, ed. John W. O'Malley and Louis A. Perraud, trans. Michael J. Heath (Toronto: University of Toronto Press, 1999), 225, that "sacrament" and "mystery" mean much the same thing; since Protestantism demotes marriage from the status of sacrament, we might then take "mystery" as Protestant for "sacrament." On Milton's reading of Ephesians 5 in *Tetrachordon,* see Rachel Trubowitz, "'The Single State of Man': Androgyny in *Macbeth* and *Paradise Lost,*" *Papers on Language and Literature* 26 (1990): 329. See also Don Cameron Allen, *Mysteriously Meant: The Rediscovery of Pagan Symbolism and Allegorical Interpretation in the Renaissance* (Baltimore: Johns Hopkins University Press, 1970) and Daniel Boyarin, *A Radical Jew: Paul and the Politics of Identity* (Berkeley and Los Angeles: University of California Press, 1994), 57–85.

14. For a collection of classical literature on friendship, emphasizing the "other self" tradition, see *Other Selves: Philosophers on Friendship,* ed. Michael Pakaluk (Indianapolis: Hackett, 1991).

15. See *The City of God against the Pagans,* book 14, chap. 24, where Augustine tries to make his notion of a penis controlled by the rational will more credible by retelling stories of men who can move their ears or their scalps and even fart and perspire at will.

16. I rely on observations and analyses here, and later, from John Guillory, "Milton, Narcissism, Gender: On the Genealogy of Male Self-Esteem," in *Critical Essays on John Milton,* ed. Christopher Kendrick (New York: G. K. Hall, 1995), esp. 209–15.

17. As I mentioned in the previous chapter, Milton probably borrows his sense of the word *cattell* here from Aristotle's distinction between the way humans live together and the way beasts live together: "Therefore a man ought also to share his friend's consciousness of his existence, and this is attained by their living together and by conversing and communicating their thoughts to each other [*koinônein logôn kai dianoias*]; for this is the meaning of living together as applied to human beings, it does not mean merely feeding in the same place, as it does when applied to cattle" (*Nicomachean Ethics,* 1170b).

18. That not all babies born are necessarily truly human is implied by Michael's teaching in *PL* 12.97–110. Presumably Ham's children were born with the face of God turned from them, justly doomed or cursed to be servants of servants with no legitimate claim to humanity. Milton was, contrary to what many modern Miltonists believe, quite comfortable with the notion of race- (or "Nation"-) based slavery. See Steven Jablonski, "Ham's Vicious Race: Slavery and John Milton," *Studies in English Literature, 1500–1900* 37 (1997): 173–90.

19. In Plato's *Symposium* (191e), Aristophanes expresses the conviction that adulterous lust was most typical of heterosexuals, those who originally were hermaphrodites; presumably homosexuals, or those from

originally male and female wholes, made more faithful partners, and in general were less moved by lust.

20. According to most classical teaching the paradigmatic human relationship was manly friendship. Milton follows Genesis, which teaches that the first and therefore paradigmatically human relationship is heterosexual marriage. In many ways, however, Milton's redefinition of marriage makes it look a lot like classical pederasty and classical friendship. In both *Paradise Lost* and the divorce tracts this had the un-looked-for effect of suggesting that women are human enough — "Manlike" enough — to serve as friends and protegés to men (*PL* 8.471). Perhaps this is why some readers find the poem mildly protofeminist.

21. Xenophon, *Symposium*, 8.11–12, in *Symposium and Apology*, trans. O. J. Todd, vol. 4, *Xenophon in Seven Volumes* (Cambridge, Mass.: Harvard University Press, 1979). Cited hereafter as Xenophon. Plato, *Symposium*, 180d–e.

22. On the homoerotic tones of Adam's conversation with Raphael, see Linda Gregerson, *The Reformation of the Subject: Spenser, Milton, and the English Protestant Epic* (Cambridge: Cambridge University Press, 1995), 171.

23. I cannot agree with John Shawcross's and William Kerrigan's speculations about a sexual relationship between the two young friends. Their relationship was certainly erotic; even a brief glance at the surviving correspondence betrays that, but their bond also involved a deep appreciation of and perhaps commitment to sexual purity. For Kerrigan, see *The Sacred Complex: On the Psychogenesis of Paradise Lost* (Cambridge, Mass., 1983), 49. For Shawcross, see "Milton and Diodati: An Essay in Psychodynamic Meaning," in *Milton Studies 7, "Eyes Fast Fixt,"* ed. Albert C. Labriola and Michael Lieb (Pittsburgh: University of Pittsburgh Press, 1975), 127–63.

24. Amor, or Cupid, appears again in *PL* 4.763–64; his "constant Lamp" distinguishes him as the fully spiritualized lover of the human soul rather than the younger son of Venus, who hides in the dark.

25. The Neoplatonist uses to which Plato's *Symposium* was put are fascinating. For example, in Aristophanes's story about where desire comes from, Neoplatonists imagined they had found a solution to the problem of the apparently divergent accounts of human creation in Genesis. Genesis 1:27 articulated the creation of a spiritual or ideal Adam, both male and female. Genesis 2:7–23 told how the corporeal Adam was formed from the dust of the ground, and the female made from a piece of his body. Milton rejected such interpretations as Jewish fables, by which I take he means traditional midrash, and insisted that Paul's teaching in 1 Corinthians settled the matter: "But *St. Paul* ends the controversie by explaining that the woman is not primarily and immediatly the image of God, but in reference to the man. *The head of the woman,* saith he, 1 *Cor.* 11. *is the man:*

he the image and glory of God, she the glory of the man: he not for her, but she for him" (*Tetrachordon,* Gen. 1:27, YP 2:589). Marsilio Ficino, *Commentary on Plato's Symposium on Love,* trans. Sears Jayne (Dallas: Spring Publications, 1985), whose Latin translation of the *Symposium* was standard throughout the Renaissance, divides up his *Commentary on the Symposium* according to the different speakers and their speeches, but the commentary is dramatically syncretistic anyway; Ficino acknowledges that the procreative love Socrates ranks as highest was homoerotic, not heteroerotic, but he says, "the genital part . . . should have been redirected from males to females" (135). See also Turner, *One Flesh,* 65–68; Philo, *On the Creation,* in vol. 1, of the Loeb Classical Library *Philo,* trans. F. H. Colson and G. H. Whitaker (London, 1929), 55–61; Leone Ebreo, *The Philosophy of Love,* trans. F. Friedeberg-Seeley and Jean H. Barnes (London, 1937), 367–73.

26. See also Turner, *One Flesh,* 70–71.

27. See Milton's frequent berating in *Colasterion* of the answerer for always having sex on his mind when Milton speaks of a "fit conversing soule" (YP 2:741–43).

28. Turner, *One Flesh,* even refers to this episode as "the normal process of sexuality" (258).

29. Halkett, *Milton and the Idea of Matrimony,* without any explanation or paraphrase, quotes lines 738–43 as evidence of the "fully sexual" nature of Adam and Eve's relationship (102).

30. Turner, *One Flesh,* notes that Luther imagined prelapsarian lovemaking as a form of worship and that Milton here realizes Luther's "wistful conjecture" (236). In this I think Turner was exactly right, but this observation does not lead Turner to conclude that Adam and Eve's coupling here is something other than "making love," as we use the term today.

31. For examples, see *Jane Anger, Her Protection for Women* (London, 1589); *Ester Hath Hang'd Haman* (London, 1617); Mary Tattle-well, *The Woman's Sharpe Revenge* (London, 1640), all reprinted in *Half Humankind: Contexts and Texts of the Controversy about Women in England, 1540–1640,* ed. Katherine Usher Henderson and Barbara F. McManus (Urbana: University of Illinois Press, 1985).

32. Turner's frequent assumption that Milton understood the rhetoric of the Song of Solomon as sensually erotic cannot stand in the face of this passage, where Milton explains the "jolliest expressions" of the Song of Songs are not about sex:

> Wherof lest we should be too timorous, in the aw that our flat sages would form us and dresse us, wisest *Salomon* among his gravest Proverbs countenances a kinde of ravishment and erring fondnes in the entertainment of wedded leisures; and in the Song of Songs, which is generally beleev'd, even in the jolliest expressions to figure the Spousals of the Church with Christ, sings of a thousand raptures

between those two lovely ones farre on the hither side of carnall injoyment (*Tetrachordon*, Gen. 2:18, YP 2:597).

33. Marcus Tullius Cicero, *De Amicitia*, trans. William Armistead Falconer (London: William Heinemann, 1927), 133.

34. Adam actually overpraises Eve much as teachers or parents overpraise their charges for making a good, but mistaken, effort: "Well hast thou motion'd, well thy thoughts imployd / . . . Nor of me shalt pass / Unprais'd" (229, 231–32).

35. Book 9, lines 57–67, appear to indicate that seven nights have passed between Eve's disturbing dream, discussed in book 5, and this separation colloquy. After leaving Eve's ear, Satan, the narrator tells us, travels around the globe, staying always in the night's darkness, "The space of seven continu'd Nights."

Notes to Chapter Five

1. David Halperin, *One Hundred Years of Homosexuality and Other Essays on Greek Love* (New York: Routledge, 1990), chap. 4.

2. Jeffrey S. Shoulson, *Milton and the Rabbis: Hebraism, Hellenism, and Christianity* (New York: Columbia University Press, 2001), 245–46. A useful treatment of the Herculean Samson is Murray Roston, "Milton's Herculean Samson," in *Modern Language Quarterly* 16 (1982): 85–93.

3. Flavius Josephus, *Jewish Antiquities, Books V–VIII*, trans. H. St. J. Thackeray and Ralph Marcus (Cambridge, Mass.: Harvard University Press, 1934), 143.

4. For a detailed analysis of the strong differences between Josephus's Hellenized Samson and the biblical Samson as interpreted by the rabbis, see Louis H. Feldman, *Josephus's Interpretation of the Bible* (Berkeley and Los Angeles: University of California Press, 1998), 461–89.

5. See the *Ordo Prophetarum*, a popular form of medieval drama wherein selected Hebrew prophets and patriarchs take turns bearing witness to Christ's Incarnation, Passion and Resurrection. See *The Procession of the Prophets (Ordo Prophetarum)*, from Limoges, ed. and trans. Fletcher Collins Jr., in *Medieval Church Music-Dramas* (Charlottesville: University Press of Virginia, 1976), 165–88.

6. Camille Slights, "A Hero of Conscience: *Samson Agonistes* and Casuistry," *PMLA* 90 (1975): 395–413, discusses Samson's highly developed sense of conscience and casuistry.

7. Mary Beth Rose, "'Vigorous Most / When Most Unactive Deem'd': Gender and the Heroics of Endurance in Milton's *Samson Agonistes*, Aphra Behn's *Oroonoko*, and Mary Astell's *Some Reflections Upon Marriage*," *Milton Studies* 33, *The Miltonic Samson*, ed. Albert C. Labriola and Michael Lieb (Pittsburgh: University of Pittsburgh Press, 1997), argues

that "slavery and passivity" do not mark the loss of Samson's heroic identity, but constitute a new heroic identity that includes being married (88–89). The argument stumbles over an attempt to regard Milton as advancing a "female heroics" with Samson in the position of a "wife." The drama, I believe, presents Samson's divorce as truly heroic, an action that initiates his salvation from the degraded positions of wife and slave. I find nothing in Milton that endorses a heroics of wifehood or slavery.

8. Robert Boling, translator of the *Anchor Bible Judges* (Garden City, N.Y.: Doubleday, 1975), notes that the name Delilah may be derived from Aramaic *dallatum*, meaning "flirt" (248 n. 4). Since the verses just before those introducing Delilah tell of Samson visiting a harlot (*zona*), Delilah is well distinguished from harlotry. Josephus, in his version of the story, identifies Delilah as a harlot. He translates the *zona* of Judges 16:1 as an "innkeeper" and then refers to Delilah as "a harlot among the Philistines" (*Jewish Antiquities*, 137–39).

9. As Rosenblatt, *Torah and Law*, 98–100, has shown, Milton's knowledge of Torah and rabbinics owes almost everything to John Selden, *De Jure Naturali*, and *Uxor Ebraica*.

10. For an analysis of Milton's deployment of Jewishness in the *Doctrine and Discipline of Divorce*, see Maria Whelan, "Jewish Metaphors and Christian Self-Definition 1630–1660"(unpublished diss., Cambridge University, 2003), 21–36.

11. Genesis 3:6 indicates that Eve sins first, but only by a moment, almost negligible: "she took of the fruit thereof, and did eat, and gave also unto her husband with her; and he did eat." Milton builds 220 lines of speculation about Adam divorced from Eve out of an almost nonexistent hint of narratological sequence.

12. Anthony Low, *The Blaze of Noon: A Reading of "Samson Agonistes"* (New York: Columbia University Press, 1974), 140; emphasis added. Joseph Wittreich, *Interpreting "Samson Agonistes"* (Princeton: Princeton University Press, 1986), goes even further to argue that insofar as typology operates in the poem, it more a "typology of difference" than of sameness (306).

13. Low, like most Milton critics until recently, often refers to the ancient Israelites as Jews. There is good reason to distinguish between ancient Hebrew religious practice and people and the Judaism that grows up in explicit rivalry with Christianity. The distinction is not perfect, but it is less confusing than projecting rabbinic Judaism back onto the Israelites of the Hebrew Scriptures. John Ulreich, "'Beyond the Fifth Act': *Samson Agonistes* as Prophecy," *Milton Studies* 17, ed. James D. Simmonds (Pittsburgh: University of Pittsburgh Press, 1983), points out that the typological associations we expect of any Samson poem are in Milton's poem repeatedly dashed "against the rock of Samson's unremittingly Judaic consciousness" (281). Kent R. Lehnhof, "Arrested Spiritual Development in Milton's *Samson Agonistes*," *Renaissance Papers* (1999): 147–67,

accuses Samson of being overly legalistic, "hardened" and spiritually "blinded," neglecting and even scorning "the workings of grace" (167).

14. See, for example, his sound discussion of the limited understandings of Manoa and the Chorus, who receive nothing like Christian enlightenment from Samson's sacrificial death (134).

15. David Loewenstein, "The Revenge of the Saint: Radical Religion and Politics in *Samson Agonistes*," *Milton Studies* 33, 168, 173. Michael Lieb, "'Our Living Dread': The God of *Samson Agonistes*," *Milton Studies* 33, 3–25, differs very little from Loewenstein. Lieb's article acknowledges that the God represented in *Samson Agonistes* is far more "archaic" than is normally acknowledged, but he fails to identify this as Milton's projection of a Hebrew (mis)understanding of God. Mary Ann Radzinowicz, *Toward "Samson Agonistes": The Growth of Milton's Mind* (Princeton: Princeton University Press, 1978), argues that the theology of *Samson Agonistes* represents Milton's most advanced thinking about God. Barbara K. Lewalski, "Milton's *Samson* and the 'New Acquist of True Experience,'" *Milton Studies* 24, ed. James D. Simmonds (Pittsburgh: University of Pittsburgh Press, 1988), 233–51, accurately surveys the range of critical opinion on *Samson* up until 1987.

16. Elisa Narin van Court, "Socially Marginal, Culturally Central: Representing Jews in Late Medieval English Literature," *Exemplaria* 12 (2000): 300.

17. Thomas H. Luxon, "A Second Daniel: The Jew and the 'True Jew' in *The Merchant of Venice*," *Early Modern Literary Studies* 4, no. 3 (January 1999), paragraphs 7–14.

18. Jeremy Cohen, *The Friars and the Jews: The Evolution of Medieval Anti-Judaism* (Ithaca, N.Y.: Cornell University Press, 1982), 20. See also Cohen, *Living Letters of the Law: Ideas of the Jew in Medieval Christianity* (Berkeley and Los Angeles: University of California Press, 1999), 19–21.

19. Barbara K. Lewalski, *Protestant Poetics and the Seventeenth-Century Religious Lyric* (Princeton: Princeton University Press, 1979), 132.

20. The strongest case for Milton's Samson as a hero of faith was made by Barbara K. Lewalski, "*Samson Agonistes* and the 'Tragedy' of the Apocalypse," *PMLA* 85 (1970): 1050–62. Her case requires that we accept that Calvinist (and Miltonic) typology regarded "Israelite and Elect Christian" as type and antitype, historically considered but essentially identical in faith and spiritual experience (1055). Evidence I have cited suggests Milton believed otherwise. Perhaps the most elaborate case against regarding Milton's Samson as a hero of faith is in Joseph Wittreich, *Shifting Contexts: Reinterpreting "Samson Agonistes"* (Pittsburgh: Duquesne University Press, 2002), esp. 67–100.

21. Marc Zvi Brettler, *The Book of Judges* (New York: Routledge, 2002), 113.

22. See David Norbrook, *Writing the English Republic: Poetry, Rhetoric and Politics, 1627–1660* (Cambridge: Cambridge University Press, 1999), 480–91.

23. Gregory Bredbeck, "Milton's Ganymede: Negotiations of Homoerotic Tradition in *Paradise Regain'd," Publications of the Modern Language Association* 106 (1991): 268–71. On this topic and the more general issue of Christian interpretations of Genesis 19 and Judges 19, see Claude J. Summers, "The (Homo)Sexual Temptation in Milton's *Paradise Regained,"* in *Reclaiming the Sacred: The Bible in Gay and Lesbian Culture,* edited by Raymond-Jean Frontain, 45–69 (New York: The Haworth Press, 1997); and John Boswell, *Christianity, Social Tolerance, and Homosexuality: Gay People in Western Europe from the Beginning of the Christian Era to the Fourteenth Century* (Chicago: The University of Chicago Press, 1980), esp. 113–14.

24. See also Tobit 3:7–17.

25. Bredbeck, "Milton's Ganymede," 273–74; Summers, "The (Homo) Sexual Temptation," 58–65.

26. Perhaps Milton wants us to think Satan is a clumsy tempter in saying he will offer no trafe and then does so, but I am inclined to believe that Milton regarded the Son as already sharing the opinion taught to Peter by God in Acts 10, that all things provided by God are clean. By this logic, everything Satan offers is trafe, not just the shellfish.

INDEX